Isolated Cases

Isolated Cases

o o o

THE ANXIETIES OF AUTONOMY
IN ENLIGHTENMENT PHILOSOPHY
AND ROMANTIC LITERATURE

Nancy Yousef

CORNELL UNIVERSITY PRESS
Ithaca and London

Copyright © 2004 by Cornell University

All rights reserved. Except for brief quotations in a review, this book, or parts thereof, must not be reproduced in any form without permission in writing from the publisher. For information, address Cornell University Press, Sage House, 512 East State Street, Ithaca, New York 14850.

First published 2004 by Cornell University Press

Library of Congress Cataloging-in-Publication Data

Yousef, Nancy.
  Isolated cases: the anxieties of autonomy in enlightenment philosophy and romantic literature / Nancy Yousef.
    p. cm.
Includes bibliographical references and index.
  ISBN 0-8014-4244-3 (cloth : acid-free paper)
  1. English literature—19th century—History and criticism. 2. Romanticism—Great Britain. 3. Rousseau, Jean-Jacques, 1712–1778—Appreciation—Great Britain. 4. Rousseau, Jean-Jacques, 1712–1778—Influence. 5. English literature—French influences. 6. Autonomy (Psychology) in literature. 7. Philosophy, Modern—19th century. 8. Philosophy, Modern–18th century. 9. Philosophy in literature. 10. Isolation (Philosophy) 11. Anxiety in literature. 12. Autonomy (Philosophy) 13. Enlightenment. I. Title.
PR457 .Y68 2004
820.9'145—dc22
                                          2003023880

Printed in the United States of America

Cornell University Press strives to use environmentally responsible suppliers and materials to the fullest extent possible in the publishing of its books. Such materials include vegetable-based, low-VOC inks and acid-free papers that are recycled, totally chlorine-free, or partly composed of nonwood fibers. For further information, visit our website at www.cornellpress.cornell.edu.

Cloth printing   10 9 8 7 6 5 4 3 2 1

To Jonah Sebastian Siegel

Contents

∘ ∘ ∘

ACKNOWLEDGMENTS
ix

Introduction
1

CHAPTER 1: Locke's Loneliness
26

CHAPTER 2: Rousseau's Autonomous Beast: Natural Man as Imaginary Animal
63

CHAPTER 3: Natural Man in the Wild: The Feral Child as Philosophical Subject
96

CHAPTER 4: "Unfathered Vapour": The Imagination of Origins in *The Prelude*
114

CHAPTER 5: Fantastic Form: *Frankenstein* and Philosophy
149

CHAPTER 6: Mill Alone
170

NOTES
198

INDEX
245

Acknowledgments

The completion of *Isolated Cases* was made possible by a year's leave from teaching funded by the Whiting Foundation and by a generous fellowship from the American Council of Learned Societies. I am happy to acknowledge the crucial assistance of these institutions.

Friends and family, sympathetic readers, and challenging interlocutors made vital contributions to this project, and it is a pleasure to give thanks for words and deeds that helped bring the many pages that follow into being. I am grateful to Steven Marcus and Michael Seidel at Columbia University for the long duration of their support. Their confidence in the relevance of writing about philosophy and literature across the lines separating the enlightenment from the nineteenth century allowed for the early formulation of questions I am still grappling with. Along with David Damrosch, also at Columbia, they fostered the comparative and interdisciplinary tendencies of my work. In its later stages the project benefited from timely and thoughtful advice. With unique intellectual grace and characteristic incisiveness, John Brenkman aided me in the search for conceptual clarity. Adam Potkay read an incomplete manuscript, written by a stranger, for Cornell University Press, and responded with remarkable generosity and salutary rigor. Individual chapters became stronger for the scrutiny of Marshall Brown and Joseph Wittreich. For their encouraging responses to my work at a number of critical junctures, I am grateful to Isobel Armstrong, Rachel Brownstein, David Clark, Stuart Curran, David Ferris, William Galperin, and Elaine Scarry. Thanks also to Bernhard Kendler at Cornell University Press for his long-standing interest in the project and the careful oversight he brought to bear over the past year.

The design of *Isolated Cases* began to take shape during a year I spent as a Harper-Schmidt Fellow at the University of Chicago, teaching wonderful books and learning a great from colleagues in the social sciences. My conversations at the time with philosophers, political theorists, and cultural historians remained with me—and continued in different form—as I worked on this book. For their companionship during that year, I am especially grateful to Eric Caplan, Peter Miller, and Andy Wallace.

Special thanks to my colleagues at Baruch College, City University of New York (CUNY). I am happy to acknowledge the support not only of the chair, John Todd, but of John Brenkman, Jackie Di Salvo, Shelly Eversley, Tom Hayes, Gary Hentzi, Gayana Jurkevich, Elaine Kauvar, Bill McClellan, and Mary McGlynn. Their encouragement and collective commitment to the idea that humanistic research and the teaching of liberal arts are absolutely interdependent have been especially heartening to me.

Parts of the work-in-progress were presented to the Eighteenth-Century Interdisciplinary Group and the Victorian Seminar, both at the CUNY Graduate Center. Thanks to Gerhard Joseph, Anne Humphreys, and James Hatch for their invitations, and their work in sustaining these genial forums for intellectual exchange within the dauntingly sprawling academic landscape of greater New York City.

Isolated Cases is about various struggles we wage against the powerful temptation to see ourselves as profoundly alone in the world. I am fortunate to feel spared from that temptation as the influence of close friends and family lingers genially about, touching me at home, abroad, in and out of the study. On the occasion of his retirement from decades of scientific research, I was recently reminded of the strong impression that my father's evident pleasure in his work made on me as a young girl. For that perhaps inadvertent gift, he has my gratitude.

This book is dedicated to Jonah Siegel, dearest, fiercest ally, closest reader of my words and silences for many years now. This work has been sustained by the resolute, but always gentle, stirrings of his will. His kindness, forbearance, and confidence, his terrific charm and love have made so much more than this possible for me.

Nancy Yousef

New York

o o o

Grants from the PSC-CUNY Research Foundation allowed work to proceed during three summers and resulted in the publication of several parts of *Isolated Cases*. An early version of chapter 2 appeared as "Natural Man as Imaginary Animal: The Challenge of Facts and the Place of Animal Life in Rousseau's *Discourse on the Origins of Inequality*," *Interpretation* 27, no. 3 (2000): 205–229, reprinted here by permission of the editors; a version of chapter 3 appeared as "Savage or Solitary? The Wild Child and Rousseau's Man of Nature," *Journal of the History of Ideas* 62 (2001): 245–263, reprinted here by permission of The Johns Hopkins University Press; a version of chapter 5 appeared as "The Monster in a Dark Room: *Frankenstein*, Feminism, and Philosophy," *Modern Language Quarterly* 63, no. 2 (2002): 197–226, reprinted here by permission of Duke University Press; and parts of chapter 6 first appeared as "'Destitute of frank communicativeness': Reading the Reserve of John Stuart Mill's *Autobiography*," *Prose Studies* 21 (1998): 51–73, reprinted here by permission of Frank Cass Publishers.

Isolated Cases

Introduction

Isolated Cases is about an imagination of human origins so counterintuitive that it meets resistance as soon as it is ventured, yet so compelling that it is formulated again and again, leaving a rich reaction in its wake. It is a well-established fact of intellectual history that a range of philosophies identified as "enlightenment" strove to define the human being as independent, free-standing, and irreducibly individual. The fraught but powerful ideal of autonomy stands among the key inventions that received opinion attributes to the enlightenment, sometimes as a celebrated innovation, but more recently as a damaging fiction needing to be exposed.[1] Yet it is obvious that human individuals are born and develop in intimate and constant contact with others, that dependence is our inescapable first condition and interaction with others necessary for our survival and formation. Banal and yet crucial, these truths about human beginnings are set aside in philosophies that assume some combination of isolation and self-sufficiency to be the basis on which more complex forms of human life—individual and social—ought to be theoretically reconstructed and examined.

Efforts to conceive the mind's autonomous workings and the individual's autonomous survival in a state outside of and prior to society hypothesize independence as the original or fundamental human condition. Hobbes offers the classic articulation of this notion, first arguing that the view of man as a "creature born fit for society though received by most, is yet certainly false," and then proposing a *presocial* "natural state of men."[2] Yet Hobbes does not begin with a "return" to nature. Rather, his starting point is a radical and overt departure from the common view: "It may seem a wonderful kind of stupidity," he concedes, "to lay in the very threshold of this doctrine such a stumbling block before the reader as to deny *man to be born fit for society*." How and why the philosopher feels compelled to overturn or somehow get behind the obvious—and to do so openly, with the confidence that what passes for obvious will not bear the scrutiny of a second glance—are vital questions that have been lost sight of in the contention over Hobbes's well-known conclusions. So while the Hobbesian view of human beings locked in a brutal egoistic struggle for survival has typically been the focus of analysis, it bears repeating that his vision opens up only by an oddly deliberate turning away from the familiar truth that "to man by nature, as soon as he is born, solitude is an enemy."[3]

Hobbes was, of course, not alone in hypothesizing a counterintuitive origin for human forms of life. His work is only the most well known example of the striking emergence of questions about the foundation of communities in late-seventeenth-century political thought. As the philosopher Charles Taylor observes, the principal innovation of theorists such as Hobbes, Grotius, Pufendorf, and Locke is a new "atomistic" starting point for reflection. Where previously "the existence of the community was something taken for granted," now it must be "justified relative to a more basic situation," one in which the individual is imagined to be "on his own."[4]

It is manifestly strange that highly influential conceptions of the individual would begin by ignoring, refuting, or setting aside the fact that human beings are born and formed in relation to others. *Isolated Cases* is about a distinct set of particularly rich and complex challenges to that initial denial. Although tightly bound to one another through intellectual history, the four well-known works of philosophy and literature at the heart of this book—Rousseau's *Discourse on the Origins of Inequality among Men*, Wordsworth's *Prelude*, Shelley's *Frankenstein*, and John Stuart Mill's *Autobiography*—hardly present themselves for consideration as a group under traditional generic or historical rubrics. The terms under which they can be seen as coherently related to one another are defined in the course of this book, but it is possible to state at the outset that each questions, criticizes, and ultimately repudiates the possibility of imagining that human beings (as minds, as political or moral subjects, as protagonists of a life history) can be conceived as essentially independent. Such a characterization of these works will itself strike some readers as odd. Do I not mean to say just the opposite, particularly about Rousseau, dreamer of the noble savage, or Wordsworth, lyricist of the egotistical sublime? In fact, I will be arguing that these works appear to propose precisely what they demonstrate to be impossible, that each *renounces* an ideal of independence. That renunciation in and of itself, surprising though it may be in some cases, is not what makes these texts unique. Their peculiarity lies in containing, acknowledging, and making sense of the drive to reject and deny the ordinary view of human "fitness" to social life that I have just touched on above in Hobbes. The authors at the center of this book eschew a straightforwardly affirmative revaluation of sociality and instead incorporate a sympathetic and unmystified apprehension and expression of the anxieties and desires that compel (and make compelling) imagination of an original self-sufficiency. In the process these writers find ways to make the obvious fact of human dependence remarkable—fragile and imperative at once—without simply reasserting the obvious and thereby simplifying the forms of human relationship.

IGNORING THE OBVIOUS; INVENTING THE PAST; REMEMBERING

Before turning to a more precise outline of these paradoxical challenges to autonomy, it will be helpful to recollect how ideals of individual independence typically associated with the enlightenment are articulated. Although introduced as conjectural or speculative, the invented origin is nevertheless inevitably accorded the same force—to explain or move or enlighten—with which we are prone to credit the past. "It is with commonwealths as it is with particular persons, they are commonly ignorant of their own births and infancies," notes Locke in the *Second Treatise of Government* (1689), preparing his readers for an entirely speculative history that is nevertheless *not* meant to be taken as fantasy. Lost to memory, but recovered in philosophical reflection, is a first period before the "love and want of society" brought individuals together. In that forgotten time and place, men dwelled in a "state of perfect freedom to order their actions . . . without depending on the will of any other man."[5] This original, albeit forgotten, era of independence and freedom becomes the basis for Locke's conception of the individual, trumping the temporal and existential priority of the most readily recognized and observed first stages of human life. The "weakness of infancy" is thereby distorted, misremembered as a transient inessential phase, an "imperfect state" that is not yet the state of being human. Every child undergoes a virtual metamorphosis after which, chrysalis-like, dependence is sloughed off: "The Bonds of [children's] Subjection are like the

Swaddling Cloths they are wrapt up in, and supported by, in the weakness of their Infancy," writes Locke, "Age and Reason as they grow up, loosen them, till at length they drop quite off and leave a Man at his own free Disposal." Only one man was ever rightly conceived from the start—Adam, the first man, whose perfection consists in having been originally independent, "capable from the first Instant of his being to provide for his own Support." Only the "man at his own free disposal" whom the child mysteriously becomes is the proper subject of philosophical reflection on the "state of nature."[6]

Locke draws on the rich confluence of political and epistemological formulations centering on individuals in isolation that preceded his work. The self-defining Cartesian *cogito* is an invention contemporaneous with Hobbes's state of nature (*Discourse on Method*, 1637; *Meditations*, 1641; *De Cive*, 1642; *Leviathan*, 1651), arrived at by an equally bold, unconcealed turn away from the received and the familiar. The work of philosophical construction (to build knowledge "upon a foundation which is completely my own") begins *after* a narrative about the impulse or compulsion to isolate oneself in order to find truth or, rather, to found the truth on one's self alone.

The discovery of the *cogito* occurs in a place "where I have been able to live as solitary and retired a life as I could in the remotest desert," but it would be a mistake to think that Descartes's reflections *begin* in solitude. The dramatization of retreat does not simply frame the epistemology; it is intrinsic to its methodology. This bears emphasizing because Descartes's account of a past in which others filled the mind with ideas can seem simply prefatory and even superfluous to his meditations. The point of his work can seem to lie solely in the results of his method, in the affirmation of self-determined truths. In fact, the philosophical reasoning that forms the substance of the *Meditations* only begins in the fourth part of the *Discourse on Method*, the first three sections of which comprise an account of Descartes's early schooling, travels, military service, and immersion in social life—experiences that shape the adult now seeking retirement. The formative role of that past is itself implied in the opening lines of the *Meditations* ("Several years have now passed since I first realized how many were the false opinions that in my youth I took to be true"); yet it is easy to forget that the philosopher "*withdraws* to solitude" from another prior place not only because the achievement of the *Meditations* has the effect of making that past seem irrelevant but also because so many subsequent philosophies of knowledge simply start from the isolation at which Descartes actually takes pains to arrive.[7]

In a subtle but critically significant variation of the Cartesian imperative to think for oneself, Diderot's concise formulation, "*l'homme est né pour penser de lui-même,*" fuses and confuses end and aspiration (to think for oneself) with origin and nature (to be born as such). This erasure of the turn away from something common, received, inherited—a crucial first methodological step in both Hobbes and Descartes—has profound implications for the theorization of independence. "The word principle," Condillac writes in an accurate but pointed etymology, "is the synonym of beginning."[8] Descartes's solitary retreat—which he himself presents as idiosyncratic—becomes the virtual cradle of human thought out of which knowledge of self and world comes to develop, *as if from a real beginning*. Locke's *Essay concerning Human Understanding* (1689/1706) presents its examination of the foundations of human knowledge as a recovery of the origins of individual mental development rather than as a heuristic speculation. Voltaire only follows the author of the *Essay* when he credits the work with offering a "history" of the soul.[9] And yet, even as (or perhaps necessarily because) the mind in isolation becomes the normative model in theories of human understanding, it is worth remarking that the nascent mind often takes inhuman form. Certainly well-known figures such as Locke's "white paper void of all characters," Condillac's fully formed statue whose senses are animated one by one, or La Mettrie's related *"homme machine"* illustrate the fundamental empiricist premise that everything we know we learn by experience. But the very artifice of these figurations masks the strangeness of their isolation and isolatability in a way that representation of human infants never could.[10] As disembodied solitary objects, these philosophically conceived models appear to belong to what the contemporary moral philosopher Annette Baier has described as a "supernatural realm," one deliberately removed from our "natural habitat as persons" which is—in Baier's deceptively simple formulation—"among other persons."[11]

That seminal enlightenment philosophies of individual origins and development entail a forgetfulness about the need for other persons has not escaped remark, but it is worth pausing briefly to note how common recognitions—such as Baier's—of the crucially ignored fact of dependence have become. In his comprehensive history of modern ethical thought (aptly entitled *The Invention of Autonomy*), J. B. Schneewind observes that most theorists of natural law simply "ignore the fact that we start as newborn babies." The substance of that remark—relegated to a footnote by Schneewind—is the focus of Tzvetan Todorov's "Living

Alone Together," an essay recently featured (along with responses) in *New Literary History*. "If we look at definitions of the human in the mainstream of European thought," begins Todorov, a widely held presupposition emerges: "the fact of living with others is generally not conceived as being *necessary* . . . we perforce accept a definition of man as solitary and nonsocial." The same neglected fact motivates the political theorist Seyla Benhabib, who proposes that any "renegotiation" of an enlightenment legacy must begin with this first principle: "the subject of reason is a human infant, whose body can only be kept alive, whose needs can only be satisfied and whose self can only develop within the human community into which it is born."[12] These remarks, ventured in different contexts for different purposes and with different degrees of emphasis, are the merest indication of the extent to which critiques of the self-determining autonomous subject that were so explosive and contentiously debated just a few decades ago have become virtually commonplace.[13] My small sampling is also indicative of how critical reflections on the philosophical history of the individual arising from different disciplines share an arresting and powerful simplicity. In spite of diverse interests and aims, Baier (a feminist, ethicist, and Hume scholar working in the Anglo-American tradition), Schneewind (a historian of eighteenth- and nineteenth-century moral philosophy), Todorov (a structuralist anthropologist), and Benhabib (a political scientist working within the framework of Habermasian discourse ethics) are all driven to observe that the social and relational matrix within which the single self arises has generally been ignored in the philosophical tradition—and do so by recalling us to the same simultaneously profound and mundane facts of infant need and dependence.

The reminder that we were infants before being persons—that we are essentially parented beings—will inevitably strike many readers as a psychoanalytic discovery or, indeed, as *the* discovery of psychoanalysis. The philosophical influences on the origins of psychoanalysis aside, it is worth considering the possibility that the confluence of psychoanalytic and philosophical critiques of autonomy might not represent a finding but (to paraphrase Freud) a *re*-finding that the individual is ineluctably, constitutively dependent on others, a *re*-finding of the pathos and implications of that dependence.[14] Contention between the two fields has unfortunately obscured and simplified the intellectual history they share, a small part of which is represented in the works that are the focus of this book. It may be important to ask *why* so much contemporary thinking about individuals recalls us to that obvious, common truth which Hobbes turned aside from, but my own question is, rather, *when* did we forget we were born and raised? The necessary presence of other persons may be something we now, again, take for granted as constitutive of individual formation, but the preparation for its recollection may go back even farther than we typically look for it, back to places where we would not expect to find it.

Philosophy with Literature, Enlightenment with Romanticism

While one need not look too far or too deeply into enlightenment philosophy and romantic literature to discover individual selves conceived as detached and independent, this book asks whether a certain dialectical formation in intellectual history itself—whereby an autonomous subject has been both positively presented as an achievement and negatively identified as an object of critique—has made it difficult to gauge the depth of the fissures within the material that history describes.[15] Is it possible for a single text to function as both paradigm and counter-paradigm of a given idea, for it to be understood in its own time or in our time as the expression of two mutually exclusive ideas? Such theoretical questions arise in interpretive practice, in the struggle to account for the detailed workings and troubling specificities of particular texts— even, perhaps especially, texts that seem familiar in advance of a first reading. At the core of *Isolated Cases* are three powerful but distinctive approaches to the problem of how to make apparent what is evaded, denied, or disowned in the claims of originary autonomy on which the most widely accepted theories of mind and morals in the period are based. Jean-Jacques Rousseau's *Discourse on the Origins of Inequality among Men*, William Wordsworth's *Prelude*, and Mary Shelley's *Frankenstein* form an arc of critical argument and imagination in the history of the autonomous subject so coincident with that history as to generally be seen as cohering with it rather than straining against it. My title is meant to gesture toward the complex evidentiary role of instances in the works I discuss and their reception. From Rousseau's natural man to Shelley's monstrous creature, from Locke's isolated philosophical mind to Wordsworth's remembrances of solitary youth, the texts in which these figures are constructed present remarkably nuanced reflections on their own conceptualizations. The isolation of my cases both allows them to be studied as discrete instances and also makes them exceptional, and therefore in need of close attention.

Rousseau's *Discourse on the Origins of Inequality amongst Men* (1755) is a locus classicus of the premise of original independence. And yet, as recent work in a variety of fields has begun to suggest, the longing for primitive life with which Rousseau was and is still so often associated is actually misconceived when it is taken either as a vision of the past or as an object of nostalgic yearning.[16] His hypothesis of an original state in which human beings lead solitary and self-sufficient lives is pursued rigorously and nonteleologically to the point of generating a crucial theoretical impasse: the movement from "nature" to "society" is not presumed to be inevitable so that the impossibility of constructing a logical or causal transition from asocial independence to social life is insistently foregrounded. The longing to "return" to a natural state is exposed as a longing for existential otherness, a longing to be something other than—rather than more essentially—human. I structure my analysis of the *Discourse on Inequality* (in chapters 2 and 3) around the complex reception of the hypothetical state described in this seminal work, in efforts to see it as somehow empirically verifiable. What might it mean to take as true what Rousseau offers as conjectural, to identify an impossible fantasy with such concrete objects of knowledge as primates, or with such spectacularly exceptional cases as the various "savage" children who were objects of fascination throughout the eighteenth century?

Wordsworth's *Prelude* (1805/1850) is both a splendid indulgence in the myth of a return to the state of nature and a definitive relegation of such an origin to the realm of lyric invention. The poet's history of the "growth of a mind" (the focus of chapter 4) recounts the enabling virtues and possibilities of imagining one's self formed apart from others, but it does so even as it makes clear the inevitable factitiousness of the kind of life story it tells, enclosing the poet's recollections within a narrative frame that insistently makes present the intersubjective context on which the poet's imagination of autonomy depends.

If Rousseau's *Discourse* and Wordsworth's *Prelude* are cases in which the questioning and repudiation of originary independence are paradoxically achieved by theoretical and imaginative indulgence in that very ideal, Mary Shelley's *Frankenstein* (1818) differs in explicitly casting its story of the birth and formation of a uniquely solitary individual as a supernatural event. The fictional structure allows for a rendering of isolated individual development that gestures toward verisimilitude while at the same time decisively reconceiving the ideal of original independence as a monstrous and aberrant version of the human. The paradox of the novel (explored in chapter 5) is one of formal displacement and estrangement whereby philosophical elements that, in another context, would be taken for a normative model of intellectual development are rendered, or exposed as, fantastic.

The figures of Rousseau's natural man, Wordsworth's "child of nature," and Shelley's monster have a critical philosophical power most apparent when set against antithetical reconstructions of individual history that would trace the development of each thought and idea back to an originally solitary and fundamentally independent mind. Accordingly *Isolated Cases* begins with Locke's *Essay concerning Human Understanding* (chapter 1) as perhaps the most influential philosophical narrative of an isolated "mind" developing from simple sensations to complex ideas, and concludes with John Stuart Mill's *Autobiography* (composed 1853, published 1873) (chapter 6), a seminal nineteenth-century life story that is at once a poignant transmission and striking indictment of the Lockean legacy.

One trajectory of the argument of *Isolated Cases* follows the self-sufficient inward subject who is the protagonist of Locke's *Essay* from an enlightenment origin as a figure of normativity, a theoretical model for all minds, to its nineteenth-century manifestations as tragic anomaly—as a monster who has the upbringing of a philosopher and as a philosopher made monstrous by preternatural cultivation of the mind alone. Shelley's *Frankenstein* and Mill's *Autobiography* are perhaps the clearest repudiations of self-determination as a starting point for reflection on individual formation, but Rousseau's *Discourse* and Wordsworth's *Prelude* are equally powerful renunciations of autonomy. This is not to say that these texts are related solely on the terms defined in *Isolated Cases*. Each of the nineteenth-century narratives included in *Isolated Cases* is informed by eighteenth-century philosophical precedents, and all are substantively engaged with topics (including education, influence, the role of literature in self-discovery and self-definition, the mutually exclusive spheres of intellectual pursuit and affectional life, the tempering of fantasies of uniqueness with fears of solitariness) that deserve to be pursued across the lines of historical periodization that the works themselves cross. The connections between individual texts, it is worth emphasizing, are both historically specific and significant: Locke is Rousseau's principal target at a crucial juncture in the second *Discourse;* Locke's *Essay* and Rousseau's *Discourse* are imaginatively transformed sources in the *Prelude* and in *Frankenstein;* Wordsworthian romanticism is presented as the saving alternative to philosophical despair in Mill's

Autobiography, even as Locke's *Essay* remains the framework for Mill's analytic psychology. Intellectual and cultural history bind these particular works together, evincing the persistence of eighteenth-century concepts of individual origins in the nineteenth century, and manifesting a dynamic and critical exchange of ideas between eras.

Without attempting anything like a broad historical narrative, *Isolated Cases* is inspired by recent efforts to think anew the relationship between the enlightenment and romanticism. The "more dialectical account" of the two periods Marshall Brown recently called for would not simply substitute emphasis on the continuities between an "eighteenth century preromanticism and a Romantic post-Enlightenment" for the more familiar stress on romantic "reactions" to eighteenth-century tendencies. It would instead recognize how particular strains of enlightenment thought are "refined and subsumed" by romantic writers. If, in Brown's Hegelian-inflected proposition, "the self-knowledge of Enlightenment is what we know as Romanticism," then recognition of the complex historical relationships between the two periods will necessarily deepen understanding of each period on its own.[17] For example, the particular shape of monstrosity Mary Shelley imagines in *Frankenstein* is both a critical inversion of enlightenment constructions of natural man *and* an acutely accurate version of Rousseau's critique of those same constructions. Neither straightforwardly opposed to its eighteenth-century sources nor straightforwardly incorporating them, the later text complicates our understanding of the material it both draws on and transforms.

As a "counter-enlightenment" *philosophe* or romantic "precursor," standing between or even overlapping the clear outlines of two periods, an undeniably pervasive and for that reason nebulous "influence," Rousseau is the necessary transitional figure at the heart of this project.[18] Posing as much a formal challenge as a historical one, the diversity of his works (including novels, philosophical essays, treatises, autobiographies, and more) demands an interdisciplinary engagement approaching that which (it is useful to recall) many of his nineteenth-century readers brought to bear. The body of his works, moreover, presents an exemplary case of the dynamic relationship between philosophical and literary writing that is typical of the period from enlightenment to romanticism. His principal subjects—solitude, nature, liberty, social structure, trust, corruption, virtue—are not separately explored in literary and philosophical texts but are diffused throughout works that mingle facts and fabulations, arguments and entreaties, appeals to reason and to sentiment.

Any student of the eighteenth and early nineteenth centuries knows that the style and subject matter of literary and philosophical works are not as distinct as they are today, or even as they would become late in the nineteenth century.[19] But to see that the boundaries between literary forms and genres, including expository or nonfictional modes, are fluid does not help us understand the relations between works which make quite different claims about their descriptive or normative value—or lack thereof. Philosophy "and" literature in this period do not amount to undifferentiated textual material but constitute a field of subtle variations in which specific formal distinctions can make significant conceptual differences.

Ironically philosophers, more than literary critics, have insisted, in recent years, on the difference that literary forms and representations can make in radically modifying theoretical approaches. Moral philosophers especially have come to look to literary texts for complex forms of representation, contextualization, and exemplification. It bears emphasizing that it is most often to nineteenth-century literature that philosophers have turned to enrich modes of ethical investigation that have their sources in the enlightenment.[20] One might speculate in passing that the persistent return to this period is itself evidence that some of the most substantive responses to, and transformations of, problems raised in eighteenth-century philosophical writing took *literary* form in the nineteenth century.

Philosophical Subjects

"Abstract," "ghostly," shaped from "loss" and "deprivation," victim of an "illusion" of its own unified integrity—these are some of the terms used by the neo-Aristotelian ethical philosopher Alasdair MacIntyre in his provocative 1981 study, *After Virtue*, to describe the kind of subjectivity constructed by enlightenment thinkers such as Locke, Berkeley, and Butler.[21] An "urge to escape the finitude of one's time and place" in a doomed attempt to "compare ourselves with something absolute": so the contemporary neo-pragmatist Richard Rorty characterizes both the scientific and transcendental aspirations of post-Cartesian philosophy.[22] "Stripped of all constitutive attachments," the "antecedently individuated subject" central to liberal political theories from Locke to Rawls, according to the communitarian political philosopher Michael Sandel, is presented as the "agent of choices [it does] not really choose," barred from the knowledge that it "move[s] in a history [it] neither summon[s] nor command[s]."[23] Though clearly resonant with the substance of French poststructuralist critiques of the subject that are familiar to literary critics, these representative revaluations of the enlightenment legacy have yet to find a firm place in literary studies. Whatever else might be said about the gap between the enthusiastic advocacy and actual practice of interdisciplinarity, I would venture to suggest that (with few exceptions) the widespread neglect and even dismissal of significant and related currents within philosophy threatens to leave literary critics constrained within strangely self-imposed limits on the ways that we pursue the implications of the paradigmatic shift in the understanding of individualism that has taken place in both fields.[24]

Isolated Cases aims, in part, to complicate the simpler forms of juxtaposition between a past commitment to an illusory autonomous self and recent demystification of that self. The critical imagination of autonomy identified through the readings presented here touches on several related but distinct developments in contemporary philosophy. The communitarian imperative to rethink individualism is clearly akin to feminist critiques of the ostensible centrality of autonomy in the philosophical tradition. To these two broad trends we must add the equally feminist identification of counterstrains within that tradition as well as the complex engagement with ethics running through a certain line of Wittgensteinian interpretation. I will touch briefly on each of these in turn, but first a note on terminology is in order.

o o o

The terms *autonomy* and *independence* share as primary definitions the idea of being "self-governing." Earliest usages of both terms in this sense—referring either to the will of a political entity or of a person— date to roughly the same period (between 1611 and 1640, the age of Hobbes and Descartes). *Independence*, with its extended definitions of freedom from authority, influence, and other forms of reliance on others, has broader application than *autonomy*, but the terms are largely synonymous. To be independent, as the *Oxford English Dictionary* defines it, is to be "self-governing, autonomous, free"; to be autonomous is to be "self-governing, independent."

Since Kant, however, *autonomy* has often been used among philosophers to refer to freedom of the will in a more narrow and specialized sense. The term is central to Kant's theorization of moral judgment as free from the contingencies of circumstances including the agent's own empirically determined needs, feelings, and inclinations. The concept of *moral* autonomy, in particular, is thus associated with a Kantian standpoint in ethical theory as it has been developed since his foundational work.[25] Nevertheless, *autonomy* has lately acquired a broader range of meaning in two contexts especially relevant for this study: the history of philosophy and evolving feminist theorization of a "relational" self.

Historians of philosophy recognize that the ideal of moral autonomy represents one development from conceptions of the individual in liberal political philosophies of the modern (i.e., post-Renaissance) period—conceptions that in turn are associated with new theories of psychology and cognition. Contention over application of the term can be seen as symptomatic of the recasting of questions about the historical and theoretical foundations of individual identity. Schneewind, whose formidable historical study traces the origins of Kantian autonomy from ideas of self-governance extending back to Montaigne, remains invested in a restricted application of the term. And yet, notwithstanding his assertion that "metaphysical, epistemological, sociological, psychological, or language-based theories of the self's nature and formation have no bearing on the validity of the idea of autonomy," the term has evidently broadened to include all the dimensions Schneewind attempts to foreclose.[26] Feminist philosophers and communitarians, in particular, have pioneered a wider usage of the term by insisting on the "nature of the connection between theories of the *self* and moral theories."[27] In its broader usage, *autonomy* frequently occurs as a negative term against which to define an alternative position; so, for example, Simon Blackburn explains "the centrality of autonomy is challenged by [those] . . . who see it as a fantasy that masks the social and personal springs of all thought and action."[28] Negative inflections aside, in selecting a title for this book, my preference has been for the term *autonomy* because it is within the interpretive frameworks made possible by its broader application among feminists and among historians of philosophy that I locate my own approach.

What is stressed in the term *autonomy* (in the wider usage it currently enjoys) are the ideas of self-sufficiency and self-determination as *constituting* the individual in some fundamental sense. Although literally synonymous with *independence*, the latter term carries with it connotations of political rights and individualism that figure in several of the texts I analyze but are not directly engaged in this study. At the same time, the concept of autonomy as an ethical principle, and especially recent philosophical efforts to reconceive moral autonomy—even Kantian autonomy—from within a social or relational matrix *are* germane to the ambivalent and anxious formulations of the ideal that are my focus.[29] In the course of the book, however, following the *Oxford English Dictionary*, I tend to use the terms *autonomy* and *independence* almost interchangeably to refer to a constitutive *absence*, or *lack* of dependence and relation, in accounts of human origins and individual development.

o o o

The communitarian argument with liberal political theories is important to this book both for its insistence on a view of the self as "encumbered" by "constitutive attachments" (by which is meant necessarily "situated" within specific historical, social, institutional, cultural, and familial milieux) and in the derivation of this view from a critical reading of enlightenment natural law philosophies.[30] The critique extends from the field of political theory to moral philosophy. In particular, feminist efforts to theorize the role of emotions, attachments, communal structures, and complex contexts in ethical deliberation implicitly identify all these areas of attention as missing or inadequately addressed by the two late-eighteenth-century models—Kantian and Utilitarian—that have framed contemporary debates in moral philosophy. This charge is especially notable because the Kantian and Utilitarian models are usually opposed to each other, and their abstractions of the moral agent and deliberative situation are radically different. Broadly speaking, the empiricist foundation of Benthamite constructions of the subject can be seen to reduce motivation to the self-centered pursuit of pleasure and avoidance of pain. Kantian emphasis on the universality and rationality of moral judgment, by contrast, can be understood as excluding concern for particular consequences, circumstances, feelings, and even desires from the deliberations of the moral reasoner. Advocates of a "relational" or "communitarian" view of the self cut through these distinctions, as they see both these dominant modern moral philosophies as failing to incorporate the basic fact of human sociability into their accounts of agency.[31]

Communitarian challenges to liberal theory coincided with a remarkable explosion of specifically feminist approaches within philosophy from the 1970s forward that similarly focused on a radical revaluation of individualism. Critics such as Carole Pateman and Christine Di Stefano have vividly demonstrated the manner in which contractarian imaginations of self-sufficient persons entering into compact with one another expunge the social origins and ties that bring individuals into being in the first place.[32] Epistemologists such as Lorraine Code, Sandra Harding, and Susan Bordo have focused on how classic constructions of a solitary, introspective knowledge-seeking mind (in Descartes, Locke, and others) fail to account for the social preconditions of learning.[33] Moreover, in identifying *isolation* itself as common to both the radical atomism of political and ethical theories and the individualistic ontologies of philosophies of mind originating in the late seventeenth century, these thinkers have also restored some of the historical connections between specialized fields or between opposed positions within the discipline.[34]

The revisionary interpretations of enlightenment texts that have become possible in the wake of varied critical examinations of autonomy are more important for *Isolated Cases* than broad indictments of the tradition. Annette Baier's studies of passion, sentiment, and trust in Hume, for example, renew attention to neglected eighteenth-century theories of moral sense and natural benevolence, while, in a radical and powerful rethinking of the grounds and implications of Kantian ethics, Christine Korsgaard interprets this most influential modern conceptualization of autonomy as necessarily embedded in and arising out of intersubjective relations.[35] These interpretive efforts identify counter-strains or counter-themes within the philosophical canon (or, in the case of Kant, within the interpretive canon built around a particular author) and are important examples of analyses that have fully absorbed the critical insights of contemporary thought while allowing those insights to enrich and complicate canonical texts rather than to define them as inevitably representative of "traditional models of subjectivity" or "Western metaphysics." That historical traditions are complex and multivalent, and that philosophical arguments can arise from and contain unsettling compromises, misgivings, and uneasy resolutions would seem to be points of departure for analysis—certainly not discoveries. Still, the observation bears repeating given unfortunate tendencies to imagine a generalized modern philosophy largely devoted to the invention and promotion of a "sovereign, rational consciousness." Seyla Benhabib is not alone in pointing to "the spell of a meta-narrative" about the history of philosophy among some "poststructuralist" critics.[36]

Critical disenchantment with traditional conceptualization of persons and minds need not preclude—and might actually even make possible—the recovery of dissident strains *within* canonical philosophical writing.

The failed resolutions, unfinished ostensible narratives, and paradoxical paths of argument I find in the texts at the heart of this book make it difficult to assimilate them to the relatively unified intellectual history of subjectivity which the most sweeping genealogical critiques tend to assume. In the case of Rousseau especially, who (along with Kant) is generally regarded as the champion of a kind of idealized solitary individualism, the challenge lies in understanding how his works belong to the main currents of enlightenment thinking about human nature while proceeding with a reading detailed enough to show why the works compel a revaluation of the very categories ("independence," "nature") through which they are most often studied.

My approach has been shaped, in part, by the "diagnosis" of traditional philosophical concerns undertaken in Wittgenstein's *Philosophical Investigations*, and its extension in Stanley Cavell's studies of philosophy and literature, both of which evoke the powerful pathos driving fantasies of autonomy. The dismantling of concepts of the self found in Wittgenstein's work has inspired comparison to the unstinting demystifications of Freud and Nietzsche, though he offers nothing so evidently systematic as the former nor anything so conspicuously bold as the latter. "When philosophers use a word—'knowledge,' 'being,' 'object,' 'I,' 'proposition,' 'name,'—and try to grasp the essence of the thing," observes Wittgenstein, "one must always ask oneself: is the word ever actually used this way in the language game which is its original home?—What *we* do is bring words back from their metaphysical to their everyday use." The remark forms part of an important series in the *Investigations* in which Wittgenstein identifies his inquiry as "grammatical" (as opposed to "theoretical" and "metaphysical"), aimed at dispelling philosophical "illusions" (such as an "ideal" of perfect clarity, an "order ... common to both world and thought," an "incomparable essence of language") by "looking into the workings of our language," by "assembling reminders" of the "familiar" and the "ordinary."[37]

Wittgenstein's challenge to the notional interiority of the mind entails showing how a sense of the ineluctable privacy of the self and its thoughts arises from and depends on the deeply shared, inherited, yet nonsystematic network of agreements underlying the use and understanding of language. The *Investigations* finds or renders incoherent the utterances of a subject sure of what goes on "inside" of himself but not of others, worried about whether words convey "real" intentions, convinced that his "unique" experiences (of colors, of pain, of love, of hope) can only be imperfectly expressed. But how does it do so? It is not through straightforward assertion of positions that Wittgensteinian argument compels. His self-described task of recovering words from their estranging philosophical uses places particular emphasis on the effort to imagine the occasion that leads the thinker astray in language. "Understanding from the inside [a view one wants to criticize] is methodologically fundamental," proposes Cavell, not only for purposes of critique but also, perhaps most importantly, so as to recover the insight, the question, the worry leading to the extraordinary, or incoherent, or mystifying view. When philosophy drives one to "abandon a certain combination of words as senseless," writes Wittgenstein, the "resignation" entailed is "one of feeling and not of intellect. . . . It can be difficult not to use an expression, just as it is difficult to hold back tears, or an outburst of anger." The orientation toward error or illusion is not one of straightforward indictment, then, but of what has been described by others as "empathic," "active reenactment of philosophical conflict," and of what Wittgenstein himself described as a therapeutic practice aimed at "resistances of the will."[38] Whether thus arriving at (being reminded of, recovering) the "language of everyday" results in the dissolution of philosophical problems, or whether it compels one to recognize certain difficulties while forswearing the temptation to resolve them, what is pressed upon us is acceptance of what Wittgenstein calls the "given," what Cavell calls "finitude," and what Cora Diamond calls the "realistic spirit."[39]

In dwelling on the limitations of explanation, the depths and subtleties of everyday practices, and in acknowledging the desires and temptations at work in philosophical argument, many readers see, in Wittgenstein's work on language, that elusive point at which ethical aspiration and psychoanalytic insight intersect. In Cavell's interpretation: "Wittgenstein wishes an acknowledgment of human limitation that does not leave us chafed by our own skin, by a sense of powerlessness to penetrate beyond the human conditions of knowledge." But as Naomi Scheman cautions, admission of finitude does not imply acquiescence: "to come to terms with the unseemly contingencies of being human [is] not to accept everything as we find it," she writes, "but to give up on the fantasy of being saved from the human condition, or of being in our truest natures not really defined by it."[40] On this view, the conditions of mortality, encumbrance, and dependence are precisely what the philosopher tries to save us from with, for example, the promise of a transcendent or "unconditioned" or autonomous standpoint (of reason or judgment). But the resistance to philosophical temptation that Cavell and Scheman understand as central to Wittgenstein's project applies equally to powerful counter-fantasies of our being doomed by the human condition—existentially defined by "lack," for example, governed by intrinsically unsatisfiable desire, destined to never really recognize or be recognized by others.[41]

o o o

The critical implications of what I have described as a Wittgensteinian approach to philosophical problems of mind and meaning and agreement are inextricably bound up with a method of dramatizing argument that elicits and requires recognition of the constitutive passions and affect shaping philosophical utterances. But why take on this task? Is analysis not compromised by the effort to indulge in and reconstruct the very perspective—perhaps even to feel the feelings—that lead to the errors one hopes to expose? The answer to these questions depends, in part, on how—perhaps also whether—the difference between the philosophical and the "everyday" is to be valued. Are philosophical fantasies of deep psychological inwardness and autonomy extraordinary metastases of everyday afflictions (evasions, for example, of the risks of disclosure and dependence)? Or are those fantasies representative of—continuous with and proportionate to—a grave avoidance of existential verities built into the "everyday" itself? One might say that one effect of Wittgenstein's method is to shift between these alternative diagnoses, and thus to keep open the question of what a philosophical illusion can bring to light.

The Anxious Imagination of Autonomy

I said at the outset that the repudiations of autonomy at the center of this study do not straightforwardly affirm dependence and relation as foundational facts against the bold, counterintuitive hypothesis that the "natural" state of human beings is—or was—other than what we commonly observe. Eighteenth-century theorists of natural sociability such as Shaftesbury, Francis Hutcheson, and Hume did indeed reassert the obvious against the Hobbesian vision of original independence. However, if repudiation of Hobbes were merely a matter of calling attention to the easily observable conditions of human infancy, then Shaftesbury's reminder that "'tis evident" that creatures physically constituted like human beings "can no more... abstain from society than they can possibly preserve themselves without it" ought to have sufficed as counterargument. The failure of such affirmations to compel, to valuably count, only confirms that Hobbes's philosophical efforts are aimed at the determination of a truth about the "natural state of men" that is fundamentally nonempirical—and if nonempirical, then what? What can count as evidence against a self-evidently counterfactual representation?

Hobbes's notorious invitation to "consider men as if but even now sprung out of the earth and suddenly, like mushrooms, come to full maturity without all kind of engagement to each other" *flamboyantly* veers away from the familiar, the recognizable, and the obvious facts of how human beings come into the world.[42] It does not ask to be accepted or denied on grounds we (think we) know but solicits our complicity in an act of imagination, an act of forgetting that we do *in fact* come to maturity with all kinds of engagement to one another. It is by means of our complicity that its surmise is verified, but how and why are we compelled? What do we learn by looking away from what we know to be true?

The power of the idea of an originally independent or self-made individual never derived from its being mistaken for a fact (insofar as it claimed that status, it was contested from the outset) but from the theoretical and imaginative implications of conceiving the individual as such, from the barely articulated needs and desires such an idea could meet, and the barely acknowledged anxieties and fears it could attempt to quell. The fears forestalled by the *idea* of coming into being without all kinds of engagement are perhaps as self-evident as the facts of childhood weakness and dependence—and perhaps related to those facts. Instead of seeing the self at the mercy of and under the influence of others, the imagination of autonomy enables the articulation of possibilities of self-determination and independence from authority, allows for a conception of those possibilities as fundamental or "natural." Freedom (of thought and action, from bondage and suasion) is inextricably bound up with the idea of self-sufficiency from Descartes's resolution "to escape tutelage" and "to search for no other knowledge than what I could find within myself" to Kant's famous definition of "enlightenment" as liberation from tutelage.[43]

A crucial and consequential obfuscation occurs when possibilities of independence and freedom that might be understood as *aims* are projected backward onto hypothetical and fantastic first stages of individual development or human history and thus become theories or myths of originary independence. Reenvisioned as actually fundamental, the ideal or aspiration to autonomy in theories of the understanding presents the individual as the self-begotten, self-sufficient hero of a narrative of coming into knowledge of the world around him, proceeding from sensation to the construction of ideas and eventually to reasoned and nuanced judgment. In the related narrative of political theory, the protagonist is a self-sufficient man reasonable enough to trade some measure of his natural liberty for greater security by voluntarily entering into a compact with other equally free and independent persons. Locke's *Essay concerning Human Understanding* and *Second Treatise of Government* are seminal examples of the slippage between the establishment of theoretical grounds and the hypothesizing of actual beginning foundations: the *Second Treatise* identifies the "State all Men are naturally in" *at first* as a "State of perfect Freedom," and the *Essay* is introduced as an inquiry into "the *Original*, Certainty, and Extent of humane Knowledge."[44]

What is the difference between independence *imagined* as an original condition and an imaginary original condition of independence? The implications of the confusion over the theoretical status of "origins" are worth pausing over. I have pointed to two stages in Hobbes's imagination of autonomy: first the invitation to make believe ("as if but now sprung . . .") in order to arrive at the real nature of human beings and, second, the arrival at a view independent of what we commonly know about how we in fact come to maturity (precisely *not* sprung spontaneously out of the earth). The first stage, proposing that the real can be approached by forgetting what we already know, establishes the terms on which to advance a view of human nature, while the second stage presents a specific view, but surely not the only one imaginable. Challenges to Hobbes, which took (and still take) the form of reasserting the obvious facts of our original dependence, fail as repudiations because they do not participate in the hypothetical reasoning through which Hobbes advances his argument. They point to a reality that Hobbes openly proposes we set aside in order to arrive at a truth that is somehow truer than what we observe daily. They remind us of what we are quite deliberately (and perhaps for good reasons) choosing to forget.

The critical visions of original independence studied in this book recognize the power of the first "as if" and stake their ground of contention there. Against the invitation to turn away from something obvious, common, but evidently worrisome and troubling, only a powerful counter-imagination can compel a turn back to the obvious. Rousseau, Wordsworth, Shelley, and Mill envisage original independence in such a way as to turn its *theoretical* gains into losses. The vital presence of other persons is affirmed in primal experiential terms (Rousseau's inventors of language are inspired to expression by the newly discovered "pleasure of not being alone," for example, and Wordsworth's "blessed babe" is indeed in a state of subjection, but one that vitally connects him to the world through the "beloved presence" of another), but more emphatically and effectively, the implications of conceiving the individual as solitary and self-sufficient are negatively imagined and inflected. The invitation to conceive of oneself as spontaneously springing from the earth, as a mushroom does, or as a seed sown on a wild field, elicits corresponding recollections of being simply cast out, belonging to and with no one. However, in Locke and in other theorists whose reflections on social and individual development are premised on isolation and self-sufficiency, the Hobbesian invitation to set aside what we commonly know is never proffered. The hypothesis of original independence proceeds as though there were no initial "as if." The deliberate turn away from the self-evident is obfuscated. The choice to forget is forgotten. Consequently, in a formidable theoretical construction such as Locke's, where independence and self-sufficiency are assumed as primary and natural first stages, the fear of being enslaved or beholden that provokes the imagination of autonomy becomes *implicit*, the repressed source of the reenvisioned origin. Clearing up the confusion between imaginary and actual origin that one finds in Locke involves not only the recasting of independence as an impossible—and indeed undesirable—origin for the individual but also involves a return to the repressed source of the confusion, to the fears or anxieties or uncertainties that compelled the turn away from the obvious.

Lockean claims to originary autonomy are repudiated in figures of an emphatically negative cast; thus instead of a (natural) man living "according to reason" while enjoying "perfect freedom," Rousseau presents an "animal" with "neither foresight nor curiosity," whose "imagination depicts nothing to him, [whose] heart asks nothing of him." In Wordsworthian terms, to be "by nature free, equal, and independent" is also to be unsupported by affection, "left alone, seeking the visible world nor knowing why." To be "dependent on none and related to none" is not to have been born perfect, as Adam, but to be monstrously incomplete, an "abortion" of the human (in Shelley's rendering). These troubled and troubling imaginations of independence emphasize something as obvious about autonomy as the freedom from bondage or tutelage it implies—an isolation that, when taken to be the prevailing condition of individual development, confines the individual within a state of lonely and insuperable incommunicability. Rousseau's natural man is doomed to dwell in the ignorance of pre-linguistic immediacy; Wordsworth defines the "point" in the soul "where all stand single" as a place words never reach; Shelley's monster is abandoned to a condition of independence that is also one of permanent exclusion; Mill understands the inexpressible privacy of his pain as the irremediable effect of his philosophical formation. It is as if, in choosing to imagine ourselves as originally independent of others, we turn away from future possibilities of relation as well, as if not needing others also means neither loving nor being loved.

The facts of subjection and attachment to others are those which a philosophy such as Locke's invites us to reimagine. In the idealization of self-sufficiency, our first love is never lost, our first attachments never broken, but then where and when and how is what Mill calls "the love of loving" ever to originate? To see Wordsworth's "blessed babe" and Shelley's abandoned creature together is to see the condition of being "dependent and related" as inseparable from the condition of being in the "beloved presence" of others. This recollection of dependence (for that is undeniably what it is) again begs the question of what compels us to accept the invitation to imagine ourselves as naturally without all kinds of social and affective bonds.

I want to suggest that it is by no means only, perhaps not even principally, the suppression of the *original* condition of dependence that allows for bold and assertive constructions of the individual as fundamentally independent, but a suppression of anxieties that afflict the mature individual even more poignantly (in some ways) than the child. Rousseau, for example, is less concerned with the origins of anxiety in childhood fear and dependence than in making manifest the connection between fantasies of autonomy and the actual anxieties bound up with vulnerabilities to longing, loss, and to love itself that afflict us throughout life. Because discussion of an anxiety associated with (though not reducible to) the dependence of infancy and childhood often arises in the following chapters, Freud's efforts to grapple with the etiology of anxiety—an affect he consistently traced back to the trauma of birth and separation from the mother—are worth recalling here, as much for their similarity to, as for their difference from, the views of his philosophical forebears. In the fluid interplay across the boundaries of phylogenetic inheritance and individual psychic experience, Freud's account of anxiety (especially in its earliest formulations in *The Three Essays on the History of Sexuality* and the *Introductory Lectures on Psychoanalysis*) reveals its debt to enlightenment theorization of the original human condition. The analysis of childhood phobias (of darkness, of solitude, and of strangers) identifies two elements: fears that may be traceable to the "behavior of prehistoric men" and that have a tenuous but not irrational connection to real dangers and needs, and a longing bound up with the actual experience of loss and disappointment. "A child is not afraid of . . . strangers because he attributes evil intentions to them and compares his weakness to their strength, and accordingly assesses them as dangers to his existence," writes Freud in an analysis that evocatively defines the fear and suspicion of others we may call Hobbesian as a cover for the anxieties attendant on childhood love and longing: "A child who is mistrustful in this way . . . is a theoretical construction that has quite miscarried. A child is frightened of a strange face because he is adjusted to the sight of a familiar and beloved figure. . . . It is his disappointment and longing that are transformed into anxiety."[45]

While Freud and his followers have accustomed us to thinking about the persistence of childhood anxieties in later life, this order is in some measure reversed in the texts that are the focus of this book. It is not so much the fact that we *were* once weak and dependent that is troublesome and that provokes fantasies of original autonomy, but a present and uncomfortable sense of vulnerability for which the figure of infantile need may well be an emblematic reminder. Wordsworth's "blessed babe" is, necessarily, a "frail creature . . . helpless as frail," but it is ultimately aloneness, not dependence, that profoundly afflicts and troubles the self imagined in *The Prelude*. The unique efficacy of the critical imaginations of origins and development at the heart of this book lies not only in how they present individuals as essentially related to and formed by others but also in their insistent articulation of the very fears that drive the denial of neediness and its reinvention as original freedom and independence. In other words, the rejection of myths of self-origination does not lead to diminution or denial of the intersubjective anxieties that generate the desire to conceive oneself as independent in the first place, but to their exposure. If, as I suggested above, the kind of confusion between imaginary and actual origin that one finds in Locke can only be cleared up by returning to its source in a repressed act of forgetting, then some of the work of clarification is performed by the reminder of the fears and risks that lead us to imagine love as a kind of bondage or subjection.[46] Hence, while "relation and dependence" are identified as constitutive of human-ness in *Frankenstein*, the novel's intercalated tales of orphans, betrayals, and the unjust execution of the law present life with and among others as itself monstrous. Written after the loss of the beloved, the longed-for openness to longing recounted in John Stuart Mill's *Autobiography* necessarily incorporates its subject's susceptibility to bereavement. Wordsworth is "saved" from moral despair by the "living help" of a friend and a sister, but the recovery of his "true self" entails recognition of an opaque world of moral relations in which we are liable to betray and fail one another, in which only the solitary can retain a "just equipoise of love."

Unlike other proponents of the constitutive force of sociality from this period, the writers and thinkers who figure prominently in this book avoid a sentimentality about the need of others that is just as implausible as the myths of robust originary independence. What troubles Shaftesbury, Francis Hutcheson, and other philosophers of moral sense is not so much the strange imagination of human origins that Hobbes's theory demands, but the consequent characterization of the individual as selfish and hostile toward others. Against this view, the naturally sociable human being is posited as innately inclined toward benevolence: the "helpless, weak" condition of the human infant, according to Shaftesbury, is itself enough to "force [us] to own" that the human being is "made rational and sociable, and can no otherwise increase or subsist than in that social Intercourse and Community which is his *Natural State*."[47] While explicit disagreement with the premise of original independence is a first principle for a significant group of eighteenth-century thinkers deeply opposed to Hobbes's vision of the state of nature, that disagreement is merely instrumental to the quite different theoretical aim of affirming a natural disposition to virtue or benevolence. A hypothesis such as Shaftesbury's works by ignoring anguishing misgivings about social existence that the myth of originally independent individuals is intended to mitigate.

Fear of others predominates in the Hobbesian state of nature, and is the basis or driving force for the aggression that is only superficially its opposite. Dread and suspicion of others are fundamental not only to Hobbes's political theory but also to a particularly individualistic conception of how human beings experience the world and acquire knowledge.[48] Mistrust, defensive hostility, and preemptive efforts at self-protection are the inevitable consequences of epistemological limitation. Human beings cannot see or know one another well enough to trust that the other is not a secret enemy. "Things desired, feared, hoped . . . are so easie to be kept from our knowledge," writes Hobbes in the introduction to *Leviathan*, and—as a necessary consequence—"the characters of man's heart [are] blotted and confounded . . . with dissembling, lying, counterfeiting." Mutual inscrutability is at once an unavoidable epistemological phenomenon and the source of moral corruption, risk, and peril. Rousseau's *Discourse* not only retains precisely this apprehension of vulnerability to others but also presents it as inescapable.[49] The end of the war of all against all that Hobbes envisions as consequent on the social contract represents not only a cessation of hostility but also a peace of mind best understood as the absence, or at least attenuation, of fear. In Rousseau's revision, "the most horrible state of war" is precisely where we are, not an original condition we have escaped.[50] His repudiation of natural independence thus proceeds in full recognition of the anxieties that shape that ideal, and the moral challenge they pose.

The *Discourse on the Origins of Inequality among Men* is central to *Isolated Cases* not only because of its pivotal position in intellectual history but also because it so powerfully represents the individual's subjection to envy, deception, and loss as the constitutive affliction of life among others while at the same time arguing with a relentless rigor that life among others is constitutive of the human being.[51] Apprehension of the painful dilemmas of sociality and of dependence is at the core of the texts under consideration here. The renunciations of originary autonomy traced in this book are uniquely poignant precisely because they also entail an imagination of the individual as weak, vulnerable, subject to betrayal, frustration, disappointment. The acknowledgment of frailty opens up the possibility of uniquely ethical aspirations and desires—imaginations of what individuals might be to one another that have no place in bold and confident assertions of independence.

CHAPTER 1

Locke's Loneliness

Locke typically depicts the world and others in it as intrusions into an enclosed mind. Objects "solicit" the senses, are "conveyed into" the mind, "impressed" on it from the outside, with the sense of the term *outside* extended so as to include the implications of the foreign, the alien, the strange. "Children, when they first come into it, are surrounded with a world of new things," writes Locke, "thus the first Years are usually imploy'd and diverted in looking abroad. Men's Business in them is to acquaint themselves with what is to be found without."[1] Remarkable in this description is not only the casting of childhood interests as adult occupation but also the narrow focus on curiosity about *things* which necessarily excludes the timidity, fear, or aversion (even when mixed with curiosity) with which children often respond to strange new people. Locke's *Essay concerning Human Understanding* nonetheless betrays an acute consciousness of being at the mercy of others, apprehensive of their loss but also wary of their approach.

Such a characterization will seem strange to philosophers and literary critics who have been used to thinking of Locke as the preeminent theoretician of modern individualism, even to those who find constraint or fragility in Locke's representation of individual understanding. The *Essay* offers so rich and sustained a development of the solitary mind's epistemological undertakings that various lines of interpretation simply take it for granted: philosophers such as Derek Parfit still find its arguments relevant to contemporary discussions of psychological continuity and personal identity; feminist theorists such as Annette Baier reprehend its construction of atomistic individualism and the long-lived influence it has had in philosophy of mind.[2] A robust individualism is also assumed by readers who see the *Essay* as failing in pursuit of the very aims it lays out. So, for example, the "stripped-down," "abstract," and "ghostly" subject that Alasdair MacIntyre finds would be present in any theory that does not begin from communitarian premises. Similarly, while Cathy Caruth rightly understands Locke to be engaged in a "project of self-understanding" designed to establish the "self-sufficiency of reason," any such project, she suggests, would be doomed to paradox from the outset by the very form of its argumentation.[3]

Other readers have seen the impasses of Locke's system as ones that he himself identifies, conclusions he is compelled to draw. On this view, the frailty of Lockean understanding appears to be intrinsic to Locke's arguments—an undesirable but unavoidable implication that comes to be foregrounded in the *Essay*. Thus historians of philosophy such as Richard Popkin find Locke espousing a "kind of semi-skepticism and stat[ing] it as if it were an answer to skepticism"; Peter Nidditch observes that Locke's "committed anti-skepticism was at odds with his chief epistemological stance." More boldly, John Richetti sees Locke as practicing a "twisting, strangling" form of analysis designed to "dra[w] a tighter and tighter circle" around the understanding, and S. H. Clark argues that the *Essay* ultimately offers no "locus of ontological permanence" within a mind struggling to conserve its ephemeral glimpses of an "otherwise unknowable reality."[4]

I will be approaching the epistemological vulnerabilities of the Lockean subject from a different angle than either those who see them as manifestations of a necessary conceptual blindness or as part of an entirely controlled commitment to skepticism. I trace them back to the *Essay*'s failure to distinguish between persons and things in the experiential life of the subject—an oversight which can, in its turn, be traced to the *Essay*'s occlusion of the role of other persons in the formation of subjectivity. Such an approach reorients interpretation away from well-rehearsed questions about the relationship between mind and world, or subject and objects, in order to begin to see the traces of philosophical thinking, or attempts to avoid thinking, about the relations between subject and subject.

"Follow a Child . . .": The *Essay* as History?

"Infants, newly come into the World," Locke observes, "are seldom awake, but when either Hunger calls for the Teat, or some Pain . . . forces the mind to perceive, and attend to it" (2.1.21). The metonymic reduction of caretaker to breast is symptomatic of the *Essay*'s treatment of subject-subject relations as a species of encounter between subject and objects. Other persons are simply a category of perceived matter to the young mind, which familiarizes itself with persons as with any other thing in its environment. "A Child knows his Nurse, and his Cradle, and by degrees the Playthings of a little more advanced Age," but nurse, cradle, and playthings are present for the child in the same way, they exist on the same epistemological plane (1.2.27). "After some time, [the mind] begins to know the *Objects*, which being the most familiar with it, have made lasting Impressions," Locke explains, "*Thus* it comes, by degrees, to know the *Persons* it daily converses with, and distinguish them from Strangers" (2.1.22; emphases added), but the differences between the child's familiarity with a parent and his awareness of familiar inanimate things pass unconsidered, untheorized.[5] Locke's own *Thoughts concerning Education* (1693–1705) offers a powerful and illuminating contrast to this account.[6] The handling of the child's growing familiarity with a caretaker is close to that of the *Essay* but is inflected with fear and apprehension of loss. The infant's "indifference" to all "objects of sight that do not hurt their eyes" is replaced with anxiety about the absence of, and delight in the presence of, the person who nurses him: "the child apprehends by coming into the arms of a stranger the being taken from what delights and feeds it and every moment supplies its wants, which it often feels, and therefore fears when the nurse is away."[7]

Human beings and inanimate things are equally and similarly "objects" of knowledge in the *Essay* not only because the theory fails to recognize a difference but also because Locke's prose works to blur the distinction, even to render it invisible. The child's gradual acquisition of knowledge is magically made possible by the abstract agency of "time." Newborn children have no ideas in their minds, but, "by degrees, afterwards, *Ideas* come into their Minds" because "things come in their way" (1.4.2); "observe the alterations that time makes, and you shall find. . . [the mind] thinks more, the more it has matter to think on" and "thus [as a result of the alterations made by time] it comes, by degrees, to know the Persons it daily converses with" (2.1.22). To identify "time" as that which effects change and development in the child's mind is precisely to omit the activity of persons in the child's environment, and the child's interaction with them. After all, "things come in their way" only if they are brought to the child, perhaps in response to cries; the child comes to know familiar persons not "by degrees" but by a continuity of experience and what Locke calls "converse." Abstract and passive formulations such as "things come" and "time alters" are subtle and deliberate omissions of parental and caretaking agency in the child's development, an exclusion all the more remarkable given how fully Locke attends to the part other persons play in making things familiar to the child in *Some Thoughts concerning Education*. Familiarity, in that account, involves the attenuation of fear "by gentle degrees," and it is the caretaker who quells fear by "bring[ing] nearer and nearer" to the child the object of his terror, by "diverting [his] thoughts or mixing pleasant and agreeable appearances with it" (§ 115). To admit that a person brings things to a child in this way is to admit the essential role of another in making things in the world not only epistemologically available, but also available as objects of pleasure and not of fear. The absence of this admission in the *Essay* is of momentous consequence to the theory of knowledge that Locke develops; it is the kind of repression bound to return.

Why does no one bring playthings to the infant of the *Essay*? What is at stake theoretically in *not* presenting the child's mind as shaped, even minimally, by the actions of others? Part of the answer is suggested by Locke's telling placement of the fact that children do indeed "receive into their Minds Propositions . . . from their Parents, Nurses, or those about them" within his discussion of "wrong assent, or error" and of the harmful associations that produce incurable phobias, intransigent prejudices, and other forms of irrational fixation (4.20.9; 2.33.3). However, insofar as *Some Thoughts concerning Education* has to do with how best to form and train the young and impressionable mind, it cannot be the case that influence itself is pernicious. The question is, rather, why only its pernicious effects are attended to in the *Essay*.

Let us first consider what is gained by omission.

If what is denied or forgotten in the *Essay* is the idea of the mind as formed in relation and response and reaction to the presence and activity of others, then what is put in its place, affirmed (perhaps even invented) is a particular idea of the individual's independence. Locke's chapter on the origins of ideas culminates in the autonomous achievement of a "footing" for thoughts that may one day "towre above the Clouds": "In time, the Mind comes to reflect on its own *Operations*" and the ideas it thus arrives at "proceeding from Powers intrinsical and proper to it self" represent the "first step a Man makes towards the Discovery of any thing, and the Groundwork, whereon to build all those Notions, which ever he shall have naturally in this World" (2.1.24). Were not time but parents or nurses named as effecting the child's development, then the protagonist of the *Essay* would seem a far less active being. His growing familiarity with the world of nurses and playthings would seem less his own accomplishment; his first steps would not be taken unsupported, the groundwork, rise, and footing for *all* his notions not laid solely by powers intrinsic to himself.

Though nothing in Locke's epistemology would seem to require the denial of a *pre*-autonomous stage of dependence on the nurture of others, the drive to conceive autonomy as the *original* condition is undeniable. It is what distinguishes Locke's project, makes the *Essay* a "history" as well as an "anatomy" of the understanding, as Voltaire famously described it in the *Letters on England:* "So many philosophers having written the romance of the soul, a sage has arrived who has modestly written its history." Voltaire credited Locke with literally "tak[ing] a child at the moment of birth and follow[ing] step by step the progress of its understanding," but insofar as Locke also writes other persons out of the account, his history must also be seen as a heroic fiction of self-determination.[8]

Kant would famously indict the *Essay* for its "fictitiously invented genealogy"; Locke shows the understanding actively ordering perceptions, but the concepts by which that ordering is achieved "show a certificate of birth quite other than that of descent from experiences." What is factitious, according to Kant, is the very attempt to trace the "claims of metaphysics" back to "origins in common experience."[9] The falsification of history that concerns me, however, involves the representation of "common experience" itself in the *Essay*, particularly the representation of the development of the understanding on its own from fundamentally *solitary* origins. "It is inconceivable how a man could, by his own strength alone," progress from "pure sensations to the simplest knowledge": Rousseau's explanation of the impossibility of intellectual progress within a state of nature in which each lives on his own is equally a challenge to a Lockean model of individual epistemic achievement.[10] A text such as Mary Shelley's *Frankenstein* participates in this philosophical conversation, affirming Rousseau's surmise by showing that it is indeed inconceivable to imagine the intellectual formation of an isolated mind and tracing the idea back to a fantastic misconception of human origins. For Kant, Locke's account of the formation of the understanding paradoxically allows for the recognition of the "pure *a priori* concepts" by presenting a theory that shows the concepts to be necessary but that cannot adequately or convincingly account for their origin.

What Rousseau's account of individual formation in the *Second Discourse* (and, in different ways, in *Emile* and the *Confessions*) shares with Shelley's imagination of monstrosity is a recognition of the constitutive role of dependence on, and relation to, other persons. Like Kant's a priori concepts, the shaping presence of other persons seems both necessary for the achievements of understanding that Locke presents in the *Essay*, and yet unaccounted for and missing at the origin. Locke's analysis of knowledge achieved thus appears to lack a key foundational element, leading to conclusions that are either distorted by the exclusion or impossible to conceive of without supplying missing parts or movements.

For Kant, the independence of the understanding is insufficiently realized in the *Essay*; the epistemic autonomy of the subject is, in a sense, even more primal, more essential than Locke would have it. For Rousseau, and even more evidently for Shelley (as I discuss in later chapters), Locke gives the idea of independence an impossible priority and thus an impossible origin. From both perspectives, the Lockean imagination of the understanding as originally independent—"proceeding from Powers intrinsical and proper to it self"—is exposed as somehow inadequate, ambivalent, unsettled. The subject conceived as originally autonomous is no more and no less than a beast for Rousseau. Shelley—who is more exclusively engaged with Locke's *Essay*—creates a subject more closely related to the one Locke imagines, not only in intellectual achievements but also in irremediable and existential loneliness. It is tempting to say that her novel contains the romance of the *Essay* but more precise to say that it imagines the emotions of the mind Locke describes, finding that, as it senses light and darkness, warmth and cold, it must also *feel* its aloneness as pain. It is to the traces of affective life that can be found in the *Essay* that I now turn, particularly to how the unacknowledged presence of others in the life of the mind can be seen to shape Locke's conclusions about the limitations of the understanding.

Alone in a Dark Room

> Only a few of the manifestations of anxiety in children are comprehensible to us . . . when a child is alone, or in the dark, or when it finds itself with an unknown person. . . . These three instances can be reduced to a single condition—namely, that of missing someone who is loved and longed for.
> Sigmund Freud, *Inhibitions, Symptoms and Anxiety*

All that the Lockean understanding achieves on its own is achieved in alone-ness. The exclusion of the influence of others from the very beginning of the history the *Essay* purports to trace not only allows for a theoretical emphasis on the mind's autonomous activity but also places the mind in a setting that can only be described in terms of confinement, apartness, and isolation. The tabula rasa remains the most well known (albeit misattributed) figure for the mind associated with the *Essay*, but its most compelling representation—and the one that, in its ambiguity, would exercise a powerful hold on scientific and literary imaginations of the understanding—is the dark room. The "true *History of the first beginnings of Humane Knowledge*" concludes and culminates with this extended metaphor of internment: "External and internal Sensation, are the only passages that I can find, of Knowledge, to the Understanding. These alone, as far as I can discover, are the Windows by which light is let into this *dark Room*. For, methinks, the *Understanding* is not so much unlike a Closet wholly shut from light, with only some little openings left, to let in external visible Resemblances, or *Ideas* of things without" (2.11.17).

If darkness is the cradle of thought, then, not surprisingly, "Children new-born . . . always turn their Eyes to that part, from whence the Light comes." Vision is the governing sense in Locke's epistemology, but that is not the only reason he emphasizes the newborn's preoccupation with light (instead of, for example, the pain of hunger, the pleasure of satiety, the discomfitures of stillness or movement). Locke does not theorize a *development* in the relative significance of the senses (beginning with smell or touch, for example), but he makes vision doubly primary—not only the most important but the *first* of the senses, an idea with the powerful implication that we are to take the notion of the mind as enclosed and separated in its own space not only as a formal or schematic model but also as a genealogical model. Light, rather than warmth or nourishment, would naturally be the original pleasure for a being conceived as *always having been* alone in darkness.

"Knowing is seeing," Locke states bluntly in *Of the Conduct of the Understanding* (§ 24), but one need not look too closely to identify the epistemological compromises that Locke's use of vision as the epitome of epistemic access to the world compels him to make. As *the* model for compellingly immediate presence, vision may offer the "greatest assurance" of the existence of things, according to Locke ("a Certainty as great, as humane Nature is capable of, concerning the Existence of any thing, but a Man's self alone, and of God " [4.11.2]), but it also unavoidably suggests the limits of certainty. If seeing is being sure, then, once out of sight, the world and others in it must be consigned to the penumbral realm of mere belief or probability—precisely the conclusion that has led many readers of the *Essay* to suggest that Locke "either did not understand or admit the radically skeptical consequences of his epistemology."[11] Given that *"Knowledge extends as far as the present Testimony of our Senses, employ'd about particular Objects, that do then affect them and no farther,"* once a thing slips out of sight, out of reach of the eye, it ceases to be (real). This is the startling implication of Locke's reasonings in the final book of the *Essay*; the Lockean individual is perpetually being left all alone in a frighteningly evanescent world.

> If I saw such a Collection of simple *Ideas*, as is wont to be called *Man*, existing together one minute since, and am now alone, I cannot be certain that the same Man exists now, since there is no necessary connexion of his Existence a minute since, with his Existence now: by a thousand ways he may cease to be, since I had the Testimony of my Senses for his Existence. And if I cannot be certain, that the Man I saw last to day, is now in Being, I can be less certain, that he is so, who hath been longer removed from my Senses, and I have not seen since yesterday, or since last year: and much less can I be certain of the Existence of Men, that I never saw. And therefore though it be highly probable, that Millions of Men do now exist, yet whilst I am alone writing this, I have not the Certainty of it. (4.11.9)

A notable anxiety insinuates itself into many of Locke's thought experiments, not gratuitously but as the affect appropriate to the patterns of reflection most characteristic of the *Essay*'s discursive "I." One such pattern involves simultaneous affirmation of the efficacy of the senses and intimation of realms of reality and certainty that lie beyond the reach of the senses. This motif is perhaps most obvious in the final book of the *Essay* where a refutation of (Cartesian) skepticism on the commonsensical ground that "no body can, in earnest, be so skeptical, as to be uncertain of the Existence of those Things which he sees and feels" is no sooner ventured than qualified by the concession that "our Faculties [are] suited not to the full extent of Being, nor to a perfect, clear, comprehensive Knowledge of things free from all doubt" (4.11.3, 8). Yet consider the specific inflections of the example above. What begins as an argument about the continued existence of "particular objects" once out of sight becomes a meditation on the fate of a particular man, the one "I saw last." That subtle shift betrays a profound appreciation of the difference between persons and things as objects of knowledge that generally goes unacknowledged in the *Essay*. The man I saw last today only "ceases to be" if he has died, and the poignancy of Locke's example lies precisely in the fact that it is true of a person in a way that it cannot be true of a table that he may cease to exist once out of sight. Implicit is a form of loss undisguised by the abstract introduction of the example ("a collection of simple *Ideas* as is wont to be called *Man*") or by the logical yet absurd generalization of the uncertainty about one man no longer present to "Millions of Men."

Locke's reflections begin with an evocation of what can only be called worry—the thousand ways that one man may cease to be—and end with an evocation of solipsistic solitary confinement, in which the condition of being "alone, writing" necessarily leads the thinker to find it logically possible that no one else now exists. The fear of having lost the other leads to the heightened sensation of isolation and, taken *this* way, the seeming depersonalization of the case (from one man to millions of men) may be read as an amplification of its affect (if he is lost, then I am alone in the world). A particular narrative and even emotional arc might be traced, along which the mind in a dark room illumined only by the presence and immediacy of visual impressions—the culminating figure in Locke's account of the "first beginnings of Humane Knowledge"—becomes father to the figure of the philosopher alone, fretting over all the ways that an other may be lost to him once out of his sight. The vulnerability exposed in this reflection on the possibility of loss intimates an intersubjective core of experience that the *Essay* largely fails to acknowledge.

The repression of the heteronomy of childhood entailed by Locke's construction of an originally independent mind returns here in the form of epistemological constraints that leave the isolated mind at once afraid of others and afraid of being alone, on its own and yet longing.[12] The presence and *agency* of other persons are given no special place in Locke's account of the "earliest era of the understanding," but how appropriate to find that involuntary memories are personified in the *Essay*—"start[ing] up in our Minds of their own accord," and "rouzed and tumbled out of their dark Cells, into open Day-light" (2.10.7), as if raised from the dead. The mind is not, after all, alone in the dark room but is vulnerable to haunting visitations from its own darkest corners. The ghostly workings of involuntary memories are related to the kind of deep impression on youthful understanding that can only be made by another person. The dormant recollections that "start up in our Minds of their own accord" are akin to the "bugbear thoughts" Locke describes in *Some Thoughts concerning Education*—"strange visions" that afflict a child made afraid of the dark and "upon any occasion [may] start up" (even in adulthood, *after* "their reason had corrected the wrong ideas they had taken in") (§ 138).

In both the *Essay* and *Thoughts concerning Education*, the fear, not of darkness itself but of "invisible beings" lurking in the darkness, receives special attention. Locke enjoins parents to protect the child's "tender mind from all impressions and notions of *spirits* and *goblins*" because they have the potential to make children afraid of the dark "all their lives after" (§ 138). Virtually the same caution appears in one of the only places in the *Essay* where the formative influence of others on the child's mind is recognized: "those who have Children, or the charge of their Education" should shield them from ideas of "*Goblins* and *Sprights*" because once a child associates these imaginary beings with darkness he "shall never be able to separate them again so long as he lives, [and] Darkness shall ever afterwards bring with it these frightful *Ideas*" (2.33.8, 10).[13] If in childhood (the "time most susceptible to lasting impressions"), the "indiscretion of a servant" attempting to awe a child (in *Education*), a "foolish Maid" telling tales (in the *Essay*) can create such irrational yet irresistible and perhaps permanent fear, then the power and influence of the affection, anger, and attention of other closer intimates on the child's mind cannot be understated.

Freud, for one, in his many discussions of childhood phobias, consistently traces the fear of darkness and solitude to anxieties born of attachment, love, and loss. Children "are afraid in the dark because in the dark they cannot see the person they love," he writes in *Three Essays on the Theory of Sexuality*; "*longing* [for a "loved person"] felt in the dark is transformed into a *fear* of the dark," he writes in the *Introductory Lectures on Psychoanalysis*; and again, in *Inhibitions, Symptoms and Anxiety*, "missing someone who is loved and longed for" manifests itself in the child's "fear of being alone, or in the dark."[14] The imbrication of a child's love and fear for those who care for him is an explicit and guiding premise for Locke in *Some Thoughts concerning Education* ("When you have planted in [the child] a particular affection for you, he is then in the state you could desire, and you have formed in his mind that true *reverence* . . . in both the parts of it, *love* and *fear* as the great principle whereby you will always have hold upon him" [§ 99]), and while it would be a mistake to say that the impact of this attachment is irrelevant to the project of the *Essay*, it would also be misleading to argue that Locke sets aside his own "great principle" of child rearing in his study of the understanding.[15] To see the associations between childhood fear of darkness, solitude, and longing for a loved one made in Locke's writing (as in Freud's) is also to find that the *Essay* is strangely consistent with the opening proposition of *Education*. That "the little and almost insensible impressions on our tender infancies have very important and lasting consequences" (§1) is true for the mind Locke describes as independently achieving its own intellectual footing in the *Essay*, openly discussed only as a form of harmful influence but implicitly present throughout in the darkness and solitude in which the understanding takes shape and remains. This is to say that while the shaping influence of other persons is only evidently present in the *Essay* as a fear, it is worth asking whether the traces of the other half of the dyad, of something like love, might also be found in the text.

Dread of invisible spirits lurking in the darkness is a trace of the powerful influence that another person might have on the mind; in the scheme of the *Essay* it is also an example of false or erroneous association of ideas. Other instances of "wrong Connexion in our Minds," particularly those involving pain, concern relation with another person: "a Man receives a sensible Injury from another, thinks on the Man and that Action over and over"; another man suffers in the very room where he saw his friend die, and can no longer bear to be in the place; a mother grieves the loss of her child (2.33.11–13). Locke's presentation of "undue connections" of ideas as "unreasonable," or "beyond the power of reason to help," and therefore a "sort of Madness" has struck some readers as problematic because these connections resist reason precisely to the degree that they *seem* reasonable (2.33.3–4). In their affective content, however, the associations evincing attachment to another differ in kind from the particular forms of self-delusion Locke attributes to prejudice and custom that are indeed powerful to the extent that they are simulacra of reason.[16] The distinction among Locke's examples bears emphasis precisely because the mind is so rarely described as subject to emotion; the very exceptionality of these cases, both in the *Essay* and for philosophical approaches to mind typified by it, is worth preserving. The fear of darkness which a grown man recognizes to be irrational, yet cannot resist, or the grieving of a mother whose pain resists the consolations of reason: the power of the nonrational in these cases does not lie in a simulation of the rational but in an indulgence of and submission to a power *other* than reason—that which Locke calls "passion."

The term *passion* makes rare but highly revealing appearances in the *Essay* (and in Locke's work generally) as a force that seizes the understanding, typically tied to intense involvement with another person.[17] Its exemplars in the *Essay* as well as in a more concise treatment of the same theme in *Of the Conduct of the Understanding* are the male lover and the bereaved mother, affection having made each vulnerable to the affliction of a loss that severs attachment but not emotion. Passion painfully outlives its object in the shape of haunting memories, involuntarily disturbed—"rouzed and tumbled out of their dark Cells," writes Locke, "by some turbulent and tempestuous Passion" (2.10.7). In this context, the scenario of the writer, alone, imagining that the man he saw last may be gone forever is both a piece of philosophical *reasoning* about the extent of certitude and a rendering of the mind in the grip of a *passion* (a "rotation of thoughts about the same object" [*Conduct*, § 45]), so engrossed with the "thousand ways" that the other man may cease to be as to be beyond the reach of reassurance. Indeed not everyone excites thought of the "thousand ways he may cease to be" since I saw him with my own eyes; we are, after all, callously indifferent to numberless such cases. The anxiety the writer betrays is precisely the kind of worry that only a loved one inspires, the foreboding that Wordsworth names "a strange fit of passion"—the sudden, unbidden thought that befalls a lover as a cloud covers the moon ("What fond and wayward thoughts will slide / Into a Lover's head— / 'O mercy,' to myself I cried, / 'If Lucy should be dead'"). This groundless dread testifies not only (and not even always) to concern for another but also to one's vulnerability to the loss of the loved one, the idea that my world would cease to exist without the other in it. The romantic lyricizes a dependence on the beloved that psychoanalysis would trace back to infancy—as if the fancied death of the lover were also the phantom trace of the anxiety that afflicts the child in the absence of the mother. Taken in *this* sense, the philosophizing mind Locke represents in the concluding book of the *Essay* bears out, and is born out of, anxieties about interdependence, about always already having been subject to the influence of others.

The reflections that culminate in admission of a thousand ways that the other may cease to be are set in motion by the apparently straightforward claim that "having the *Idea* of any thing in our Mind, no more proves the Existence of that Thing, than the picture of a Man evidences his being in the World, or the Visions of a Dream make thereby a true

History" (4.11.1). Typically Locke's prose draws no distinction between "any thing" and "a Man" as ideas in the mind, but the instance is revealing. The picture of a man offers no reassurance that he lives, but why does one look at a picture if not to recall him, to recollect him, to wish him present? The picture offers no evidence of his (now) being in the world but does at least evince his having been; in any case the picture may be all that remains of the man and it is that which the mind struggles to retain. Whether it is the working of reason or of passion, the uncertainty that the philosopher must own in his isolation—that haunting possibility that another "may cease to be since I had the testimony of my senses"—betrays an attachment to others that compromises the detachment of his vantage point, the apartness that constitutes his autonomy.

The intransigent fear of not being alone in the dark, the writer left alone to take the measure of his aloneness, the sudden revival of memories that had lain buried in the mind's dark cells: these extensions and unfoldings of the initial figure of the mind in the dark room all have the effect of weakening the sense of that room as a secure and private enclosure. Goblins, spirits, and involuntary memories are frightening and unwanted inmates, the absence of the man no longer in sight an agitating preoccupation. Tales told in childhood may be impossible to forget, and so trouble evermore; the picture in my mind that is all I have left of a dead man may itself fade away, or never fade and so become an incurable sorrow; what I think I have put to rest and forgotten may suddenly come upon me. In this way, through oblique evocation of pain and trepidation within, the "art" of the *Essay* achieves the difficult task Locke assigned it at the outset; it "makes [the understanding] its own object," *both* by endeavoring to articulate its limitations, to imagine what it cannot see ("the man I saw one minute since," "men I never saw," "millions of men") *and* by evoking the pangs of a subject apprehensive about being on its own, suffering the absence of others.

o o o

I have thus far attempted to trace a narrative of passionate attachment, or a narrative of attachment as passion, unfolding along with the philosophical narrative of the *Essay* and, in that way, to locate the presence of intersubjective anxieties and longings in Locke's writing in spite of the effort (perhaps even as a result of the effort) to write the formative influence of others out of the history of the mind. As representative of the independent activities of the understanding, the infant and child described in book 2 are necessarily related to the writer of book 4, the figure of the dark room of the mind to the solitary scene of writing. Also related to each other are doubt about the existence of persons out of sight (presented as the sober conclusion of philosophical reflection) and fear of invisible beings in the dark (presented as a false but irresistible association insinuated into a young mind): the mind is alone in each case, its thoughts controlled directly or indirectly by a heightened awareness of aloneness which betrays an anxiety ultimately traceable to the impact of another person. I also suggested that these fears (of aloneness, for another) bear traces of love, or at least of longing for lost attachments. The writer is concerned with the loss of the other, the thousand ways he may cease to be; the child's fear, in itself the product of influence, is also the response to the loss, or absence of a loved protector.

However, it would be a mistake to say that fear and love are intermingled everywhere that the *Essay* evokes other persons. Dread of others is often irreducible, untinged with longing, in the conclusions and implications of arguments that are more obviously paradigmatic of the epistemological scheme laid out in the *Essay* than is that moment of doubt in the existence of millions of men. Put another way, if the longing for others as expressed in the *Essay* involves philosophizing the personal (turning groundless worry for a loved one into reasonable doubt about the existence of objects), then the dread of others involves personalizing the philosophical in a way that ultimately shifts the inquiry away from epistemology. Intersubjective anxieties arise at those points in the argument where, in spite of the *Essay*'s failure to distinguish persons from things as objects of knowledge, a distinction insistently reasserts itself—indeed inevitably asserts itself, since it is based on the *Essay*'s own imagination of the mind as an interior space.

Once persons materialize in the argument as distinct from things, the investigation of knowledge unavoidably confounds epistemological questions (How do objects stand before the understanding?) with ethical problems (How do I stand before others?). This confusion is rich and consequential but easy to lose sight of, because the history of philosophy in the eighteenth century is, in part, the history of the emergence of ethics as a domain separate from investigations of the mind. To understand what is gained and what is lost by the clarification of Locke's confusion, I turn briefly to Hume's *Treatise of Human Nature* (1739–1740) as the seminal enlightenment text separating the impasses of empiricist epistemology from the problems of morals.

In the ending of the first book, "On the Understanding," Hume famously arrives at an unresolvable skepticism that is also often understood as taking Locke's analysis to its logical conclusion: "The understanding, when it acts alone, and according to its most general principles, entirely subverts itself, and leaves not the lowest degree of evidence in any proposition."[18] Locke's relatively restrained presentation of the devastating conclusion that "though it be highly probable that Millions of Men do now exist, yet whilst I am alone writing this, I have not the Certainty of it" is openly dramatized in Hume, not only through deployment of emotional rhetoric but also in a convergence of voices or roles whereby the philosopher speaks as if *from* the place where his analysis has left the mind. "I am at first affrighted and confounded with that forelorn solitude, in which I am plac'd in my philosophy," Hume begins, "and fancy myself some strange uncouth monster, who not being able to mingle and unite in society, has been expell'd [from] all human commerce and left utterly abandon'd and disconsolate" (311–312). The affect expressed here—fear, confusion, and desolation—evidently concerns a loss of place among others, imagined now as unfitness, as not belonging (being some strange monster to men), and again as desertion or banishment. Anticipated reaction to the results of Hume's analysis is the ostensible cause of this alienation ("I have expos'd myself to the enmity of all"), but these meta-reflections on the philosophical activity that has led to such "forelorn solitude" also coincide with, or are presented as homologous with, the condition of the mind as "plac'd," that is, as defined by, philosophy (the understanding acting alone, subverting itself). Hume is speaking as a philosopher, anxious at espousing ideas he knows will be regarded as anathema, but his topic is unavoidably also the anxieties coincident with a specific form of philosophical reflection. "The *intense* view of these manifold contradictions and imperfections in human reason has so wrought upon me, and heated my brain, that I am ready to reject all belief and reasoning," says Hume of the "present feeling and experience" of his thought (316). In this state, metaphysical questions arise in the same train as ethical concerns: "Where am I, or what? From what causes do I derive my existence, and to what condition shall I return? Whose favor shall I court, and whose anger must I dread?" But where, on this continuum, do Hume's final questions—"What beings surround me? and on whom have I any influence, or who have any influence upon me?"—belong? (316).

When all these questions arise together, Hume explains, he imagines himself as "inviron'd with the deepest darkness" (316), inhabiting the philosophical place that houses the Lockean understanding. But Hume famously sustains neither the despairing mood nor the skepticism that arise in this darkness; the conclusions drawn in what Hume, like Locke, calls the "closet" are fleeting, "vanish[ing] like the phantoms of the night on the appearance of the morning" (507). At the end of book 1 the spell of melancholy is broken by moving from the solitary chamber to the sociability of a drawing room in which conversation and amusement among friends banishes fear and confusion. In the wake of that change of mood, Hume introduces a series of distinctions that the *Treatise* as a whole builds on—"reasoning and philosophy" versus "the pleasures of life," the "currents of nature," "the common affairs of life," and the "commerce and society of men."[19]

The conclusion of Hume's book on the understanding has been taken to exhaust the empiricist model of the isolated mind and shift the ground of judgment—especially practical judgment—from reasoning in isolation to reflections on the passions that necessarily and congenially attach individuals to one another; principal among these is the "natural sympathy" that is the "true origin of morals" (discussed below). But in thus dividing the irresistible (skeptical) conclusions of reason from what will be presented as equally irresistible workings of passion, Hume creates a division between philosophical approaches that cuts out anxieties traversing both fields of inquiry.

The estrangement and fear Hume expresses in the climax of his book on the understanding and the philosophical questions corresponding to that mood are all equally present in Locke. But ethical questions that Hume clearly formulates as such (Whose favor shall I court? Whose anger shall I dread?) are, in Locke, only ever articulated in the form of questions that waver between the ethical and the epistemological (What beings surround me?). Precisely for this reason, and in the wake of Hume, the uncertainties Locke arrives at can easily be interpreted as being confined to skepticism about *existence* (what we *really know*). The ethical implications of Locke's arguments are hidden to the extent that their intersubjective aspect is obscured. To allow them to appear is to see what occurs when Hume's resolution does not present itself, when the philosopher is compelled to remain in the dark room.

o o o

Readers who maintain that the *Essay* leads to radically skeptical conclusions must do so in spite of the fact that Locke does not explicitly present the understanding as subverting itself. On the contrary, Locke consistently maintains that the faculties serve "our purpose well enough"—even as he shows that I can only ever think it *probable* that I am not alone in the world when others are not immediately present. Indeed, the *Essay* insistently defines the *limits* of knowledge precisely in order—positively—to determine its grounds and possibilities. That there are limits (of the senses, of demonstration, of certainty, of language) is repeatedly emphasized throughout and notably foregrounded in the first chapter: just as "'Tis of great use to the Sailor to know the length of his Line, though he cannot with it fathom all the depths of the Ocean," so it will be useful to "examine our own Powers" of understanding so as not to "let loose our Thoughts into the vast Ocean of *Being*" (1.1.6–7).[20] The goal of the *Essay*, then, is to determine what does lie "within reach" of the understanding, "how far the Understanding can extend its View" given the "narrowness of our Minds" (1.1.4–5). What appears to be *pre*determined however, is the happy outcome of the investigation.

"Questions" and "disputes" doomed to irresolution and leading inevitably to the skeptical "Despair of knowing any thing" arise not because our knowledge is without adequate grounds, according to Locke, but because of a failure to remain within its bounds. Out of ignorance men "le[t] their Thoughts wander into those depths, where they can find no sure Footing," or succumb to a despair born of arrogance when they "boldly quarrel with their own Constitution," "peremptorily, or intemperately requir[ing] Demonstration and demand[ing] Certainty" where none is to be had (1.1.5–7). No matter how limited the reach, the limits are drawn so that "we may learn to content our selves with what is attainable by us" and thus more capably "govern [our] Opinions and Actions" (rather than surrender to what Hume terms "melancholy and delirium") (1.1.4, 6). Nevertheless it is impossible not to notice how the *Essay* strains against the limits of the perceptual faculties it defines, defending them as serving our purpose well enough while dwelling on what eludes them. I turn now to several places in the argument where the unknowable realm to which Locke gestures (which he defines as beyond our grasp) is also the realm of the intersubjective (of a mind in relation to other minds, other persons, other animate bodies) because it is there that the epistemological humility (its complacence, its common sense) of the *Essay* is beset by urgent ethical questions, and where the contentment Locke promises comes to seem unattainable, the beliefs on which action must be based perilously ungrounded.

The Desire to See Through

> One might say of someone that he was blind to the *expression* of a face. Would his eyesight on that account be defective?
> Ludwig Wittgenstein, *Philosophical Investigations*

Assuring us that the "testimony of the Senses" provides "Evidence... as great as we can desire" and "beyond which we have no concernment, either of Knowledge or Being," Locke simultaneously affirms the efficacy of the senses and conjures up the possibility of inaccessible aspects of being (4.11.8). This double movement, whereby assurance and certainty are accompanied by a gesture toward the unknowable, is a recurrent and critical dynamic in the argument of the *Essay* and the focus of contention, in Locke's time as much as our own, about the coherence of empiricism itself. Locke theorizes that the "essence" of a thing ("that real constitution of any Thing... on which [its] Qualities, and their Union, depend") is inaccessible to us: "a blind Man may as soon sort Things by their colours... as by those internal Constitutions which he knows not" (3.6.6, 9). Thus essences are the very ground of the real (things would fall apart without them) but not of the reality we experience, and the question is whether this concession constitutes an idealist core at the heart of empiricism. Some readers have seen the repeated gestures at a domain "beyond" our reach as intimating a realm that transcends the empirical bounds mapped out in the *Essay*.[21] Others argue that Locke's admissions of our ignorance about the substance of things do not amount to a theory of what we cannot, in principle, ever know, but have to do with contingent limitations to be overcome by scientific and technical advances. Not surprisingly the interpretive debate arises from tensions within the *Essay* itself, which at times seems to present that which escapes our senses as a priori unknowable, and at other times unknowable because *unsensed* by us.

I am less concerned with the nature of the unknowable in Locke than with assessing his repeated assurances that what we cannot know does not concern us, and I want to approach this matter by focusing on those rhetorical and figurative representations of what lies "beyond our concernment" that do not obviously exceed the bounds of an imagination of what might be given in experience—that, in fact, rely on an imagination of the senses. For example, when Locke reasons that, "had Mankind been made with but four Senses, the Qualities then, which are the Object of the Fifth Sense, had been as far from our Notice, Imagination, and

Conception, as now any *belonging to a Sixth, Seventh, or Eighth Sense*, can possibly be," the gesture is precisely not "beyond" experience to an extrasensory realm (2.2.3). Rather, the effort to convey all that the five senses delivers of the world is compromised by the prospect of eight senses and all we must surely fail to notice, imagine, and conceive without them.[22]

Even more firmly set within the realm of experience than the evocation of other kinds of sensory capacity is Locke's use of vision itself to illustrate all that we do not see. "Blood to the naked Eye appears all red," Locke explains, "but by a good Microscope, wherein its lesser parts appear, shews only some few Globules of Red, swimming in a pellucid Liquor; and how these red Globules would appear, if Glasses could be found, that yet could magnify them 1000, or 10000 times more, is uncertain." Though quick to concede that "microscopical" perception would "be inconsistent with our Being, or at least well-being in this part of the Universe," Locke's expansiveness on the subject betrays an imagination tantalized by all that a man with such acute vision might see: "things several millions of times less than the smallest Object of his sight now . . . he would come nearer the Discovery of the Texture and Motion of the minute Parts of corporeal Things . . . get *Ideas* of their internal Constitutions" (2.23.11–12). Corpuscular theories to which Locke would have subscribed held that looking more closely at a thing would reveal the minute fundamental elements of its composition, and Locke's attention to the structure of objects (gold, pounded glass, hair, blood) visible under a microscope has frequently been set in the context of those debates and related to his discussion of unknowable "essences."[23] However, for my purposes, the rich rhetorical confusion between microstructure ("minute parts of corporeal things") and "internal constitution" in this section of the *Essay* suggests a significant difference between invisibilities.

I have said thus far that Locke's reversions to the theme of the unknowable frequently conjure up *sensible* realities: the invisibly minute structure of a thing such as a blood sample is one category; the invisible inside of an enclosed object such as a machine is another. One calls for a fantasy of magnifying vision, the other for penetrating vision; Locke's example is a man "sharp-sighted enough to see the Configuration of the minute Particles of the Spring of a Clock" (2.23.12). Concluding that such a man's discoveries would be "admirable" but of no real benefit for telling the time, Locke nevertheless cannot seem to resist offering a final example of acute perception. The "extravagant conjecture" he proposes concerns the "ways of Perception in Beings above us" (such as angels) whom Locke imagines to be liberated from a fixed set of faculties, able to alter their "Organs of Sensation or Perception." "What wonders would he discover," writes Locke, "who could so fit his Eye to all sorts of Objects, as to see, when he pleased, the Figure and Motion of the minute Particles in the Blood ... as distinctly, as he does, at other times, the shape and motion of the Animals themselves" (2.23.13). Recall that Locke has already drawn our attention to "minute particles of blood" under a good microscope and to "minute particles" in "motion" on the inside of a clock. This is one of the few places in the *Essay* where "bodies" are explicitly *animated* corporeal beings, but what difference does this make? How is the animal different from the clock Locke had imaginatively penetrated and which, like the animal, is composed of "minute particles" in "motion"? What (more) is there to see "inside"?

The questions about the reach of human senses that are raised by this digressive shift of focus from inanimate things to living embodied creatures are not the same as those about the invisible microstructure of objects, even though the language of Locke's analysis seems to apply indifferently to each. Locke speculates, "were our Senses alter'd, and made much quicker and acuter, the appearance and outward Scheme of things would have quite another Face to us," and the term *face* itself insinuates a distinction that the *Essay* generally fails to draw (2.23.12). What difference would it make to think of the "face" in this context as belonging to a thing (a clock face, for example) or to a person? If to look beyond the "outward" "appearance" of the clock would be, in Locke's terms, to "discover the secret contrivance of [its] parts," then what (analogous?) discovery is made of the human face? For one thing, peeking inside to see the mechanism of the clock in motion will not change the time registered on the face or, rather, will not result in the discovery that the clock has been fooling us with its expression of ten o'clock. Presumably that is just the kind of discovery that is meant when we say we see another face or side of someone (we find them to be other than they seem, we have been taken in or suddenly enchanted or struck by a resemblance or a flash of insight). To see another face, then, is to notice something previously unseen. But then what it means to notice or to see seems not different in intensity and degree ("quicker and acuter") when applied to a person rather than a thing, but different in kind. The very concepts of "seeing" and of "sensation" differ in these cases.[24] "Face" in this context is the most evident sign of the intersubjective experience that is an unacknowledged, or repressed, part of the history traced in the

Essay, but, once glimpsed, the limits of the analogy between knowing things and knowing persons resonate throughout this discussion of the relative fitness of our faculties. If to see acutely is to look as closely as possible, to look keenly, penetratingly, deeply and, in that way, to discover what a thing "really" is, then such rhetoric acquires a poignancy and pathos when applied to persons rather than things. Taken as such, Locke's imagination of more acute and more penetrating senses, for keener vision, points to a yearning for a more intimate knowledge of others.

The *Essay*'s construction of the mind as an interior enclosed and divided from the outside necessarily makes other minds a separate and problematic category for the knowing subject. What is really going on "inside" another mind is hidden from view. Although Locke repeatedly protests that, in denying us such vision, "God has no doubt made us so, as is best for us in our present Condition... fitted us for the Neighbourhood of the Bodies, that surround us, and we have to do with," central portions of the *Essay* reveal how ill-fitted the Lockean subject is to judge of the neighborhood of embodied minds around it (4.23.13). The repeated protestations that we have sufficient "insight," faculties well enough "suited" for "our business in this world," do not apply equally well to persons and to things.

Monsters and Men

I have said that although the *Essay* blurs and fails to distinguish persons and things as objects of knowledge, persons nevertheless emerge as a separate and problematic epistemological category. On the one hand, insofar as persons are like any other object, no special mode of perception different from what suffices for objects is theoretically called for. On the other hand, insofar as other minds are structured like that of the subject of the *Essay*, then the vital activities and characteristic features of other persons lie beyond the reach of perception (behind the face, say). Problems necessarily emerge when the *explicit* asymmetry between Locke's figuration of the knowing subject and his representation of objects of knowledge has to be considered at one and the same time as the *implicitly* assumed equivalence among persons (as each in possession of a mind, and of each mind as inside the body). It is precisely at such points in the discussion that the *Essay*'s commitment to define and remain within the "bounds" of the understanding seems most troubling, most evidently perhaps in Locke's investigations of the object most like the subject of the *Essay* itself: "man."

Given that minds exist inside opaque bodies that our eyes cannot penetrate, the shape of the human body turns out to be the crucially recognizable feature of "man." The quite literal superficiality of this basis for recognition is something Locke acknowledges as troubling but must concede to be confirmed by experience. "Scarce any one will allow this upright Figure, so well known, to be the essential difference of the *Species*," he observes; nevertheless "'tis not the *Idea* of a thinking or rational Being alone that makes the *Idea* of a *Man* in most People's Sense; but of a Body, so and so shaped joined to it" (3.6.26; 2.27.8). Not only does the appearance of the body determine recognition of others, but also—and paradoxically—that outer form is somehow intrinsic to our idea of the human being: not the idea of a rational being alone but *necessarily* joined to "a Body, so and so shaped." Thus the measure of another's interiority is bound to outward shape and, insofar as such a claim insists on the embodiment of the human subject, it verges on healing the conceptual separation of mind and body, making a kind of epistemological peace with phenomenological response to the human shape.

In fact, the concession to the body Locke makes here remains vexatious precisely because it does *not* modify theoretical structures already firmly in place in the *Essay*. The crucial role of the body in (re)cognition of other persons is troubling because it seems, in the case of man, that the accidental is essential. Yet, in itself, this should not pose a problem; in the scheme of the *Essay* we know most objects through the "accidents" of their appearance. Considered as an object or, in this case, as an animal like any other, the outward appearance of the human being is necessarily the sole criterion of identification: "As in Vegetables and Animals,'tis the shape . . . we most fix on, and are most led by" (3.6.29). So "if several Men were to be asked, concerning some oddly-shaped *Foetus*, as soon as born, whether it were a *Man*, or no,'tis past doubt, one should meet with different Answers" because nature has not drawn "precise and *unmovable Boundaries*" between species, but the trouble here goes beyond taxonomy. "So uncertain are the Boundaries of *Species* of Animals," observes Locke, and "the certain Boundaries of that *Species* [man] are so far from being determined . . . that very material Doubts may still arise" about individual specimens (3.6.27).

Empirical judgment comes into uncomfortable proximity with moral judgment. If it is true that a rational creature that "partaked not of the usual shape of a Man ... would hardly pass as a *Man*," then unusually shaped human beings will be unrecognizable—their humanity contested, affirmed by some, denied by others (3.6.29). The consequences of misidentification concern no more and no less than this life, and the next: "None of the Definitions of the word *Man*, which we yet have, nor Descriptions of that sort of Animal, are so perfect and exact, as to satisfy a considerate inquisitive Person; much less to obtain a general Consent, and to be that which Men would every where stick by, in the Decision of Cases, and determining of Life and Death, Baptism or no Baptism" (3.6.27). Attempting to avoid this grave implication, Locke introduces a distinction between definitions of "physical" and "moral" man: "whether a Child or Changeling be a *Man* in a physical Sense, may amongst the Naturalists be as disputable as it will, it concerns not at all the *moral Man*, as I may call him, which is this immoveable unchangeable *Idea, a corporeal rational Being*" (3.11.16). In such a distinction lies the germ of what Kant recognized as the "utmost necessity" to free moral philosophy "from everything which may be only empirical and thus belong to anthropology," but, given the epistemological constraints of the *Essay*, the distinction only leads Locke's argument into unresolved contradiction.[25] "A Monkey, or any other Creature to be found, that had the use of Reason" would, according to Locke, "no doubt be subject to Law, and, in that sense, be a *Man*, how much soever he differ'd in Shape from others of that Name" (3.11.16), but Locke elsewhere, repeatedly, and more consistently, argues just the opposite: "however some Men seem to prize their Definition of *Animal Rational*, yet should there a Creature be found, that had Language and Reason, but partaked not of the usual shape of a Man, I believe it would hardly pass for a Man, how much soever it were *Animal Rational*" (3.6.29).[26]

This confusion in which the human body both must be and cannot be the basis for the attribution of humanity is the logical consequence of Locke's figuration of the human *subject* as an enclosed mind. As an object of knowledge, the human being is necessarily perceived as a human shape; as a knowing subject, the human being is necessarily defined as a reasoning creature. The problem is that these two understandings do not match up: no shape reliably corresponds, or can reliably be vested, as the sign of rationality. What offers good enough knowledge in the case of objects turns out to be not good enough in the case of man because of the particular kind of object another subject is. The outward shape does not give us enough to go on: both the need for—and the absence of—some other criterion are examined one last time, when Locke returns to the topic of identifying and naming species in the final book of the *Essay*. His cases are symptomatically bizarre and unlikely but are helpful in exposing the tension between epistemological access to persons and things that we have been exploring.

The prospect of misrecognition, that a man might be taken for a monster, or a monster for a man, unfolds in a thought experiment designed "to shew that according to the ordinary way of Reasoning in this Matter, People do lay the whole stress on the Figure, and resolve the whole Essence of the Species of Man (as they make it) into the outward Shape." This pattern of "thoughts and practice" is traced through a series of images:

> The well-shaped *Changeling* is a Man, has a rational Soul, though it appear not; this is past doubt, say you. Make the Ears a little longer, and more pointed, and the Nose a little flatter than ordinary, and then you begin to boggle: Make the Face yet narrower, flatter, and longer, and then you are at a stand: Add still more and more of the likeness of a Brute to it, and let the Head be perfectly that of some other Animal, then presently 'tis a *Monster*; and 'tis demonstration with you, that it hath no rational Soul, and must be destroy'd. Where now (I ask) shall be the just measure; which the utmost Bounds of that Shape, that carries with it a rational Soul? (4.4.16)

The failure to distinguish between persons and things as objects of knowledge returns here as a menacing blindness. Recall that in arguing that essences are inaccessible, Locke also insists that the senses provide a "good enough" basis for identifying things. So, for example, although whatever may be essential to a tree is unknown to me, I can nevertheless recognize a tree; my seeing the tree as a tree does not (unless I hold some totemic faith) ordinarily hinge on the idea of something (essential) "carried inside" its shape. The distinguishing feature of a human being (be it reason, mind, or soul), however, has consistently been imagined as something "inner," "hidden," "invisible" in the *Essay*, and it turns out that I do not have "evidence as great" as I can desire to judge whether there is "such an inhabitant within" a given body. When Locke asks, "Shall a defect in the Body make a *Monster*; a defect in the Mind (the far more Noble, and, in the common phrase, the far more Essential Part) not?" (4.4.16), the answer, however disturbing, must be yes, because, as was earlier established, "ingenuous observation puts it past doubt, that the *Idea* in our Minds, of which the Sound *Man* in our Mouths is the Sign, is nothing else but of an Animal of such a certain Form" (2.27.8).

"Just measure" of another soul entails not simply accurate measurement but measurement that does justice to the other. Locke uses fanciful cases to explore his concern with the "utmost Bounds of [the] Shape that carries with it a rational Soul," but how deformed must a shape be in order to arouse suspicion of some monstrosity "carried within"? The imaginary metamorphosis of man into monster conducted in the thought experiment and ending with the melodramatic imperative to destroy the figure initially taken for a human being lays bare the ethics at stake in the epistemology—but does so "inside out," so to speak.[27] The problem, after all, is not that we cross paths with so many weirdly shaped bodies that might contain reasoning fellow souls but that we may be capable of imagining or perceiving human features in such a way as to deny them their humanity, to not take their "just measure," and therefore do them injustice.

The question that motivates Locke's thought experiment ("Shall a defect in the Body make a *Monster*; a defect in the Mind . . . not?") is not only about the possible disjunction between an outward shape that cannot be seen as human and the human soul carried within it; it is also about a more common—and so more threatening—disjunction between an outward shape one does not hesitate to see as human and a monstrous soul lurking invisibly within it. Just as we earlier saw the *Essay*'s renderings of inaccessible knowledge take the form of surreally intensified perceptions that could *also* be seen as occluded representations of ordinary limits of intersubjective knowledge, so here the repeated use of rare physical deformities to illustrate the difficulty of identifying human beings might also be seen to evoke the common risks involved in recognizing others, especially but not necessarily exclusively strangers.

Some of the "most obvious Things that come in our way," Locke reminds his reader, "have dark sides, that the quickest Sight cannot penetrate into," but this common-sense concession carries sinister overtones when the "essence" inaccessible to us is that of another human being (4.3.22). Locke's confidence "that God hath fitted us for the neighborhood of bodies that surround us" amounts to the belief that we see only far enough to recognize the possibility that a monster may be hidden beneath the mask of a human face or that a fellow human being may be trapped within the body of a monster. Moreover, we are equally at the mercy of such imaginings, equally at risk of being unjustly measured by others. Both secluded and concealed in its dark room, the Lockean mind is at once liable to be suspicious and the object of suspicion. The notion of being alone among monsters or being mistaken for a monster follows inexorably from the initial conception of the mind as an enclosed interior, but so, too, do political and ethical conjectures that have less frequently been seen as strange or surreal, such as the notion that human beings naturally and with good reason are wary of one another. Indeed, the subject of Locke's epistemology appears afflicted with "Hobbesian fear"—the suspicion, wariness, and vulnerability to attack that make man miserable in the solitary state of nature.[28]

Language is supposed to bridge the gap between minds, but as we shall see, because Locke remains committed to defining the mind as enclosed and independent, fear and suspicion of others is not overcome but is reproduced in other terms. In Locke's account, language makes it possible for human beings to live together, but sociability is itself radically limited. The picture of society implicit in book 3 looks like a cohabitation of strangers in which intimate acquaintance is unattainable, the depth of agreement impossible to fathom. Locke arrives at this picture in a way that helps illuminate how the intransigent epistemological impasses of the *Essay* inevitably entail moral and political implications, and thus keep together that rich confusion of questions about intersubjective knowledge and relations that Hume would attempt to resolve by simple separation.

Language and the Incommunicability of Thought

Concern with the means and possibility of sharing ideas distinguishes book 3, "Of Words," as the only place in the *Essay* where the fact that the Lockean subject inhabits the world with other subjects becomes both unavoidably relevant and explicitly problematic. The mind in the dark room fantasizes about senses that would more acutely penetrate other minds but does not possess faculties acute enough to see *inside*. Just as the animal is animated by "blood and other juices" coursing beneath the surface of the skin, so does man "have a great variety of Thoughts," writes Locke, "yet they are all within his own Breast, invisible, and hidden from others, nor can of themselves be made to appear" (3.2.1). The individual thus constituted is ill-suited to society, but "God having designed Man for a sociable Creature," according to Locke, provides language as "the great Instrument, and common Tye of Society" (3.1.1).[29]

Words, then, are the means by which the Lockean subject breaches the solitary confinement of his dark room. We "bring out" our ideas, "lay them before the view of others," thereby exposing what is "hidden and invisible"—not only thoughts but also the humanity evinced by thought. Although God is credited with providing the instrument of communication, the focus of Locke's discussion shifts from the efficacy of language to its limitations as a means of literally expressing or exteriorizing what is inside the mind.

Even as Locke endeavors to explain how ideas are exchanged by the common use of words, there is a rapid slippage, in his argument, from the communicative instrumentality of words to the likelihood that meanings are not, after all, shared. For example, a confident assertion that "the Knowing, and the Ignorant, the Learned, and the Unlearned, use the Words they speak (with any meaning) all alike" is weakened by a proceeding comparison of a child's use of the word *gold* and an adult's, compelling the conclusion that while "each of these uses equally the Word Gold . . . [it] is evident, that each can apply it only to his own *Idea*" (3.2.3). Common usage of a word and signification of the same idea are thus, in the space of a paragraph, dissociated from each other. Words have a common currency but also have private, incommunicable meanings. Words are "external sensible Signs" of our inner ideas, but the "sensible Marks" of thoughts do not reveal their full signification; words have a "common usage" but also "secret reference" to private, inexpressible meanings (3.2.1–4). It does not take Locke long to move from the initial proposition that man is a "sociable Creature . . . with an inclination, and under a necessity to have fellowship with those of his own kind" to the development of an argument widely taken as a classic paradigm of the theory of "private language" 3.1.1).[30] Ultimately Locke is driven to the radical conclusion that shared meaning is an assumption we necessarily, but groundlessly, make about words. Human beings "suppose their Words to be Marks of the *Ideas* in the Minds also of other Men, with whom they communicate: For else they should talk in vain," but nothing justifies this supposition, for "whether the *Idea* they, and those they discourse with have in their Minds, be the same" cannot be determined (3.2.4). The implication is that common meaning is taken for granted, that if the matter were more carefully examined we might discover how little, rather than how well, we understand one another.

The argument is not that individuals necessarily use the same words while meaning different things but that it is not possible *to know* whether the ideas in two separate minds match up. One would have to literally inhabit the other's body to know his thoughts: the "same Object should produce in several Men's Minds different *Ideas*," according to Locke, but "this could never be known: because one Man's Mind could not pass into another Man's Body, to perceive, what Appearances were produced by [his] Organs" (2.32.15). Language cannot make public an experiential life that Locke has imagined to be irreducibly, existentially private. As a consequence of this epistemic individuality, incommunicable meaning may stand behind even those words used to signify what Locke calls "simple ideas" (those "got by [the] impressions Objects themselves make on our Minds," such as the taste of pineapple or the color of violets) (3.4.11). So, for example, a word like *sugar* may have a commonly accepted range of reference while also being a secret mark of sugar-as-I-experience-it.[31]

If language is taken to refer to essentially private experience, then it becomes difficult to avoid the conclusion that "we can never really know what another means."[32] However, there is no necessary incommensurability between asserting the radical diversity of inner experience and the efficacy of language so long as words (also) have a public, instrumental signification—a point Locke is always careful to emphasize.[33] When first introduced in book 3, the disturbing implications of the idea that words "often fail to excite . . . the same ideas" in different speakers are obscured by two qualifications that run in both directions: a reminder that convention ensures communication ("long and familiar use" establishes "general meaning") and an insistence that, although words do fail to "excite the same idea" in two minds, that failure is because of a freedom no one would (or can) relinquish: "every Man has so inviolable a Liberty, to make Words stand for what *Ideas* he pleases, that no one hath the Power to make others have the same *Ideas* in their Minds" (3.2.8). Taken together, the emphasis on convention tempers what can seem a radical claim of "irrepressible linguistic individuality," and most readers of book 3 agree that Locke does not mean that each individual can use words as he wills.[34] What appears to be at issue here is not so much the *use* of words but the privacy of the ideas behind them—the fact that, in spite of conventions, words *"stand for nothing, but the* Ideas *we have in our own Minds"* (3.2.2).

The notion that thoughts remain hidden in spite of efficacious linguistic communication would seem to cast Locke's account back to its original problem (*because* thoughts are "hidden" and "invisible" we need language). Instead the problem itself is recast—the hidden-ness of thought presented as protecting the individual rather than obstructing exchange. Not incidentally, an analogy to politics defines the advantage: "The great *Augustus* himself, in the Possession of that Power which ruled the World, acknowledged, he could not make a new Latin Word: which was as much as to say, that he could not arbitrarily appoint, what *Idea* any Sound should be a Sign of, in the Mouths and common Language of his Subjects" (3.2.8). Locke is, in fact, making two different points here: Augustus cannot dictate the conventional use of words (he cannot make a new Latin word), but Augustus also cannot dictate the *ideas* behind any individual use of words. The "inviolable liberty" of the language user as Locke presents it in the *Essay* is related to the liberty Locke affirms as natural to the human being in the *Second Treatise:* "The *Natural Liberty* of Man is to be free from any Superior Power on Earth, and not to be under the Will or Legislative Authority of Man."[35] The confluence of these formulations suggests the freedom from tutelage at stake in conceiving the individual as originally on his own—politically and epistemologically—and takes us back to the question raised at the outset about the erasure of the role of others in shaping the mind described in the *Essay*. Inviolability implies both impenetrability and security from assault or trespass—dangers readily imaginable in the context of a political discussion but perhaps less clear in the context of the *Essay*. It is worth asking what threat the Lockean speaker faces or, rather, what threat his liberty (to make words stand for his own ideas) protects him from.

The "inviolable liberty" of the language user assures his freedom to think for himself rather than conform to or rely on the authority of others, but this boon requires a disowning of origins, of inheritance, of all that is received by transmission. To be sure, Locke concedes that "in communication with others, it is necessary that we conform" to common usage and that "Common use *regulates the meaning of Words* pretty well for common Conversation," but he is also anxious to insist that "no body [has] an Authority to establish the precise signification of Words, nor determine to what *Ideas* any one shall annex them" (3.9.6–8). To imagine that "What liberty *Adam* had at first to make any complex *Ideas* [such as "obligation," "gratitude," "liberty"] . . . by no other Pattern, but by his own Thoughts, the same have all Men ever since had . . . The same Liberty also, that *Adam* had of affixing any new name to any *Idea*; the same has anyone still" requires forgetting (or overcoming) ever having been indebted to others, as a child is, for the meanings of words (3.6.51).[36] The *Essay*'s avoidance of influence presents itself here again. If Locke would have us imagine the child finding his own intellectual footing, then it is only a matter of logical consistency to endow each individual with the capacity to name the ideas he arrives at in the private space of the mind. An anxiety or fear of influence would appear to be obviated and avoided by theoretical insistence on an original condition of independence (the child as autonomous thinker, each language user naming his own world as Adam), but anxieties and fears about others logically arise from and afflict the subject in his newly imagined autonomous form. Just as the exclusion of the influence of others was earlier linked to both a positive emphasis on the mind's autonomous activity and a negatively inflected confinement and isolation, so here the "inviolable liberty" of the language user derives from the same construction of mind and experience that produces a comfortless view of communicative possibilities.

Locke's emphasis on communicative efficacy, on the one hand, and a positive, politically inflected emphasis on liberty and independence, on the other, obscures but cannot eradicate the implications of the notion that words might not excite the same idea in two speakers. It is not so much that Locke's theory of language undoes his opening proposition that human beings are made for society and that language is designed to serve that purpose. Rather, the *Essay*'s fundamental claim is that the language we use—like knowledge of which we are capable—is sufficient to our needs; it works well enough as "the common measure of Commerce and Communication" (3.11.11). However, because the possibilities of social life are literally defined by language, the isolation of the Lockean subject *from other subjects* is more evidently entailed by Locke's conception of mind here than elsewhere in the *Essay*; its epistemic limits are more obviously intersubjective limits. The question is how the intersubjective aspect compels revaluation of Locke's insistence that we are "fitted well enough with Abilities, to provide for the Conveniences of living," for "our Business in this World," "for the Neighbourhood of the Bodies that surround us" (2.23.12–13).[37] Indeed, it is precisely in its consistency with the epistemic possibilities and conditions laid out in the *Essay* that the theory of language runs counter to and limits the force of the initial claim about the sociality that language makes possible. It is easier to imagine, however, that we do not *need* to know the "real essences" of objects than it is to imagine that we do not need to know the real meaning of another's words.

It is important to bear in mind that, in the *Essay*, the notion that a word such as *sweet* has a "secret reference" follows from the same premise as readily accepted claims about the disparate, relative, even irreconcilable meanings of a large category of words. *Glory, gratitude, murder, sacrilege, honor*—and *man*, of course—are among the "moral words" Locke instances in arguing that names of "compound *Ideas*, such as for the most part are moral Words, have seldom, in two different Men, the same precise signification" (3.9.6).[38] If the "Comfort and Advantage of society [are not to be] had without Communication of Thoughts," it is hard to imagine what that comfort and advantage consists of if a word such as *promise* will not necessarily "excite the same idea" in different speakers (3.2.1).

The political and moral implications of Locke's discussion of language are inescapably bound up with his epistemological premises. Consider the Lockean questions that Hume does not raise in his important discussion of promises in the *Treatise*, where the *epistemic* challenge of knowing the other's mind does not complicate exchange: "When this common sense of interest is mutually express'd, and is known to both, it produces a suitable resolution and behaviour ... The actions of each of us have a reference to those of the other, and are perform'd upon the supposition, that something is to be perform'd on the other part" (541–542). Both history and nature create the conditions under which two individuals "know" that their interest is "common" and are able, rationally, to form expectations of the other's actions. The deep agreement underlying the promise keepers' suppositions of each other "arises gradually, and acquires force by a slow progression, and by our repeated experiences of the inconvenience of transgressing it" (542). The liberty retained by the Lockean subject is thus curtailed, not by the authority or influence of a single man or ruler, but by the combined force of many in the form of historically established conventions. In itself, this argument is not necessarily at odds with the *Essay* (cf. 3.6.51), but conventions and the mutually expressed and understood interests underlying them proceed, in Hume, from a presupposition about the transparency of one mind to another mind that is at odds with the entire epistemic edifice in which Locke encloses the mind.

Grave political and moral implications follow from epistemological premises that leave the individual on his own, in a state of isolation literally inherent to physical individuation. Even when Locke embraces the premise that human beings are made for society—as in the discussion of language in the *Essay*—his emphasis falls on isolation. In spite of the admission (in the *Second Treatise*) that "God ... made Man such a Creature, that, in his own Judgment, it was not good for him to be alone, [and] put him under strong Obligations of Necessity, Convenience, and

Inclination to drive him into *Society*" (§ 77), Locke gives temporal and conceptual priority to a condition of individual independence that somehow precedes the social life to which the human being is destined. The theoretical work of the *Treatise* begins with the assertion that "we must consider what State all Men are naturally in, and that is, a *State of perfect Freedom* to order their Actions and dispose of their Possessions, and Persons, as they think fit . . . without asking leave, or depending upon the Will of any other Man" (§ 4). Ultimately the original human condition of independence and liberty is superseded by entry into civil society because that initial condition of autonomy is recognized as vulnerable; "however free," the state of nature "is full of fears and continual dangers," making the "enjoyment" of natural liberty and self-possession "unsafe," "uncertain," "unsecure" (§ 123). At particular risk in the *Second Treatise* is "property," by which Locke means not only possessions but all that is proper to the subject, including his very life, so that we must imagine not simply lands but minds and bodies as "constantly exposed to the Invasion of others" in the state of nature. Although the mind conceived in the *Essay* is certainly conceptually akin to man in the state of nature, there is no comparable movement away from the condition of independence in which Locke originally places the mind because there is no comparable *explicit* recognition of how epistemic autonomy might be compromised or vexed by fear or danger. Nevertheless, the *Essay* comes to grief over the effort to sustain the individual's secure independence—inventing a history and imagining a space in which the individual develops on his own, only to find the vulnerabilities that autonomy ought to preclude transposed into intransigent philosophical problems. Surrounded by bodies that may or may not be fellow human beings, as liable to mistake a monster for a friend as to be mistaken for a monster oneself, free to hold his own idea of what "love" means but bound never to know if another shares the same idea, ultimately certain only of his "self alone and of God"—however free the thinking subject is in the *Essay*, his condition, like that of his equally free and independent counterpart in the state of nature, must also be understood as "full of fears and continual dangers."

Locke's Dark Room, Hume's Mirror, Sade's Bedroom

"To discover the true origins of morals," Hume explains in the concluding book of the *Treatise*, it is necessary to "begin by considering anew the nature and force of *sympathy*. The minds of all men are similar in their feelings and operations ... As in strings equally wound up, the motion of one communicates itself to the rest; so all the affections readily pass from one person to another, and beget correspondent movements in every human creature" (626). In proposing that "the minds of men are mirrors to one another" (414), Hume insists on a difference between knowing objects and knowing persons that remains occluded in Locke, but he also assumes an easy epistemic access to others that forecloses rather than resolves the questions raised in Locke's more troubling account of minds hidden inside opaque bodies, behind inscrutable faces.

Humean sympathy ensures an intersubjective communicability and response undreamt of in Locke's *Essay:* "No quality is more remarkable, both in itself and in its consequences, than the propensity we have to sympathize with others, and to receive by communication their inclinations and sentiments, however different from, or even contrary to our own" (367). No more and no less than the "true origin of morals" is staked on this remarkable capacity precisely because it resolves a crucial epistemological obstacle to moral judgment. Access to the interiority of the other is central to an ethics that values intention rather than the mere performance of right: "the external performance has no merit," and therefore "we must look within to find the moral quality," writes Hume (530). Yet the terms *internal* and *external* beg the very question ("What beings surround me?") that the hypothesis of natural sympathy does not so much resolve as will away. The potential cleavage between what the other is (on the "inside") and what the other seems to be inextricably binds together epistemological mystery (What do I know of others?) and moral difficulty (Whom can I trust? Who is the other to me?).

Hume's assertion of "correspondent movements" of affections between persons cannot fully overcome the tendency to transform disappointments and risks of relation with others into a general epistemic limitation. The presumption of sympathy is vulnerable to straightforward negation, not by a counterpresumption of natural malevolence or antipathy, but by a fundamental empiricist and materialist agnosticism about the similarity of sensation (and hence of experience) in different bodies. Locke, for example, concludes that because "one Man's Mind could not pass into another Man's Body, to perceive what appearances were produced by [his] Organs," we cannot know if we have been similarly impressed by the same thing. The "diversity of our reception," as Hobbes earlier put it, "in respect of different constitutions of body ... gives everything a tincture of our different passions."[39] Essentially the same contention is to be found in Sade (among others): "there is no possible comparison between what others experience and what we sense," explains Dolmancé, the advocate of libertinism in *Philosophy in the Bedroom* (1795). Sade's insistence on intersubjective distance is rendered in empirical terms (your experience ... my sensation), but its ethical implication is immediate—"the immense sum of others' miseries ... cannot affect us."[40] Humean emphasis on "resemblance," "similarity," and "parallel" among subjects is thus inverted. The mirror reflecting other minds in our own is broken so that indifference is the utmost to be expected from the other.

In freely borrowing the basis of its arguments from Hobbes's *Leviathan*, Sade's *Philosophy in the Bedroom* serves as a reminder that claims about what individuals know of one another and how individuals act toward one another still, at the end of the eighteenth century, typically sought their justification in a conception of human origins and development. Completing the thought that "there is no possible comparison between what others experience and what we sense," Sade's philosopher invokes the evidence of our first state: "Are we not all born solitary, isolated? I say more: are we not come into the world all enemies, the one of the other, all in a state of perpetual and reciprocal warfare?"[41]

Back to Nature?

Anti-Hobbesian thinkers frequently reassert the facts of human dependence and sociality as evinced by the infant's need of others for survival against Hobbes's deliberately imagined state of nature in which men "come to full maturity ... without all kind of engagement to one another."[42] "A *human Infant* is of all the most helpless, weak, infirm," according to Shaftesbury, "forc[ing man] to own that he is purposely ... made rational and *sociable,* and can no otherwise increase or subsist, than in that *social* Intercourse and Community which is his *Natural State*."[43] Later in the century Adam Ferguson similarly observes: "Every infant is born into the society of his own family" and thus "to be in society is the physical state of the species."[44] Hume himself reasons that because physical weakness would make it "utterly impossible for men to remain any considerable time in that savage condition which precedes society," the "first state and situation may justly be esteem'd social."[45]

The reminder that dependence is the original condition of human beings is ventured not solely—not even principally—against the

Hobbesian fiction of natural independence but against the implications about moral disposition that arise when the individual is seen (as if) "born solitary, isolated." Against Hobbes's view of essentially egoistic and self-preserving persons, theorists of natural sociability proposed a view of human beings as naturally benevolent, deriving that *ideal* of moral inclination from the readily observable *facts* of infantile weakness and parental succor. Not only "conjugal Affection and natural Affection to parents" but also "Love of a common City, Community, or Country" are all "deduc'd" by Shaftesbury from the neediness of infancy.[46] Hypotheses of natural human fellowship and good will, however, cannot simply follow from general observations about the dependence and caretaking required by human infants—any more than general observations about aggression can support a hypothesis about a primordial state of enmity and hostility.

Disagreeing in point of fact with a Hobbesian view of the first state—and with the view of human nature extrapolated from that fiction—Hume nevertheless recognizes the futility of reasoning from even the most self-evident observations of human origins. Admission that the facts of the matter (sexual appetite, infantile dependence, parental sacrifice) do not necessarily matter philosophically, or may be set aside for philosophical purposes, is precisely what distinguishes Hume from the theorists of natural sociability with whom he is associated. Even as he clearly asserts the original sociality of human beings, Hume notes that this fact "hinders not, but that philosophers may, if they please, extend their reasoning to the suppos'd *state of nature*; provided they allow it to be a mere philosophical fiction, which never had, and never cou'd have any reality" (544). On this reading, the Hobbesian who places the individual in conditions of "extreme necessity," "implant[ing] in the human breast . . . perfect rapaciousness and malice," presents a vision no more realistic than the "extreme abundance" and "perfect humanity" of the poet's Golden Age.[47] It is against both these fictional extremes that Hume represents his own view of natural moral inclinations as the judicious and realistic middle way, clearly disavowing a Hobbesian pure egoism, but also seeming to resist the opposite tendency to affirm an unbounded benevolence. I say *seeming* because, even though Hume refrains from extending the principle of sympathy to an implausible universal benevolence and admits selfishness to be fundamental to "our natural temper," Hume's emphasis always falls on the affections binding individuals to one another.[48] Moderately expressed, geniality exceeds narrow self-interest: "tho' it be rare to meet with one who loves any single person better than himself, yet 'tis as rare to meet with one, in whom all the kind affections, taken together, do not overbalance all the selfish" (538). In forceful terms, sympathy is the dominant, commanding passion: "Whatever other passions we may be actuated by; pride, ambition, avarice, curiosity, revenge, or lust; the soul or animating principle of them all is sympathy" (412).

o o o

It is a mark of Hume's sophistication and complexity that he does *not* conceive of sympathy in relation to speculations about human origins.[49] The detachment of the concept from a genealogical account of human relations shields it from corrosively skeptical moral reasoning. Against the suggestion that "ties of love, of friendship, of gratitude" naturally arise among beings who need one another, for example, Sade's philosopher argues that neither moral obligation nor moral sentiment can logically be derived from the mere fact of having been cared for in infancy: "we owe nothing to our parents, not the least thing . . . the rights of birth establish nothing, are basis to nothing."[50] However, this very argument demonstrates how the notion that human beings are not bound and engaged with one another can withstand the refutation of the initial surmise that we are "born solitary, isolated." Ultimately individual "freedom" from obligation and even from affective involvement with others is an implication derived from an epistemological premise about human beings rather than a conjecture about human origins. According to Sade's philosopher, pity is dangerous because the mind is "frail," "miscalculates," and cannot reliably judge others: "far better for you to refuse a person whose wretchedness is genuine," the philosopher advises, "than to run the great risk of giving to a bandit, to an intriguer."[51] The idea that "we are born solitary, isolated" seems like the foundation of an argument that ultimately turns individuals into mutual threats; it is that, but it is also a reassuring surmise, for the individual who is thus imperiled by others is also defined as essentially "free, equal, and independent" of others. Hume's natural sympathy shields the individual against the same dangers. Assuming the dissolution of tensions between persons in reliable intersubjective correspondence makes it relatively uncomplicated to admit the natural-ness of the need to live with one another, but the reassuring operation of fellow-feeling is as obvious a turn away from the risks of dependence as the myth of solitary origin.

The hypothesis of originary autonomy ideally would shield the individual from the dangerous vulnerabilities of relational existence, and we have seen how those vulnerabilities impinge on Locke's *Essay* in occluded but recurrent forms (in the wishful speculations about penetrating vision or in disturbed misgivings about the line between recognizable humanity and monstrosity). Hume's hypothesis of sympathy answers to the danger Sade defines and the anxieties that trouble Locke by allowing a "remarkable capacity" to feel for others to compensate for limitations of knowledge. Thus even though Hume disassociates sympathy from any fact (or fiction) of a "first state," the concept is nevertheless bound up with the existential status of solitude and isolation. It is not an idea of the irreducible *selfishness* of human beings that sympathy opposes but an idea of fundamental solitude and epistemic isolation. The literal openness of minds to one another as Hume imagines it could not more strikingly reconfigure Locke's dark enclosure "with only some little openings" to let in the "resemblances" of things without. Between Locke's dark room and Hume's mirroring minds, however, lies the opacity and instability of an ever shifting and changeable boundary between what Rousseau calls "being" and "appearing"—precisely the instability that an advocate of willful egoism such as Sade exploits.

o o o

Humean sympathy answers to a need for others never explicitly acknowledged in Locke's *Essay* and thus makes it possible to own the individual's dependence, the existential fact that "man is altogether insufficient to support himself" (402).[59] But the acknowledgment or admission is itself made possible only *given* the reassuring assumption that human need and dependence reliably inspire response and support. Not by evincing the real history of the individual against the fiction that "we are born solitary, isolated," then, but by imagining a remarkable capacity for intimacy (for literally entering into the life of others) does Hume counter the idea of constitutive aloneness and independence. But the danger and risk of intersubjective distance remains just as readily *imaginable*—and perhaps all the more threatening—once we concede that we are, in fact, bound and dependent on one another. In Rousseau, as we shall see in the next chapter, neither a myth of essential autonomy nor a conviction in reliable sympathy will mitigate the vulnerability to others that is the necessary corollary of dependence.

CHAPTER 2

Rousseau's Autonomous Beast

NATURAL MAN AS IMAGINARY ANIMAL

Il serait peu curieux de savoir ce que sont les bêtes, si ce n'était pas un moyen de connaître mieux ce que nous sommes.
CONDILLAC, *Traité des animaux*

"*Borné au seul instinct physique, il est nul, il est bête: c'est ce que j'ai fait voir dans mon* Discours.*"*
ROUSSEAU, *Lettre à Christophe de Beaumont*

To paraphrase the opening assertion of Condillac's *Traité des animaux*: it would not be especially interesting to know what beasts are if it were not a means of better recognizing what we ourselves are. The question is precisely *how* animals help us to know ourselves. "*Imaginative* elaboration of the difference between ourselves and animals," according to the philosopher Cora Diamond, is a characteristic form for the "imaginative re-shaping of what it means to be human, and thus of the concept 'human being.'"[1] So, for example, to assert that reason or language or laughter distinguishes human beings from all other animals is to identify the capacity to reason or to speak or to laugh as constitutive of human-ness; it may be conventional to advance such claims about human-ness by drawing a contrast with animals, but the contrast needs to be understood as resting on conceptual rather than factual grounds.[2] Emile Durkheim credited Rousseau with the discovery that "if we take away from man all that issues from society, nothing would remain but a being reduced to sensation and more or less indistinct from an animal." The category of animal in such a formulation is a generic and theoretical one that marks the absolute difference between "man," on the one hand, and, on the other, the "nothing" he becomes when conceived apart from social life.[3] Rousseau's "natural man" is indistinct from the animal not because he is like any actual animal—an ape, for example—but because he has none of the faculties that are imagined, or conceived, as distinctively human.

Although Rousseau himself bluntly declared that natural man "*est nul . . . est bête*," such an understanding has failed to displace alluring images of the creature he described in the *Discourse on the Origins of Inequality*. Enjoying the abundance of the earth's natural fertility and a robust constitution, nurtured in the wild, unburdened by possessions, Rousseau's natural man "is at peace with all nature."[4] Enlivened solely by the "sentiment of his own present existence," the solitary inhabitant of the state of nature has been seen as the locus of metaphysical nostalgia for a prior and forever lost tranquility and equilibrium. Dwelling in the perfect stasis of autonomy and self-sufficiency, he "breathes nothing but repose and freedom, he wants only to live and remain idle" (198, 192). So desirable does his contentment seem, particularly in contrast to the man in society who "sweats, scurries, constantly agonizes in search of still more strenuous occupations" (198, 192), that it has been easy to overlook the considerable critical tradition that views Rousseau's natural man not as an idealized, unalienated version of our socially enslaved selves but as a creature entirely, and most *un*-ideally limited to an animal existence.

To insist on the animal condition of natural man is not to ignore the powerful critique of social structures and relations in the *Discourse*; rather, it is to suggest that, in spite of that critique, the *Discourse* does not sustain a straightforward opposition between "nature" and "society" as human habitats. Certainly the specific forms of civil society described in part 2 of the *Discourse* produce misery, alienation, anxiety, and corruption. Nevertheless, a range of distinctively human faculties (reason, language, conscience, self-consciousness, forethought, awareness of mortality) that *exceed* the limitations of the animal existence described in part 1 *only* develop within social life, and thus man only becomes recognizably and distinctly human outside the state of nature. Durkheim is not alone in pressing the implications of Rousseau's own representation of "nascent man" as leading the "life of an animal . . . restricted to pure sensations" (170, 164). In his magisterial study of Rousseau's social and political writings, and their relation to the principal philosophical theories of the period, Victor Goldschmidt argues that the condition of social man in the *Discourse* is to be contrasted to "the *animal condition*" of natural man. More recently Victor Gourevitch, English translator and scholarly editor of both *Discourses* and of the *Essay on the Origin of Languages*, straightforwardly identifies natural man as "man in the animal state or condition," concluding that "he may be said to have left the animal state ... insofar as he becomes sociable." Similarly Heinrich Meier (translator and editor of the German standard edition of the *Discourse*) contends that insofar as the life of natural man is the "life of a beast," an "animal obtuseness ... underlies the self-sufficiency of the individual."[5]

If natural man stands on the other side of the conceptual boundary dividing the human from the nonhuman, then in what sense is the *Discourse* a study of origins? And why is the figure of natural man still so easily taken to be an object of nostalgic yearning? This chapter focuses on the concept of natural man in relation to knowledge of animal behavior in the *Discourse on the Origins of Inequality among Men* and among contemporary readers of that text, examining the role of fact and evidence in philosophical argument in order to illuminate the complexity and distinctiveness of Rousseau's account of sociality.

Reading Rousseau through Ethology: Facts for Theory

Les sciences abstraites ont occupé trop longtemps et avec trop peu de fruit les meilleurs esprits ... les mots se sont multipliés sans fin, et la connaissance des choses est restée en arrière ... Les faits, de quelque nature qu'ils soient, sont la veritable richesse du philosophe.

DIDEROT, *Pensées sur l'interprétation de la nature*

Among those readers who have understood natural man to stand in need of a humanizing development or progress out of the state of animality, some have gone so far as to propose that the *Discourse* offers an anticipation of Darwinian evolution in which natural man serves as the conceptual "missing link" between beast and man. Others have sought to locate the origins of anthropological and even bio-anthropological thought in the *Discourse*, tempted by the uncanny accuracy of many of Rousseau's theoretical speculations in the light of contemporary scientific research on primates and hominids.[6] Robert Wokler, for example, in an influential series of articles, has traced the startling affiliations between Rousseau's natural man and the animal now classified as the orangutan. Citing the characteristics of vegetarianism, the absence of long-term sexual or familial attachments, and an "essentially solitary and indolent" life, Wokler contends that Rousseau's natural man represents a more accurate portrait of orangutans "than any description of the animal's behavior for a further two hundred years or so"—"a fact all the more remarkable because there is no reason to suppose that he ever actually saw one."[7] It is a question, however, how far such an accidental similarity between philosophical speculation and later scientific observation can take analysis. After all, not only is it the case that natural man is nowhere identified *as* an orangutan in the *Discourse*, but, as Wokler himself knows, even if Rousseau's startling conjecture that orangutans may be a species of savage man were taken to underwrite the speculation that natural man is indeed constructed in the image of that animal, the eighteenth-century term *orang-utan* is not limited to the animal identified by that term today but refers instead to anthropoids of all kinds. Access and opportunity to examine primates were so infrequent (indeed, the gorilla was not even classed as a distinct species until the late nineteenth century) that one cannot assume any correspondence between the eighteenth century's use of the names of particular species (not only orangutan, but also chimpanzee, monkey, ape) and current usage.[8] Possible historical confusions aside, such associations raise the question of what is at stake in making natural man *natural*, a part of the animal world.

Orangutans happen to be the *only* primate species that appears *not* to dwell within a relatively complex social structure; as such, they are a particularly problematic point of reference for Rousseau's natural man, for the precise trait orangutans happen to share with natural man is also the very characteristic that differentiates them from the way that other primates (including human beings) live. Indeed, others who have studied Rousseau's state of nature in relation to contemporary ethology and sociobiology—whether to confirm or contradict the conjectures of the *Discourse* by recourse to empirical evidence—run into difficulty precisely because our nearest animal ancestors do *not* lead lives of indolent solitude. Roger Masters, for example, admits that "contemporary natural scientists are virtually unanimous in rejecting Rousseau's image of solitary man in the pure state of nature" and further observes that archaeological research on australopithicenes and other early hominids confirms that "humans are a far more social species than Rousseau recognized." And yet, even as Masters concedes that the "best scientific data" available to us attest to the formative evolutionary role of sociality and cooperation (even brain size and structure "may be the *result* of cooperation"), he also marshals other "data" that would appear to affirm the plausibility of the asocial form of the state of nature: "for example, among the marmots, woodchucks have been shown to live in a solitary way which greatly resembles Rousseau's pure state of nature."[9]

Arresting as the behavioral details about the lives of woodchucks and orangutans may be, it is worth exploring in greater depth just how empirical information about the life of animals is made relevant in the context of analyzing a document such as the *Discourse on the Origins of Inequality*. After all, not only is it the case that the use of sociobiology in discussions of morality and politics makes it a particularly important site for ideological controversy, but many of the elements in contention are the direct inheritance of the eighteenth century. Wokler proposes that the *Discourse* ought to occupy a "prominent place . . . in the history of empirical primatology" because of the uncanny accuracy of its speculations. Defending his argument against the objection that "it is an accidental feature of Rousseau's thought that the product of his conjectural experiment, which he calls an orang-utan, corresponds to what is now zoologically specified as such," Wokler is quick to concede the generic use of the term *orang-utan* in eighteenth-century scientific and philosophical discourse. He nevertheless insists that Rousseau's speculations about natural man, confirmed by their apparent correspondence to facts, are, *by virtue of that facticity*, able to bear theoretical fruit. It is worth quoting at length in order to draw attention to the ideological inflection of the "facts" and "discovery" at issue in the discussion.

> Because orang-utans in the wild show very few of the characteristics—such as hierarchical social structures, territorial control and aggression—which some ethologists now attribute to all animal species in an attempt to show that man cannot escape from his zoological roots . . . the frugivorous, peaceable, solitary, nomadic orangutans Rousseau portrayed seem to be the most vital missing link in a natural chain which is taken to imply that social inequality and competition are inescapable. . . . Of course Rousseau hit upon this discovery quite by chance, since the creature he called an orang-utan is nothing more than an abstraction. . . . Yet it was a most extraordinary discovery just the same . . . remarkable even today, when our animal qualities are falsely regarded by many commentators as evidence of the fact that our lives have been destined by Nature to be nasty, brutish, and short with individuals perpetually at each other's throats, or else held in check by intimidation.[10]

Wokler's allusion to the Hobbesian state of nature as that which Rousseau's opposes appropriately returns the *Discourse* to the theoretical context of its own period, while at the same time pointing to the manner in which eighteenth-century philosophical disputes about the nature of human beings and of social structures continue to shape contemporary debate, and even to influence contemporary interpretation of the zoological "data." It may be easy enough to confirm by observation that meat is not a part of the diet of a particular species, but what comparable form of observation would count as confirmation that a particular species is "peaceable"?

The characteristics Wokler cites as facts about orangutan behavior challenge what, in the early 1980s, he perceived as sociobiological orthodoxy about the competitive nature of the species. That orthodoxy itself has since been challenged by studies of the critical role of cooperative and altruistic behavior in primate social groups. Ironically the noncompetitive autonomy Wokler would celebrate in Rousseau's text and in the behavior of orangutans might appear, in this new context, as consistent with, rather than as a challenge to, an underlying ideological investment in atomistic individualism that has obscured the role of sociality and interdependence in the study of primate behavior (and, by implication, in human behavior and social organization). For example, in Frans de Waal's recent study of altruism and empathy in a number of primate species, Rousseau's natural man appears as the ideological ally—not the opponent—of Wokler's modern Hobbesians. The *Discourse*'s image of a creature whose "independence was not even compromised by love making," who thrives in a "total absence of social connectedness," still exercises a powerful influence, according to de Waal, having become "an article of faith among economists, who describe society as an aggregation of Robinson Crusoes" and rights theorists who "ignore the ties, needs, and interdependencies that have marked our existence from the very beginning." That de Waal is a zoologist, not a political theorist or intellectual historian, makes his sensitivity to the powerful effects of ideological preconceptions on empirical investigation particularly striking. He does not, for example, present his arguments about empathy as the "discovery" of hitherto unknown facts about primates but, rather, as a *re-description* of frequently observed behavior. If explanations of animal behavior must necessarily attribute states of mind or intention (or deny them), and there is no consistent agreement about what counts as evidence for a particular state of mind in an animal, then something other than empirical observation guides the use of anthropomorphism in accounts of primate behavior. So, for example, while terms such as *threat, greeting, courtship,* and *dominance* have been widely accepted, terms such as *succor* or *reconciliation* might encounter resistance. And while anthropomorphism is unavoidable in the study of animal behavior (indeed, to refrain from it is to run the risk of anthropocentrism), underlying its use are presuppositions about what counts as thinking or intending (for example), as well as ideological convictions about the nature of *human* behavior (as inherently self-interested or competitive, for example).[11]

The use of sociobiological research to illuminate a text such as Rousseau's *Discourse* would appear to be circular, for to suggest that Rousseau (to use Wokler's phrase) "had been right all along" in some sense about the peaceable nature of the species or that Hobbes was "wrong" because of the way that the behavior of some primate species has most recently been characterized is to ignore the extent to which the conflicting theories of human nature advanced in the work of Rousseau and Hobbes (and Locke and Mandeville and others) have themselves shaped interpretation of animal behavior, particularly the behavior of those animals that stand in close evolutionary relation to *Homo sapiens.*

Animals as Evidence in the Discourse: More Facts for Theory

> One must start out with error and convert it into truth. That is, one must reveal the source of error, otherwise hearing the truth won't do any good. The truth cannot force its way in when something else is occupying its place. To convince someone of the truth, it is not enough to state it, but rather one must find the *path* from error to truth.
> Wittgenstein, "Remarks on Frazer's *Golden Bough*"

The recourse to ethology and sociobiology in order to illuminate aspects of Rousseau's *Discourse* may be problematic, but it is an approach invited by the *Discourse* itself, given the recourse to scientific rhetoric and sources both in the body of the text and in the essayistic notes. If some contemporary interpreters have deployed what are understood to be *facts* about animals in order to serve varying *theoretical* purposes, the license to do so would appear to lie in the *Discourse*'s own interest in aligning its conjectures with available fact. However, both the use and the status of fact are far from straightforward in the *Discourse.*

Information about animals (whether accurate or not) frequently, and often at key moments, is not adduced as evidentiary support but is rather exploited as an opportunity to investigate the status of evidence within a philosophical investigation. For example, the provocative claim that intrigues Wokler, namely, that orangutans may very well be a type of savage man, is ventured through a reading of travelers' reports made in such a way as to demonstrate both the inadequacy of the source and the role of bias in its observations. Rousseau thus adduces material evidence while simultaneously challenging its evidentiary effectiveness. "The small number of lines comprising these descriptions permits us to judge how poorly these Animals have been observed and with what prejudices they were seen," writes Rousseau, all but concluding that his age simply has *no* reliable source of information about them, for "good Observers" are unlikely to be found among the sailors, merchants, soldiers, and missionaries who most commonly travel extensively (217–218, 211). The complicated and ambiguous nature of contemporaneous sources of information on anthropoids is made evident in the work from which Rousseau quotes at great length—the *Histoire générale des voyages, ou Nouvelle collection de toutes les relations de voyage par mer et par terre qui ont été publiées jusqu'à présent dans les différentes langues de toutes les nations connues* (1746–1789). Within the multivolume *Histoire*, the text Rousseau draws on is a translation of Samuel Purchas's *Pilgrimage; or, Relations of the World and Religion Observed in All Ages* (originally published in London in 1613), which does not, in fact, contain Purchas's observations of orangs but those of Andrew Battel, an Essex neighbor whose experiences in Africa while working for the Spanish governor of Angola were set down by Purchas upon the former's return to England and drawn on for the *Pilgrimage*'s description of the Congo. To complicate matters further, the *Histoire*'s presentation of Purchas's record of Battel's account also refers to other seventeenth-century chronicles that support or offer material for the embellishment of Battel's observations. Among the texts alluded to in Rousseau's page-long quotation are the Dutch physician Olfert Dapper's *Description de l'Afrique* (1686) and the Italian missionary Jerome Merolla's *Breve e succinta relatione del viaggio nel Regno di Congo* (1692). So Rousseau's source on "orang-outangs" is not in itself an eyewitness account but a translation of a report of an eyewitness account with additional observations drawn from documents about other parts of Africa, all pulled together on the assumption that they report on the same species of creature.[12] The long quotation Rousseau offers concludes with a peculiar claim: "in a word, it is quite likely that [the orang-outang]

70   Isolated Cases

is the satyr of the Ancients," an observation that captures the tension between fabulism and fact in many early descriptions of anthropoids. If, on the one hand, the suggestion is taken to explain that the creature of pagan fiction is a real animal (i.e., Satyrs don't exist, but anthropoids do), on the other, that seemingly judicious, de-mythicizing conclusion rests on the shaky ground of "strange tales told by negroes" about the orangs "tak[ing] women and girls by force."[13] Moreover, this report of the animals' rapacity appears both incongruous and gratuitous following as it does on a touching description of an orang (now thought to have been a chimpanzee) who, on the sea voyage from the Congo to Holland, was observed walking upright, "gracefully wiping its lips" after using a drinking vessel, sleeping in a bed, and "covering itself so skillfully that it might have been mistaken for a human being." The conjecture about satyrs in Rousseau's text would be a strange and estranging detail to include if the purpose of this note were to illustrate the claim that orangutans are a species of savage man rather than to draw attention to the ways that descriptions of these creatures are tinged by myth and preconception.[14]

The quotation from the *Histoire* does not provide evidence about anthropoids that might be used to illuminate features of the life of natural man as it is developed in the *Discourse*; rather, it provides an occasion to challenge the very status of such evidence. The challenges come from an unexpected angle; doubt is not cast on the reliability of the observations contained in the account—which include quite fantastic accounts of anthropomorphic behavior[15]—but on the guiding assumption that the creatures variously called pongos, quojas-morros, orangutans, and mandrills are animals and not men. The provocative claim that—*based on available accounts*—orangs may be savage men is the opening gambit of this discussion, not its end game. The notion that the "humanity" of these creatures might have been misconstrued, indeed altogether missed, by unreliably "coarse travellers" may be inspired by the creatures' alleged "exact resemblance to man," but the force of the note in which this discussion takes place is not spent supporting that conjecture. Instead, the possibility that interpretation of the *behavior* of anthropoids (not of their appearance) may rest on presupposition and superstition leads to an appeal for the testimony of observers on whom it would *not* "be simple-minded to rely," and the note concludes by calling for a "Montesquieu, a Buffon, a Diderot, a Duclos, a d'Alembert, a Condillac, or men of that stamp, travelling with a view to instruct" and undertaking, "with the greatest care," a description of the world's wild regions (220, 213–214). What might these philosophers *see* differently? It is certainly not the physical appearance of "orang-outangs" or mandrills or monkeys but perhaps the challenge of understanding how that physical resemblance signifies.

The extent to which the behavior of anthropoform animals must necessarily pose complex interpretive challenges is made clear when a single observed fact of animal behavior is separated from the conclusion it was taken to support. Paraphrasing Purchas's record of Battel's observation, Rousseau writes that "the Pongos gather around the fires lit by the Negros once these have left, and they in turn leave once the fire has died out; *that is the fact*; here, now, is the *observer's commentary*: 'For although they are very dextrous, they have not sense enough to keep the fire going by adding wood to it'" (emphases added). Against this commentary, Rousseau proposes an alternative explanation, one that may equally well fit the given fact: "I should like to guess how Battel, or Purchas, his compiler, could have known that the Pongos' departure was an effect of their stupidity rather than of their will," suggesting that, in a climate so warm as that of Loango, the fire serves the native inhabitants as a means of frightening off predators rather than keeping warm and that the Pongos, needing the fire for neither warmth nor defense, merely approach the fire out of curiosity or to be "cheered by the flames" before returning to forage (217, 211). Rousseau's interpretation of the given fact here is certainly no more plausible than Battel's (or Purchas's), but that may be precisely the point: such facts do not lend themselves to indisputable, incontrovertible interpretations, and, indeed, the facts in question here are themselves of dubious status, contained in a textual pastiche of secondhand accounts, hearsay, adventurers' tales, and legends. Better, as it were, in this case, to set the "facts" aside and instead determine what is at stake in the prejudices or theoretical inclinations that guide interpretation of them.

The *Discourse*'s treatment of available facts about anthropoid animals of distant lands is consonant with its handling of information about more familiar species, for even as the behavior of commonly observable animals (goats, birds, horses) is occasionally invoked in support of one point or another (on the diet of natural man, for example, or on the lack of competition for mates), attention is consistently drawn to what I would call the conceptual or conjectural status of the facts.[16] The discussion of Locke's use of the breeding and nurturing behaviors of frugivorous and carnivorous animals offers perhaps the most open challenge to fact in philosophical argument in the *Discourse*. The argument (made largely in note 12, discussed at greater length below) is critical to the insistence in the *Discourse* that sociality cannot evolve from the asocial stasis of the state of nature, for it contests the idea that, insofar as the survival of human offspring requires dual parenting, the family naturally and necessarily develops as the earliest form of social organization. Rousseau quotes Locke's argument at length:

> "The end of society between Male and Female," says this philosopher, "being not barely procreation, but the continuation of the species; this society ought to last ... so long as is necessary to the nourishment and support of the young ones ... till they are able to shift and provide for themselves. This rule ... we find the creatures inferior to man steadily and precisely obey. In those animals which feed on grass, the Society between male and female lasts no longer than the very act of copulation; because the teat of the Dam being sufficient to nourish the young, till they be able to feed on grass, the male only begets, but concerns not himself for the female and young.... But in beasts of prey the Society lasts longer: because the Dam not being able well to subsist herself and nourish her offspring by her own prey alone ... the assistance of the male is necessary.... The same is to be observed in all birds."[17] (221, 214–215)

Rousseau objects to this reasoning on a number of grounds, asserting that (1) not all animals of prey remain coupled for the purpose of parenting their young (invoking the dog, cat, bear, and wolf); (2) "it would seem" that grazing animals would be more likely to need assistance in the nurture of their young than animals of prey so that, "in order to draw Locke's conclusion, his argument would have to be turned completely upside down"; (3) the number of teats in frugivorous species limits the number of offspring to no more than the mother can successfully nourish on her own; (4) frugivorous pigeons remain united for long periods of time while carnivorous ducks do not; and (5) even if, in other species of birds, the two sexes share in caring for the young, "it is because Birds, since they cannot fly at first and the Mother cannot suckle them, are much less able to do without the Father's assistance than Quadrupeds, where the Mother's teat suffices, at least for a time" (223, 216).

Are frugivorous species more or less likely to couple for longer periods than carnivorous species? Is there even a consistent and relevant correlation to be drawn between the diet of a species and its nurturing practices? Locke's "facts" meet only Rousseau's "counter-facts," and no supplementary evidence or supporting text that would settle the dispute in Rousseau's favor is cited.[18] The parturient and nurturing behavior of animal species becomes a moot point in this discussion, for it is clear that different facts about animals can be used selectively, perhaps misused, perhaps misinterpreted, in order to advance arguments that run in entirely different directions. Thus attention is focused all the more closely on the theoretical form of Locke's argument, its internal coherence and consistency, its "reasoning" and "dialectic," the conceptual "mistake" it shares with other philosophical states of nature—the imaginative failure to think "beyond the centuries of society . . . beyond those times when men always have a reason to remain close to one another" (225, 218).

The dissolution of apparently empirical observations about animals into speculative detail within a theoretical framework is perhaps most clear—to a modern reader at least—in those places where Rousseau's characterization of animal behavior is clearly *wrong*, as when he asserts that "it is impossible to imagine why, in that primitive state [the state of nature], a man would need another man any more than a monkey or a wolf would need his kind" (158, *151*). Given that monkeys and wolves (unlike, say, Masters's woodchucks and Wokler's orangutans) are among the most sociable of creatures, what is (inadvertently) an error of *fact* illuminates what is perhaps the most consistent feature of Rousseau's imaginative construction of animal life: the solitary existence of the animal.

In the *Discourse* the essential differentiation between human being and animal is made at a theoretical level that particular facts and counter-facts do not affect in any simple sense—be they the speculations of eighteenth-century naturalists or the discoveries of our contemporaries.

Autonomous Beasts and Perfectible Humans: Natural Man as Imaginary Animal

> He who is unable to live in society, or who has no need because he is sufficient for himself, must be either a beast or a god.
> ARISTOTLE, *Politics*

In tracing some of the ways that the complex relationship between seemingly empirical fact and theoretical design present in the *Discourse* itself has been replicated in scholarship, I have drawn attention to the persistence of eighteenth-century disputes about the "nature" of human beings in contemporary debates (on, for example, competition and aggression) and to the deployment of an array of zoological information to support varying analyses of Rousseau's text. When facts about animals bear the burden of confirming, grounding, somehow "proving" a philosophical conviction about the nature of human beings—be it a conviction about what distinguishes us from all other species or about what we share with animals, and hence of the "naturalness" of a particular characteristic—the "facts" adduced are no less likely to be shaped by interpretive bias than those Rousseau and others cited in the eighteenth century. In suggesting now that it might be best to set all such facts aside in order to arrive at an understanding of the internal consistency of the *Discourse*'s insistence that natural man is an animal, I want to shift attention away from the correspondence or lack thereof between the *Discourse*'s claims about animals and the empirical facts about them (be they the facts available to the eighteenth century or those amassed since) and to focus instead on the *Discourse*'s *construction* of the animal as the nonhuman, as the creature that cannot become human. To do so is to resist the application of what is an anachronistic post-Darwinian assumption of continuity between the human and the animal in analyses of the *Discourse*, to consider the possibility that the construction of absolute distinctions between the categories of human and animal may bear with it powerful theoretical implications.

What is emphatically and repetitively stressed, as something common to the life of animals (as *imagined* in the *Discourse*) and the life of natural man, is solitude, radical asociality, and self-sufficiency. Solitary autonomy constitutes the essence of animality in this text, and serves, paradoxically, to isolate relationship and interdependence as intrinsic to human forms of life. Perfectibility is the key difference between the human and the animal in the *Discourse*, a quality absolutely lacking in the animal and entirely inactive in the animal called natural man because he lacks involvement with others of his kind.[19] Perfectibility may be understood to differentiate natural man from the category of the human rather than from the category of the animal and thus to further differentiate the solitary creature, who looks just like us, from the social creature, who acts just like us in part 2 of the *Discourse*. Significantly, in a text careful with such specifications, perfectibility belongs to "man," rather than "natural man" or "savage man." A human being is unlike an animal, according to Rousseau, because the "animal is at the end of several months what it will be for the rest of its life and its species is after a thousand years what it was in the first year of those thousand" (149, 142). *By that very definition*, natural man is, and is destined to remain, precisely *like* the animal: "generations multiplied uselessly, and as each one of them always started at the same point, centuries went by in all the crudeness of the first ages, the species had already grown old, and man remained ever a child" (166, 160). Vast lapses of time are used figuratively in the *Discourse* to dramatize the theoretical distance between two given points rather than to imply a long progressive development. In this case, the "centuries" during which the species of natural man grows old while "man remains ever a child" and the "thousand years" during which animal species undergo no change are conceptual equivalents. The absolute and insurmountable impossibility of development links natural man to the animal and separates him from the human. The first part of the *Discourse* concludes with the claim to "hav[e] shown that perfectibility, the social virtues and the other faculties which Natural man had received in potentiality could never develop by themselves" (168, 162), indicating that insofar as perfectibility is inoperative in the state of nature so is any putative, essential distinction between natural man and other animals. Far from distinguishing natural man and animal, the concept of perfectibility further confounds them, because as long as man remains in the state of nature the very faculty that would humanize him remains dormant and thus makes no difference.

Natural man remains un-human, un-perfected, for want of needing, desiring, and dwelling with others. The constituent feature of natural man's *animal* existence is also that which limits and defines his experiences and his prospects: his aloneness in the world. While that very quality, understood as autonomy or independence, has often been taken to represent an originary, unalienated wholeness of being, it in fact represents the limitation of being—not its essence, but its diminution to the purely physical instincts that Rousseau understands to rule the life of animals. Consider the catalogue of deficiencies that sums up the experience of this creature:

> wandering in the forests *without* industry, *without* speech, *without* settled abode, *without* war, and *without* ties, *without* any need of others of his kind and *without* any desire to harm them, perhaps even *without* ever recognizing any of them individually, subject to a few passions and self-sufficient, Savage man had only the sentiments and the enlightenment suited to that state. (166, 160; emphases added)

The manifold absences and lacks in this passage amount to a single, key element: the state of unbreachable solitude. The underlying condition for the possibility of the development of industry, speech, shelter, war, and peace lies in having ties ("*liaisons*") with others. Setting aside, for a moment, the rhetorical emphasis here and elsewhere in the *Discourse* on all that natural man lacks, what does he possess? What are the few passions to which he is subject? What are the sentiments and enlightenment suited to the state of self-sufficiency?

"Savage man," writes Rousseau,

> deprived of every sort of enlightenment, experiences only the Passions of the latter kind [i.e., of the kind inspired by the "simple impulse of nature"]; his desires do not exceed his Physical needs; the only goods he knows in the Universe are food, a female, and rest; the only evils he fears are pain, and hunger; I say pain, and not death; for an animal will never know what it is to die, and the knowledge of death and its terrors was one of man's first acquisitions on moving away from the animal condition. (150, 143)

Even as the *Discourse* defines the capacities of natural man (in this case his capacity to feel pain, to fear, and to desire), it does so by pointing to a lack (of other fears, pains, and desires inconceivable without "enlightenment") associated with animality. Here, for example, to be *without* consciousness of mortality is to partake of an animal condition. Emphasis on privation again serves to describe the sentiment and enlightenment of natural man in the note appended to this passage, where Rousseau reiterates that there can be "nothing . . . so calm as his soul and nothing so limited as his mind" (221, 214). The tranquility of the creature blissfully unaware of its own mortality depends on a vacuity of consciousness that can only be defined in terms of stasis, negation, and deficiency.

> His imagination depicts *nothing* to him; his heart asks *nothing* of him. His modest needs are so ready to hand, and he is so far from the degree of knowledge necessary to acquire greater knowledge, that he can have neither foresight nor curiosity. . . . His soul, which *nothing* stirs, yields itself wholly to the sentiment of its present existence, with no idea of the future, however near it may be. (150–151, 144; emphases added)

Stressing metaphysical emptiness rather than plenitude, this rhetoric of negation circles inexorably around the singular lack of need and desire for others in the state of nature. The autonomy of natural man yields nothing but this emptiness of heart, mind, and imagination so that autonomy itself comes to seem, ironically, a state of privation. The solitary self-sufficiency of natural man is itself an incapacity, and the possibility of imagining something other than the emptiness of this animal condition will entail the loss of an autonomy that the *Discourse* constructs as lack and limit.

> The more one meditates on this subject, the greater does the distance between pure sensations and the simplest knowledge grow in our eyes; and it is inconceivable how a man could, by his own strength alone, without the help of communication and without the goad of necessity, have crossed such a wide divide. (151, 144)

"His own strength alone" is, under this description, precisely his weakness; the "help [*secours*] of communication" is bound up with the "goad [*aiguillon*] of necessity" so that relief from the "nothing" that fills the mind of natural man is only conceivable if need (for others) replaces self-sufficiency.[20]

The faculties and acquisitions that natural man lacks are consistently reduced to the single category of "*liaison*" with his kind; his alone-ness is repeatedly offered as the principal explanation of his failure to develop. The lack of need for others—self-sufficiency conceived as defect—blocks every possible avenue of evolution beyond what the *Discourse* calls the animal state. "What progress could Mankind make," Rousseau asks, when describing the impossibility of intellectual or technical development "scattered in the Woods among the Animals? And how much could men perfect and enlighten one another [*se perfectionner, et s'éclairer mutuellement*] who, having neither a fixed Dwelling nor any need of one another, might meet no more than twice in their life, without knowing and speaking to one another?" (152, 146). This is an open declaration of the problem of isolation which is only disguised as an apparent boon in other instances, such as when Rousseau addresses the absence of enmity in the state of nature: "men were not prone to very dangerous quarrels since they had no dealings of any kind with one another.... They did not even dream of vengeance except perhaps mechanically, on the spot like the dog that bites the stone thrown at him" (163, 157). The inconsequentiality of natural, physical inequalities has a similar source: "What advantage would the more favored enjoy at the expense of others in a state that allowed for almost no relations of any sort between them?" (167, *161*). What Rousseau describes as the solitary animal independence of natural man results in a key paradox, the impossibility of conceiving an origin of language:

> I leave to anyone who wishes to undertake it, the discussion of this difficult Problem: which was the more necessary, an already united Society for the institution of Languages, or already invented Languages for the establishment of Society?
>
> Whatever may be the case regarding these origins, it is at least clear from how little care Nature has taken to bring Men together through mutual needs and to facilitate their use of speech how little it prepared their Sociability. . . . Indeed, it is impossible to imagine why, in that primitive state, a man would need another man any more than a monkey or a Wolf would need his kind, or, assuming that need, to imagine what motive could induce the other to attend to it, or even, if he did, how they might agree on terms. (157–158, *151*)

In this context it is clear that sociality—and not perfectibility—constitutes the difference between human beings, on the one hand, and natural men, monkeys, and wolves, on the other. However, if in making man an isolated self-sufficient creature, "Nature" does not arrange for sociability and all the faculties that owe their development to mutual interaction, then "Nature" itself—as a theoretically constructed origin—will have to be changed from a site in which individuals are capable of living independently of one another into a site in which individuals are shaped by the need for one another and by the succor of commerce with one another. The condition of being in need of others does not represent a loss of autonomy in this text because autonomy does not lie at the theoretical foundation of meditation on "*human* nature." By the logic of the *Discourse*, the becoming-dependent of natural man coincides with his being-human.

Perpetuating Perpetual Asociality: Sex and the Single Mother

The *Discourse* does indeed contrive to change "Nature" so as to bring men together, but it does not present any progression from animal to human condition. If, as I have argued, it is the lonely self-sufficiency of natural man that blocks his development from animal to human in the *Discourse*, and if, as others have argued, the autonomy of natural man represents an originary human condition, then why is every potential movement from solitude to sociality explored only to be obstructed? This paradoxical frustration of what is apparently a tale of origins may best be understood if the solitary animal condition of natural man, so fully elaborated in the *Discourse*, is *not* taken as a representation of the human being in a primitive or original condition but rather as a refutation of the possibility of taking autonomy to be the natural condition against which all others seem to be fallings away, compromises, losses.

It is important to appreciate Rousseau's insistence on the permanence of natural man's incarceration in the state of solitary self-sufficiency. The consistency with which the *Discourse* blocks all possible avenues of evolution from solitariness to sociality is perhaps most effectively evinced by its treatment of the most obvious situation in which natural man would need another of his kind. Infancy in the life of an animal physically identical to the human being clearly entails dependence and prolonged interaction with an other and thus would seem the most logical point at which to imagine a starting point for social life, and yet this developmental stage receives only scant attention in the *Discourse*. Indeed, when childhood and parenting are addressed, they are presented not as formative periods in the life of natural man or woman, but as exceptional and fleeting phases within the static continuity of isolated individual existence. The insistence on the persistence of an asocial form of life, in spite of the exigencies of child rearing, is particularly remarkable given that, in part 2 of the *Discourse*, where "Nature" is imagined to bring human beings together, Rousseau will claim that "the habit of living together gave rise to the sweetest sentiments known to man, conjugal love and paternal love" as "each family became a small society" (173–174, *168*). Thus two key related questions about part 1 arise: Why does the sexual drive itself not constitute grounds for conceiving of some sustained interaction between individuals? And why doesn't the parent-child relationship constitute grounds for conceiving the origin of family (and hence society)? That is: Why do the biological facts of prolonged infantile dependence and the sexual intercourse necessary for reproduction of the species *not* lead to that very "habit of living together" and the sentiments it engenders in the state of nature?

The dependency of infancy, as imagined in the *Discourse*, is neither particular to natural man—for there are a "hundred other species whose young are for a long time not in a condition to forage for themselves" (144, 137)—nor identical to that of our own day because "there are many good reasons to believe that [children's] strength and their organs develop later among us than they did in the primitive state" and that, consequently, "they could walk, act, and fend for themselves much earlier" (223–224, 217). Natural woman, meanwhile, does not lose her self-sufficiency when she becomes a mother; she easily provides for the infant on her own: "carry[ing] her child with her everywhere, she can feed it much more readily than can the females of a number of animals, forced as they are to wear themselves out going back and forth, in one direction to find their food, in the other to suckle or feed their young" (144, 137). The emphasis on the mother's autonomy is so insistent in the *Discourse*, and yet at the same time the account of infancy and parenting is so uncharacteristically sketchy, that some readers have been provoked to supply supporting details that might lend plausibility to the representation. Francis Moran, for example, attempts to fill out Rousseau's picture of infancy by citing sources (such as Andrew Battel's account of an infant pongo clinging to his mother's body rather than being carried in her arms) and pointing to contemporaneous illustrations of Hottentots that show an infant "able not only to cling to its mother's back but to be suckled in this position." While Moran plausibly reasons that the "ability to transport and nurse a baby in this fashion would seem to be a considerable advantage to natural woman since it would allow her to retain relative freedom of movement of both arms and legs," and that possibly Rousseau also imagined that human females in the state of nature could have been similarly endowed, the very need to supplement and embellish begs the question: What is theoretically at stake in imagining the physical possibility of a woman independently foraging, nursing, and protecting a newborn infant?[21] Whether or not images consistent with that of Rousseau's self-sufficient mother are to be found in the eighteenth-century literature on anthropoids and Hottentots, it is certainly the case that the *logical* structure of the state of nature as the state in which men (and women) live isolated from one another *requires* the imagination of such a female. Moreover, it requires the imagination not only of the *physical* capacity to mother a child independently but also the more challenging imagination that this same woman soon abandons her child to its solitary fate.

The absence of affective consequence or intellectual impact in both infant and parent—rather than any physical obstacle—is perhaps the weakest link in the conjectural chain that the *Discourse* designs to keep individuals isolated from one another, their hearts and minds filled with nothing. The hardly sentimental Voltaire, offended at the absence of emotional engagement in this account, would contend—in explicit opposition to Rousseau—that "by a dominant instinct, the coarsest of men love the child who is yet unborn, the womb which carries it, and the mother who swells with love for him from whom she has received in her bosom [*sein*] the seed of a being akin [*semblable*] to herself."[22] Reflection on infantile dependence and maternal bonding as formative of human nature is indeed common in eighteenth-century writing, and one might find in Shaftesbury, in Hume, and even in Locke and Mandeville, an admission of this element that the first part of the *Discourse* actually seeks to avoid including.[23] Given that the second Nature devised in the *Discourse* counts conjugal and parental bonds as the "sweetest sentiments," it is difficult to understand why the same ground remains uncultivated in part 1 of the *Discourse*—unless it is, in fact, crucial to the argument of the text that there is no exit from the state of asociality, not in the physical fact of infantile dependence and certainly not in the prospect of affective attachment on the part of a parent. Nursing of the infant is initially driven by the woman's "own need," and the utmost conceded to the formation of a maternal bond is that nursing continues even after her own need has been met: "habit having made [her children] dear to her, she nourished them because of theirs" (153, 147). However, the habit is short-lived and easily broken, for "as soon as they had the strength to forage on their own, they left even the Mother; and since almost the only way to find one another again was not to lose sight of one another in the first place, they soon were at the point of not even recognizing each other" (153, 147).[24] Lest this losing sight of one another be misunderstood as a deeper type of loss, something that might lurk in the heart of natural woman, the *Discourse* contends that "the child no longer meant anything to the mother as soon as it could do without her" (170, 164). The inevitable estrangement of parent and child without impact on the sentiments of either also arrests any possible development of the mental faculties or culture: "If he by chance made some discovery, he was all the less in a position to communicate it as he did not recognize even his Children. The art perished with the inventor; there was neither education nor progress, generations multiplied uselessly" (166, 160).

If no continued relationship between individuals in the state of nature is to be derived from childhood dependence and parental succor, then it should come as no surprise that the physical need that brings the sexes together also provides no basis on which to construct the development of sustained interaction: "males and females united fortuitously, according to chance encounters, opportunity, and desire . . . they parted just as readily" (153, 147). The note appended to this passage argues at length—principally against Locke—that no "permanent union" evolves from these occasional couplings. Physical need alone determines and limits the kind of knowledge that male and female have of each other.[25] "Devoid of any sentiment of the heart," the "blind inclination" to perpetuate the species "produced only a purely animal act" and once the "need [is] satisfied, the two sexes no longer recognized each other" (170, 164). Deprived of the knowledge of—and hence also the desire for—affective attachment or relationship, nothing "humanizes" intercourse in the state of nature. There are sexual relations, but there is no love; offspring are produced, but no families are formed. The elaboration of sex and reproduction in the state of nature is austerely consistent with the passional and intellectual limitations of natural man.

> Once the appetite is satisfied, the man no longer needs this woman, nor the woman this man. He has not the least worry nor, perhaps, the least idea of the consequences of his action. One goes off in this direction, the other in that, and there is no likelihood that at the end of nine months they will remember ever having known each other: For the kind of memory by which one individual manifests preference for another individual for the act of procreation requires, as I prove in the text, more progress or corruption of the *human* understanding than it can be assumed to have in the *state of animality* that is here at issue. (224, 217; emphases added)

Given what natural man knows (or, rather, given all that he does not know), would he see any relation at all between himself and a child, any child? Between the sexual act and the production of offspring? In the passage from the *Second Treatise* that Rousseau addresses in note 12, Locke represents the necessity of prolonged partnership as a fact of human biology: "The chief, if not the only reason, *why the Male and Female in Mankind are tyed to a longer conjunction* than other Creatures, *viz.* because the Female is capable of conceiving, and *de facto* is commonly with Child again, and Brings forth too a new birth, long before the former is out of dependancy . . . whereby the Father, who is bound to take care for those he hath begot, is under an Obligation to continue in Conjugal Society with the same Woman longer than other Creatures, whose young [are] able to subsist of themselves."[26] We have already seen how Rousseau disputes the argument based on analogy to "other creatures" by supplying his own facts about animal behavior. More important, however, is the pressure Rousseau here brings to bear on the "obligation to continue in conjugal society." Locke reasons that the longer the society between male and female, the more likely are subsequent pregnancies and births, which in turn create ever more lasting bonds. The more enduring society formed depends not only on the fact of the physical dependence of human infants but also on an understanding of the causal relation between sex and procreation. The question then, as Rousseau asks, is why a man in the state of nature would help a woman "rear a child he does not even know is his, and whose birth he neither willed nor foresaw?" "Obligation" aside, Locke at the very least must presuppose knowledge about procreation that natural man cannot possess: "It is not a matter of knowing why a man remains attached to a woman after birth, but why he gets attached to her after conception" (224, *217*).[27] And although posed as a question about natural *man*, the presupposition exposed here applies to both sexes. Indeed, the argument is almost meticulously egalitarian in its insistence on the mutual indifference with which male and female regard each other after appetite has brought them together. Without instinct for or custom of cohabitation, without need that exceeds the physical appetite for sex, without the knowledge of physiological cause and effect that would connect an act of intercourse to a slowly swelling belly and, nine months later, a birth, neither female nor male have reason to abide with each other. A woman in the state of nature may know, from previous physical experience, that a child grows inside her, but surely the origin of this child is a mystery to her. It is not just natural man, after all, who neither wills nor foresees conception and procreation as the consequence of copulation.

"There is, therefore, no reason for the man to seek out the same woman, nor for the woman to seek out the same man" (224, *218*). As everywhere else in this "state of animality," there is no occasion or motivation for isolated, self-sufficient individuals to prolong their occasional, intermittent moments of encounter. To seek, in the physical appetite for sexual intercourse, an origin for what Locke calls "conjugal society" involves a specious introduction of humanizing sentiment into the autonomous animal that inhabits the state of nature. "All of that philosopher's dialectic," Rousseau concludes, "has not protected him against the error Hobbes and others committed." The error lies in imperceptibly compromising the state of isolation and autonomy that is the theoretical starting point of philosophical speculation on the nature of human beings.

> They had to explain a fact of the state of Nature, that is to say of a state where men lived isolated, and where one particular man had no motive whatsoever to remain near some other particular man, nor perhaps, which is far worse, did men have any motive to remain near one another; and it did not occur to them to transport themselves beyond the Centuries of Society, that is to say beyond those times when men always have a reason to remain close to one another, and when a particular man often has a reason to remain by the side of a particular woman. (224–225, *218*)

The fact in need of explanation here is boldly clear and simple: How could natural men ever come to "remain close to one another" (the French is *demeurer*, to dwell or reside) from "a state where men lived isolated," if that isolation is rigorously and non-teleologically theorized? The argument has implications beyond the correction of Hobbes and other philosophers, though they provide the immediate provocation for Rousseau's investigation into a state of nature he notoriously identified as one that "no longer exists, which perhaps never did exist, which probably never will exist." The fact that we do dwell with one another stands, powerful and unshakable, over against and in defiance of this hypothetical state, though each path of potential development from the theoretical origin of autonomy to the actuality of interdependence is obstructed. The *Discourse* does not purport to be an investigation of why or how human beings come to dwell with one another, but it is this question that the first part of the *Discourse* repeatedly asks and cannot answer. To think "beyond the Centuries of Society" is not, in the *Discourse*, to think of a time *prior* to the establishment of society; rather, it is to imagine a space that is perfectly asocial rather than necessarily *pre*social. If nothing compels a movement from isolated animal existence to social life and the development of the distinctively human capabilities contingent on it, then the conceptual foundations must shift; the ground zero of reflection on the "nature" of human beings can no longer be a state of (animal) independence.

Theoretical Leaps and Factual Gaps: Remaking "Nature"

The *Discourse* presents no simple evolutionary model of human development. The transition from "state of nature" (synonymous with state of isolation; or state of animality, as Rousseau defined it) to a state in which the "natural habitat"[28] of human beings is among other human beings occurs as rupture and re-beginning rather than as development or evolution, because, without a radical reconstruction of the original condition, natural man will never acquire those faculties that humanize him. "Nature" itself must be transformed from a "state where men lived isolated" to one in which individuals always already exist in a state of mutual need. "Singular and fortuitous combinations of circumstances," "foreign causes which might never have arisen," "contingencies," "facts that are unknown," "long barren years," "a volcano," "some happy accident"—these are some of the vague and conjectural events that allow for the passage from the solitary animal existence of the first part of the *Discourse* to the phases of human society traced in the second part. The inadequacy of this transition in the *Discourse* has inspired numerous critical efforts to provide the missing links between parts 1 and 2, and to construct an orderly evolution between them. Such lines of interpretation risk replicating the very error the *Discourse* identifies in previous theories of the state of nature, for in spite of the text's caution against mistaking its conjectures for "historical truths" about "genuine origins," many readers have persisted in treating the sketchy "concatenation" of "circumstances that might never have arisen" as a satisfying historical explanation of the origin of societies. The various, unspecified *"hasards"* are elevated to the status of "causes" when described in terms that only the past century of evolutionary theory has made available.[29] Yet so insistent is the *Discourse* on the unknowability, uncertainty, and contingency of the "accidents" that change the state of nature from a place where individuals live in isolation to a place of mutual needs as to suggest that the absence of a cause is more than a weakness in the argument. There is no historical development out of the state of nature because human history does not begin there.

Having concluded that natural man "would eternally have remained in his primitive condition" in the absence of the "fortuitous concatenation of foreign causes that might never have arisen," the *Discourse*'s discussion of the state of nature concludes with this meditation on transition:

> When two facts given as real [that is, the fact of the asocial state of nature, on the one hand, and the fact of the social state of humanity, on the other] are to be connected by a sequence of intermediate facts that are unknown or believed to be so, it is up to history, if available, to provide the facts that connect them; in the absence of history, it is up to Philosophy to ascertain similar facts that might connect them. (169, 162–163)

History, in this case, be it anthropological, archaeological, or evolutionary, is unavailable, and thus philosophical conjecture must fill in, as best it can, the missing link of coherent causation. But what if a fact "given as real" is not real at all but is itself conjectural in status and theoretical in aim? What if there is no first fact (the state of nature conceived as the state where men live isolated) to connect to the second (the state of sociality)? The accidents and contingencies invoked at the end of part 1 of the *Discourse* may be understood as philosophical disclosure of that which history could never disclose: that the first given fact, the asocial state, is now, and always was, philosophical fiction.

Natural Supernaturalism

The *Discourse*'s initial image of natural man is of a creature "conformed as [we] see him today," fully grown, erect, "using his hands as we do ours, directing his gaze over the whole of Nature." But let us not be fooled by physical appearance. "By stripping [*en dépouillant*] the being, so constituted, of all the supernatural gifts he may have received, and of all the artificial faculties he could only have acquired by prolonged progress," Rousseau imagines a solitary animal (141, 134). The procedure is neither one of restoration nor of recovery but of metamorphosis *via* subtraction and negation. Of all the meanings of the verb *dépouiller* (to denude, to plunder, to cast off, to dispossess), its primary denotation—to skin (as in remove the hide of an animal)—is perhaps most evocative in this context, for it captures the sense in which the "supernatural" and "artificial" do not line up in simple opposition to the categories of the "natural" and "authentic." With rare exceptions, after all, the skin of an animal only becomes extrinsic to it when it ceases to live.

That which is "supernatural" and "artificial" to the constitution of Rousseau's "man" is not necessarily superadded or extraneous but may be tightly bound up with its "natural" form, as is skin to an animal.

As we have seen, reason, forethought, knowledge, and self-consciousness are among the faculties Rousseau strips from his imaginary animal. The condition for the possibility of all these intellectual capacities is language, which must also be counted as a "supernatural" endowment because, like all the others, Rousseau's attempt to account for its origins in the state of nature ends with an unanswerably circular question implying the impossibility of doing so: "Which was the more necessary, an already united Society for the institution of Languages, or already invented Languages for the establishment of Society?" Having catalogued all that must be accounted for in accounting for language (the invention of "numbers, abstract words, aorists, and all the tenses of verbs, particles, syntax . . . propositions, arguments . . . the entire logic of discourse"), Rousseau confesses himself "frightened by the increasing difficulties, and convinced of the almost demonstrated impossibility that languages could have arisen and been established by purely human means" (157, 151). Jean Starobinski identifies this moment as a grand concession made to those who contend that language is divine in origin, one "conjured up as a last resort, less for itself than because of the failure of the preceding hypothesis." The concession carries with it certain unavoidable implications: "to accept without reserve the divine foundation of language would at the same time be to renounce the notion of savage man, the entire presocial history and thus to ruin the theoretical construction of the *Discourse*."[30] Yet, as others have argued, Rousseau's construction of the state of nature may be precisely designed to illustrate its implausibility. "The demonstration that every attempt to assign an absolute beginning to language—or to mutual understanding, or to moral relations—is inevitably circular," writes Victor Gourevitch, "serves as a conclusive *reductio ad absurdum* of the premise of wholly isolated, self-sufficient, speechless individuals and so of the pure state of nature." The aporia with which the discussion of language concludes is characteristic of a text in which the "difficulty of origins repeats itself everywhere" and in which human beginnings remain a "metaphysical puzzle" *so long as* isolation is the assumed origin.[31] Involvement with other persons must be seen as the most significant of the "supernatural gifts" Rousseau strips from his hypothetical man of nature.

If the intertwined, untraceable origins of language and society implicitly entail the "supernatural"—understood as something more than, or other than, what is found in the state of nature—then it is perhaps not surprising that Rousseau's insistence on the impossibility of "returning" to the state of nature that he has described rests on the impossibility of escaping the force of a "supernatural" vision—understood as inspiring and obligating individuals toward ideal forms of relations with one another. Only those "to whom the celestial voice has not made itself heard," he writes, could "go into the woods" without fear of "debasing [the] species." But who has heard this "celestial voice"?

> Those who were honored in their first Father with supernatural lessons; those who will see in the intention of giving from the beginning a morality to human actions which they would not have acquired for a long time, the reason for a precept indifferent in itself and inexplicable in any other System; those, in a word, who are convinced that the divine voice called all Mankind to the enlightenment and the happiness of the celestial Intelligences; they will, all of them, try, by practicing the virtues which they obligate themselves to perform as they learn to know them, to deserve the eternal prize they must expect; they will respect the sacred bonds of the Societies of which they are members; they will love their kind and serve them with all their power. (213, 207)

The unmistakably Christian tone and enigmatic allusion to an unidentified "precept" in this passage (added while the *Discourse* was in press) has puzzled readers. While many agree that the precept to which Rousseau refers is the injunction not to eat of the tree of the knowledge of good and evil, the ethical practice prescribed, particularly that of loving one's kind, leads others to suggest the command to love one's neighbor as most appropriately related to the context of this passage.[32] In either case, the "supernatural lessons," which, once learned, cannot be forgotten, entail the moral possibilities of human relations, the challenges and aspirations of which necessarily assume a social context.

The "sad and constant experience" of Life among Others

Taken together, Rousseau's two *Discourses* are best known as uncompromising indictments of the moral failings and corruption that are endemic to "civilization." The long endnote that culminates in the reminder of "supernatural lessons" about our "sacred bonds" begins with the famous dictum that "Man is good but men are wicked," and, in a recapitulation of themes from the *Discourse on the Arts and Sciences*, proceeds to chronicle the disadvantages of technology, the pernicious effects of culture, and the depravities of luxury. Although the wickedness of men is presented as increasing and spreading relative to "progress," wickedness itself appears to arise from the mere fact of men being together rather than apart from one another.

"Society" as such "moves men to hate one another in proportion as their interests cross" (208, 202), but conflict between individual interests is not the fundamental problem in Rousseau's imagination. Rather, the covert, hidden nature of conflict appears insuperable: men render one another "apparent services" while intending and doing one another actual harm; a "private person's reason" dictates something contrary to what "public reason" advocates; heirs "secretly wish" their parents dead; "frivolous displays of beneficence" mask "what goes on in the recesses of men's hearts" (208, 202–203). If Rousseau graphically imagines that, driven by ever greater needs and desires, "my hero [the successful man in society] will end up by cutting every throat until he is sole master of the universe," then the truly grave threat is not posed by the excesses of this striver but by his representing the "*secret* aspirations of the heart of *every* civilized man," by his being a figure for the socialized human being as such (209, 203; emphases added). Consumed by ambition and greed, the mind and heart of civilized man is filled with "secret jealousy" and "black inclination" toward others: "To be and to appear became two different things" and from that cleavage arises the possibility of "display," "deceit," "disguise" (180–181, 174).

Rousseau presents the "state of things where all men are forced to both caress and destroy one another" as a culminating point in human history, but it is important to understand that the power to dissimulate and the corresponding vulnerability to deception imply an *inherently limited* capacity to apprehend intentions and thoughts that afflicts all persons living together at all stages of civilization. While in the *First Discourse*, the cleavage between being and appearance is indeed presented as a consequence of refinement, a tragic change from simpler times ("Before art had fashioned our manners . . . men found their security in how easily they saw through one another [*se pénétrer reciproquement*]," but now "one no longer dares to appear what one is" [6, 8]), the *Second Discourse* imagines no moment in which individuals could "see through" one another. The discernment of artifice would seem, logically, to assume some preexistent authenticity, corruption to imply a prior purity, but this is not the case in the *Discourse on Inequality*.

The nostalgic rhetoric of the *Discourse on the Arts and Sciences* assumes the loss of a capacity that perhaps never existed; all that is "no longer" in the *First Discourse* ("sincere friendships," "real esteem," "well-founded trust") never really comes to be in the *Second Discourse*. Even after the "fortuitous concatenation of circumstances," when Rousseau represents human origins as social ("each family became a small society"), even as the "habit of living together gave rise to the sweetest sentiments known to man," the bitter possibilities of human sociality are equally present: "jealousy awakens together with love," delight and admiration also engender "vanity and contempt," "shame and envy," "injury," and "contempt" (175, 169).[33] But for a brief and incompletely imagined instant when a "tender and sweet sentiment steals into the soul," animosity also finds lodging there, albeit hidden under a "mask of benevolence." "One never really knows with whom one is dealing," writes Rousseau in the *First Discourse*: it is precisely this *not knowing* that both engenders and leaves one vulnerable to suspicions, offenses, fears—and that the individual must react to and defend himself against in what the *Second Discourse* describes as the "sad and constant experience of social life."

Rousseau's speculative history ends where Hobbes's investigations begin, culminating in repeated and intensified emphases on the hiddenness of thoughts, desires, and motivations.[34] It is worth recalling that Hobbes's confidence in the similitude of human passions (to "read thyself" is to know mankind) is immediately qualified (in the introduction to *Leviathan*) by the proposition that "things desired, feared, hoped, are so easie to be kept from our knowledge that the characters of man's heart" are "blotted and confounded . . . with lying, dissembling, counterfeiting." The notion that "ambition, anger, and avarice" are lodged deep within the human heart is derived from the epistemic limitation that makes it easy for individuals to keep things from one another.[35] In the previous chapter I suggested that anti-Hobbesian moralists such as Shaftesbury countered this threat by hypothesizing a natural inclination to benevolence and that Hume more directly attempted to obviate (if not resolve) the epistemological problem of knowing others by assuming a natural "transparency" of minds. In Hobbes, the possibility of being "deceived by too much trust" (83) is not resolved, but the danger is attenuated through the social contract and submission to sovereign power. In Rousseau, the problem is obdurate and inescapable because it is coincident with the very sociality that also makes possible language, forethought, self-consciousness, and the other specifically "human" faculties.

The opacity of individuals to one another is the deforming constraint and misfortune of social life and of the human nature *necessarily* formed in social life as Rousseau conceives it in the *Second Discourse*. While the moral implications of that opacity are predominant in Rousseau's argument, and in the context of the political and ethical theories with which the *Discourse* is in dialogue, the epistemological implication of the idea that being and appearing are two different things is perhaps more critical to an understanding of the continuity of concerns linking the *Discourses* to his other writings. The human being described in part 2 of the *Discourse* is one whose survival involves a set of adaptive traits designed to exploit the difficulty of knowing and being known by others among which might be counted the cultivation of privacy, of hidden interests, motives, desires, and hostilities, and hence the advantage of regarding others with suspicion. These are moral habits and attitudes that arise from and make use of the fact that intersubjectivity is epistemically limited. If the human relations described in the *Discourse* are ones in which the limits of intersubjectivity are exploited by all and suffered by all, then the human relations prescribed in the utopian works that follow the two *Discourses—Letter to d'Alembert* (1758), *La Nouvelle Héloïse* (1760), *Emile* (1761), and *Social Contract* (1762)—are designed to restrict the possibility of exploiting and suffering from that vulnerability. Each of these works takes on the task of imagining forms of social life that would engender different adaptations to our insecure knowledge of one another. Thus Emile is brought up in conditions which ensure that he "does not think of dissembling," "does not know what use there is in deceit," but his honesty is not strictly moral in the sense of engaging the will. His virtue consists of being credible, being a wholly knowable object: "not a single movement takes place in his soul which his mouth or eyes do not reveal."[36]

Emile's appearance and being reliably correspond. Rousseau's imagination of the possibility of that correspondence generally entails the elimination of privacy and particularity, the (re)formation of individuals as predictable and exposed members of an inescapably public realm.[37] Thus at the appropriately named "Clarens," the utopian estate over which Wolmar presides in *La Nouvelle Héloïse*, "one moral precept take[s] the place of all the others . . . : never do or say anything that you do not want the whole world to see and hear." But the very idea of "not wanting" the whole world to hear and see cannot arise in worlds like Clarens or the Swiss communities described in the *Letter to d'Alembert* that are designed to keep individuals revealingly before one another, "always in the public eye."[38] The epistemological certainty guaranteed by such public forms of life is perhaps most explicit in the courtship rituals Rousseau describes in the *Letter to d'Alembert*. Young men and women are given "occasion to get a taste for one another and to see one another" at feasts or dances where "the eyes of the public are constantly open and upon them." "Can a more decent way of not deceiving one another (*ne point trompé autrui*) be imagined?" Rousseau asks—or a better way of "show[ing] themselves off (*se montrer*) to the people whose interest it is to know them before being obliged to love them?" (128, 271). To know *before* being obliged to love, knowledge as the precondition of love: the criteria for this knowing ("to get a taste of," "to see") entail the sense impressions on which empiricism relies for its knowledge of objects so that an epistemological ambition or ideal—the founding of human relations on a secure basis of knowledge—is here combined and confounded with a moral aspiration or ideal—a "decent way of not deceiving" and of never being deceived. The citizens and lovers inhabiting Rousseau's utopias do not, or cannot, exploit to their advantage the cleavage between being and appearing. They behave with the consistency and predictability associated with a stable world of things. Emile is formed so that he does not "take a step without your having foreseen it . . . [nor] open his mouth without your knowing what he is going to say" (120, 363). At these points Rousseau approaches Locke's wishful reflections on the wonders of vision that could penetrate the surface of the body to see the animating flow of life within; both fantasies betray a desire to ascertain the correspondence between being and appearance. The wish the later philosopher articulates is that of giving human relations the same "inflexibility" as the laws of nature, so that "dependence on men would then become dependence on things" (85, 311).[39]

The epistemological ideal is melodramatically dismantled, however, in the ruin of the two unions at the romantic heart of Rousseau's utopias. In *La Nouvelle Héloïse*, Julie literally perishes from an intensifying fear of her own potential for infidelity. Espousing the duty to be a reliable object of her husband's trust, the doubt that only she can spare her husband becomes a doubt she casts on herself. "I have lost the right to depend on myself," Julie confesses near the end, "I dare pride myself in the past but who can answer to me for the future? One more day, perhaps, and I might be guilty," she decides (741). Self-suspicion is a wound she inflicts on herself; the sudden spasms of doubt she suffers culminate in fatal illness. In the unfinished sequel to *Emile*, *Emile et Sophie, ou Les Solitaires* (composed in 1762), the ideal spouse designed both to be and "to be judged to be faithful by her husband, by those near her, by everyone" abruptly announces "another has soiled your bed; I am pregnant" ("*un autre a souillé votre lit; je suis enceinte*").[40] The feared suspicion of betrayal that Sophie had been painstakingly constructed to forestall is thus suddenly, inexplicably confirmed. The vulnerability at the heart of human relations makes itself felt in spite of how fully or how well the other is known. Ultimately the fantastic disappointment Rousseau contrives for Emile, the fantasy of such an ending to the union he had imagined, suggests that the overcoming of epistemic limitations is a misguided conceptual effort.[41] Emile does not, after all, suffer the consequences of being deceived or mistaken in his apprehension of his wife but, rather, of discovering himself no longer loved by her: "*Elle ne m'aime plus, la perfide! Ah! c'est là son plus grand crime*" (902). What knowledge of the other can protect one from such crime?

The utopian thought experiments fail insofar as their subjects remain at the mercy of others, vulnerable to injury and betrayal, but Rousseau does not ever fully abandon the epistemic diagnosis of this vulnerability. Loving remains contingent on knowing—such is the foundation on which Rousseau continues to build and which repeatedly collapses. What unites the final autobiographical trilogy—*Confessions* (composed 1764–1770), *Dialogues, Rousseau juge de Jean-Jacques* (composed 1772–1776), and *Reveries of a Solitary Walker* (composed 1776–1778)—if not successive and cumulative failures of trust, disappointed affections, unexpected ruptures of attachment? The life history Rousseau recounts in these works repeatedly confirms the discovery of the *First Discourse*; the cleavage between being and appearing means that "one will ... never really know with whom one is dealing," that "suspicions, offenses, fears, coolness, reserve, hatred, betrayal, will constantly hide beneath [the] uniform and deceitful [*perfide*] veil of politeness" (6, 8).

o o o

To see the persistence of epistemic uncertainty about other persons through Rousseau's works is to appreciate the intransigence of the intersubjective anxieties he describes in the *Discourse on Inequality*. "Secret aspirations" and "black inclinations" and the miserable wariness that are the "sad and constant experience" of sociality appear to be intrinsic to human forms of life in Rousseau's imagination. What is most remarkable and seldom fully appreciated is that Rousseau's unstinting admission of the vulnerabilities of living among others occurs alongside, as part of, a powerful repudiation of a theoretical definition of human beings that would obviate those vulnerabilities. "Mutual dependence" and "reciprocal needs" are, in Rousseau, the origin of troubling weakness but are also inescapably necessary conditions for the development of language, knowledge, passion, reason, and a range of other faculties considered specifically human.

The heuristic purpose of prior philosophical constructions of the state of nature—particularly those of Hobbes and Locke—concerned establishing how and on what terms individuals enter—or contract—into social and moral relations with one another from a position of essential independence. Rousseau's state of nature is consistent with such constructions—presenting a solitary, independent "natural man"—but also, and pointedly, radically opposed to them—allowing for no passage from "nature" to "society," showing the creature who comes to maturity in isolation to be incompletely human.

The notion that it is impossible to imagine human beings as other than dependent on and related to one another is not unique to Rousseau. But the yoking together of conviction of the necessity of living among others with acknowledgment of the irremediable unease and fragility of attachments and associations engenders an idea of dependence that is too complex and dark to be assimilated among other enlightenment theories of natural sociability. As we shall see in the next chapter, by the end of the eighteenth century, for all its ubiquity and remarkable influence in culture, the meaning of the *Second Discourse* had become so indeterminate that the very arguments—indeed the very words—Rousseau used to repudiate original independence would be employed, paradoxically enough, in refutation of his own purportedly idealized representation of natural man. The demystification of isolation and independence as realistic—even as idealistic—bases for thinking about being human will be the ongoing concern of subsequent chapters, as will the acknowledgment of the moral and epistemic challenges of life among others that is the particularly Rousseauvian demand met in the works of Wordsworth, Shelley, and Mill.

CHAPTER 3

Natural Man in the Wild

THE FERAL CHILD AS PHILOSOPHICAL SUBJECT

L'Homme Sauvage, livré par la Nature au seul instinct . . . commencera donc par les fonctions purement animales. . . . Ses desirs ne passent pas ses besoins Physiques. Les seuls biens qu'il connaisse dans l'Univers, sont la nourriture, une femelle, et le repos.

[Savage man, left by Nature to bare instinct alone . . . will then begin with purely animal functions. . . . His desires do not exceed his physical needs; the only goods he knows in the Universe are food, a female, and rest.]
  Jean-Jacques Rousseau, *Discours sur les origines et fondements de l'inégalité parmi les hommes*, 1755

Livré par la nature au seul instinct, cet enfant n'exerce que des fonctions purement animales . . . ses désirs ne dépassent pas ses besoins physiques. Les seuls biens qu'il connaisse dans l'univers, sont la nourriture, le repos, et l'indépendance.

[Left by nature to instinct alone, this child performs only purely animal functions . . . his desires do not exceed his physical needs. The only goods he knows in the universe and food, rest, and independence.]
  Pierre-Joseph Bonnaterre, *Notice historique sur le sauvage de l'Aveyron*, 1800

By the end of the eighteenth century, Rousseau's natural man comes to occupy a singularly paradoxical position in culture. The *Discourse on Inequality* is both read as the paradigmatic expression of an ideal of solitary, savage, uncorrupted being and used as an important source for arguments and rhetoric aimed at discrediting that ideal. The aura of contradiction surrounding this important text is itself unsurprising given that it contains an elaborate and seductive construction of the very hypothesis it aims to dismantle. Nevertheless, the paradoxes posed by Rousseau's *Discourse* not only troubled the recourse to animals discussed in the previous chapter but also complicated approaches to living human "examples" of the hypothetical original condition.

I argue, in chapter 4, that the essential attributes of the independent mind and man described in Locke's philosophy—solitude, self-sufficiency, and freedom from influence—are used by Mary Shelley to define an absolute and monstrous deviation from the human. But the normative premises of eighteenth-century psychology are not suddenly revealed to be fantastically unworkable and abortive in a flash of post-enlightenment insight. Tentative and small shifts in perspective on human formation make possible Shelley's transvaluative revision of natural man as monster. The present chapter is a case study intended to bring that shift into focus by examining scientific writings that borrowed liberally, and for contradictory purposes, from Rousseau's *Discourse* in order to understand and diagnose the array of impairments presented by Victor of Aveyron, one of the most famous of the so-called wild children—unfortunate isolated cases that it sometimes seems eighteenth-century philosophy would have needed to invent had circumstances not brought them to public attention.

"A Child Cut off from all of Society . . . Scrutinized Down to the Slightest Movements He Might Make"

The "discovery" of Victor of Aveyron may be seen as the sensational climax of the eighteenth-century fascination with rare cases of children abandoned to the wild.[1] Classed as a separate species of human being by Linnaeus, *Homo sapiens ferus* represented a tantalizing and uncanny blurring of the conceptual lines separating man and beast. Interest in these cases had always been far in excess of reliable information about them, however. Of the ten instances itemized by Linnaeus in the thirteenth edition of *Systema naturae* (1788), all but Peter of Hanover and the wild girl of Champagne are shrouded in the mystery created by historical distance and sketchy accounts, and even those cases are not nearly so well documented as that of Victor of Aveyron, who ultimately became the charge of a medical and scientific community acutely aware of the potential significance of the case for the progress of human knowledge.[2]

The philosophical self-consciousness that characterizes the reports on Victor's case offers an extraordinary example of the interpenetration between theories of human nature and scientific study during a period in which political theory, biology, linguistics, and anthropology were compounded under the single term *human science*. Philosophical figures for the acquisition of knowledge such as Locke's "white paper void of characters," Condillac's gradually animated statue, and Rousseau's natural man made it possible to imagine that Victor might present a pure model for the study of individual development. Reporting on Victor's arrival in Paris for the *Gazette de France*, the Abbé Sicard (director of the Institute for Deaf-Mutes that would eventually be responsible for evaluating Victor's condition) captures the intellectual excitement surrounding the case, eagerly anticipating that the child would now be "the object of observations by true philosophers," that he would be

> visited promptly by those who have long desired to raise a child cut off from all of society and all intellectual communication, a child to whom no one had ever spoken and who would be scrutinized down to the slightest movements he might make to express his first sensations, his first ideas, his first thoughts.[3]

While Sicard accurately expressed the level of interest in the subject of this "forbidden experiment," he nevertheless managed to make a number of telling descriptive errors in his eyewitness account. Sicard's observation that Victor "occasionally seems touched by the care he is tendered, and he offers his hand of his own accord to those who express any interest in him," contradicts more credible accounts of his behavior which describe the boy "express(ing) no kind of affection for those who attended upon him" and even "biting and scratching" individuals in the throngs who pressed upon him. "The most brilliant but unreasonable expectations were formed by the people of Paris respecting the Savage of Aveyron, before he arrived," writes Jean-Marc-Gaspard Itard, the doctor who would undertake Victor's education. "What did they see? A disgusting, slovenly boy, affected with spasmodic, and frequently with convulsive motions, continually balancing himself like some of the animals in the menagerie . . . indifferent to every body, and paying no regard to any thing."[4] Sicard's sentimental misreporting of Victor's sociability is no stranger than his speculations about the boy's state of mind. "Nothing can console him for the loss of freedom and his earlier way of life," Sicard confidently asserts. The Abbé not only presumes that the boy's efforts to escape signify a yearning for an independence and liberty that can only be had in the wild (and not, for example, fear of the strangers who had suddenly, incomprehensibly become his captors), but in so doing he also conflates the very real mountains and forests around Aveyron with a purely hypothetical and idealized state of nature. Both the notion that the boy could interact with his caretakers with ease after years of isolation and the idea of his prior state as one of freedom—and not deprivation—cloud Sicard's perception of the mute, malnourished, convulsive child who arrived in Paris on July 20, 1800.

If prior assumptions about the nature of the individual and about human origins render Sicard in some sense unable to see the extent of Victor's impairment, it is also the case that Victor's condition could *only* be seen through the lenses shaped by those very philosophers (Locke, Condillac, Rousseau, and others) for whom "a child cut off from all society . . . to whom no one had ever spoken" could serve as a model for studying the development of sensations, thoughts, and ideas. Both the degree and the permanence of Victor's impairments would modify, and in some cases overturn, the very theoretical assumptions that many looked to his case to confirm—principal among them the idea that a child who had endured Victor's years alone could be in any way a normative model of human beings in their "natural" condition.

In his own day, and more recently, Victor has been seen to represent a powerful "countermyth" to Rousseau's natural man—an extremely degraded rather than uncorrupted and original form of the human. "I would really like to see J. J. Rousseau here, with all his rantings against the social state!" exclaimed the poet La Harpe on witnessing a disturbing display of Victor's "untamed" behavior.[5] The comment is typical of both the inevitable association between natural man and the wild child in the cultural imagination of the time, and of the tendency to see Victor as a living refutation of the philosopher's hypotheses. My interest here lies not in observing how the man of nature and the wild child are placed in opposition to each other but, rather, in showing how the reading and misreading of Rousseau can itself lead to a more complex understanding of the philosopher's state of nature. It is worth recalling, for example, Rousseau's own anticipation of the line of criticism to which La Harpe's comment belongs: "What then! Must we destroy societies . . . and return to live in the forests with bears?"—a conclusion, he adds, that could only be drawn "in the style of my adversaries."[6] Indeed, it is because Victor matches rather than contradicts the philosopher's expectations about man in a state of isolation that the *Discourse* became a source from which all the principal investigators of the case drew in order to describe the child's limitations and weaknesses.

Scientific documents adopted the language and reasoning of the *Discourse* in order to describe and understand the unusual case of an individual profoundly damaged in his capacity to learn, to communicate, and to interact effectively with others, and thus Rousseau's image of original human nature came to serve as a diagnostic template for the severe linguistic, cognitive, and affective impairments associated with such rare cases of extreme isolation. The investigators' writings thus beg the question of what kind of model the philosopher's natural man was supposed to offer. The three principal documents detailing Victor's initial physical, emotional, and intellectual condition are the *Notice historique sur le sauvage de l'Aveyron* (1800) by Pierre-Joseph Bonnaterre, professor of natural history at the *école centrale* of Aveyron and the scientist who studied the boy during his first six months out of the wild, prior to his transfer to Paris; the *Dissertation sur un jeune enfant trouvé dans les forets du département de l'Aveyron, avec des remarques sur l'état primitif de l'homme* (1800), written by the important naturalist Julien-Joseph Virey who based his account on Bonnaterre's report as well as on his own examination of Victor soon after the child's arrival in Paris; and *De l'éducation d'un homme sauvage ou des premiers développements physiques et moraux du jeune sauvage de l'Aveyron* (1801) by Jean-Marc-Gaspard Itard, the young doctor who undertook Victor's education from 1801 to 1806.[7] Each of these reports provides a detailed description of Victor's physical condition and behavior, and each supplements its observations and diagnoses with introductory and concluding reflections on the philosophical significance of the case. They also each borrow, at times virtually verbatim, from Rousseau's *Discourse on the Origins of Inequality*. Collectively these documents represent a critical revaluation of the significance of natural man—but one that turns out to be fully consistent with the argument regarding the formative role of socialization implicit in Rousseau's text.

"Primitive Simplicity" or "Vacuity and Barbarism"?

Parallels between the scientific reports on Victor's condition and the condition of natural man as Rousseau had imagined it in the *Discourse* are not limited to mere incidental details regarding, for example, the relative development of the physical senses (crudeness of touch, sophistication of scent); a Rousseauvian framework underlies the scientists' ambitious efforts to draw general truths about the nature of human beings from this exceptional case. The notion that there could be a creature of human form but without a human essence is that which the *Discourse* conjures up in its image of an animal bearing an exact physical resemblance to man but stripped of his "supernatural" qualities (among them language, foresight, and memory), and it is precisely such an uncanny figure that the scientific reports on Victor construct. "If it were not for his human face what would distinguish him from the apes?" asks Virey. "He is truly and purely an animal, limited to simple physical sensations; he does not yet have anything beyond that. What enormous barriers separate him from us!" (G, 247; L, 47).

In the *Discourse* the terms *animal state* and *animal condition* are used to signify a simplicity of existence that effectively constrains natural man's development. The tranquil "sentiment of being" he enjoys is characterized by a profound inertia and emptiness of mind.[8] The Rousseauvian underpinnings of all three scientific reports on Victor are most obvious when they deploy this notion of animal limitation in order to infer the inner state of the feral child. Victor "reflects on nothing," writes Bonnaterre, and "consequently, he has no discernment, no imagination, no memory." The child's limited physical needs in turn delimit the activity of his mind; "where it is not a matter of meeting his natural needs or satisfying his appetite," Bonnaterre explains, "we find only purely animal functions: if he has sensations, they do not give rise to ideas" (G, 206; L, 41). Similarly Itard asserts, "His whole existence was a life purely animal" because the boy is apparently sufficiently satisfied simply "to sleep, to eat, to do nothing, and to run about in the fields." The doctor concludes that, insofar as "all his intellectual faculties are rigorously circumscribed within the narrow sphere of his physical wants," Victor demonstrates the general principle that "in the earliest stage of his infancy, and in regard to his understanding, man appears not as yet elevated above other animals" (G, 289, 310; M, 103, 127).

The sense of Victor's existence as *reduced* to the satisfaction of mere physical appetites leads Virey to conclude that it is only in physical form—in face and body—that Victor resembles a human being, that he would otherwise be indistinguishable from an animal—"one vastly inferior," according to Itard, "to the more intelligent of our domestic beasts" (G, 299; M, 114). His apparent inability to move beyond the highly circumscribed "animal" needs and satisfactions—to evolve—is perhaps a graver sign of his limitation. "Nothing that does not have a direct bearing on nourishment and self-preservation will ever be repeated by a creature occupied solely with his own needs," Virey theorizes. "It is for this reason that one remains in the state of nature so long as nothing impels one to leave it" (G, 228; my translation).

Virey's final pronouncement that "enormous barriers separate" Victor from the species he belongs to in appearance only is followed—strangely enough—by a labored apostrophic conclusion in which he imaginatively follows the boy's passage from his natural, animal independence to a social world that will both humanize him and bind him in chains of dependence: "Go forth, poor youth, on this unhappy earth," he enjoins,

> go forth and lose in your relations with men your primitiveness and simplicity [*ta primitive et simple rudesse*]! You lived in the bosom of ancient forests; you found your nourishment at the foot of oaks and beech trees; you quenched your thirst at crystal springs; content with your meager destiny, limited by your simple desires, satisfied with your way of life beyond which you knew nothing. (G, 247; L, 48)

This image, too, is drawn from the *Discourse*, from the initial glimpse of natural man, "sating his hunger beneath an oak, slaking his thirst at the first stream, finding his bed at the foot of the same tree that supplied his meal" (141, 135), but the image appears incongruous and inconsistent here, for its bucolic vision of a nurturing natural world is belied by the *Dissertation* itself—not only by the "animal-like" limitations of mind that Virey himself repeatedly remarks on but also (as we shall see more fully below) by the evidence of the boy's body itself, testifying not to "protective dryads who watched over" him (as Virey imagines) but to a severe wilderness endured and barely survived. Itard closes his first report with a decisive refutation of nostalgic yearnings for such "*rudesse*." Among the "important inferences relative to the philosophical and natural history of man that may be deduced" from Victor's case is a final resolution of questions regarding man's original state:

> Man is inferior to a great number of animals in a pure state of nature [*pur état de nature*], a state of vacuity and barbarism [*état de nullité et de barbarie*], although it has been unjustly painted in colors the most attractive, a state in which the individual, deprived of the characteristic faculties of his species, drags on miserably, equally without intelligence and without affection, a life that is every moment subject to danger, and confined to the bare functions of animal nature. (G, 320; M, 138)

These opposing conclusions are not in disagreement about Victor's "natural state" of arrested development (indeed, while lamenting the boy's "exchange of freedom for dependence," Virey at least looks forward to his enlightenment, to the "new ideas [that] will germinate in your young head"), but Virey's rhetorical flight and Itard's tendentious conclusion do point to the contrary interpretations and profound ambiguities surrounding the state of nature Rousseau hypothesized. The mere fact of Victor's apparently self-sufficient existence in the wild could be seen (following Virey) as an original, uncompromised natural liberty, while at the same time (following Itard) his numerous disabilities belie the unnatural-ness of such a way of life and thus expose the state of nature as a chimerical fallacy. If Victor's condition is taken to refute the myth of natural man's serene, sylvan, solitary existence, it nevertheless also begs the question of whether—apart from those images of a fertile earth evoked by Virey—the state of nature is in fact "unjustly painted in colors the most attractive" in the *Discourse*.

In reproducing Rousseau's conjectures about the underdeveloped mind and narrow passions of natural man in order to assess the wild child's mental state, the literature on Victor of Aveyron would *appear* to redound on its source, exposing what has been called the "animal obtuseness" of the frequently idealized figure, but the extent to which Itard, Bonnaterre, and Virey draw on the formulations of the *Discourse* indicates that—far from being confounded by Victor's condition—Rousseau's conjectures about natural man are remarkably well suited to the case. The "*mental* equality between the boy and the brute," which Itard and the others identify, is precisely consistent with the condition of natural man as described in the *Discourse*. Yet this consistency is obscured and confused by the fact that, even as the scientists draw on and adapt Rousseau's text for their analyses of Victor's limitations and impairments, they also understand the *Discourse* to present the existence of natural man as desirable; thus Virey ends his report by invoking "freedom" as the locus of a nostalgia for the boy's original condition, while Itard more ambitiously views Victor's "confinement" to pure animal functions as a decisive demystification of any such longing.

The site of the simple freedom whose loss Virey laments is not the forests of Lacaune but those pictured in the *Discourse*, while the miserable existence Itard depicts rests on evidence of the distinctly less benign natural environment from which Victor emerged. It is principally in the *actual* conditions of the natural world—and what survival in them would entail—that Victor's state of nature differs from that of Rousseau's natural man, but that difference does not amount to a contradiction. The constitutive feature of the *Discourse*'s state of nature is not the ease of abundance but the constraint of solitude; it is this that natural man most significantly shares with the feral child. Whether the setting is a locked room, a remote island, a barren waste, or a fertile wood, the effects of prolonged and extreme isolation are remarkably consistent with the limitations of Rousseau's hypothetical natural man.[9] Indeed, evidence of the harsh environment Victor survived ultimately points to the crippling consequences of his isolation—and it is precisely the solitariness of natural man that the *Discourse* does not "paint in colors the most attractive." Let us look, first, at what the scientific reports reveal about the adversity Victor encountered while in the not-so-nurturing "bosom" of the forests, and then return to the question of how his life in the wild stands in relation to the one imagined by Rousseau.

The Physical Evidence: Scars Natural and Unnatural

Where the *Discourse* promises a history drawn, "not in the Books . . . but in Nature, which never lies" (140, 133), Victor presented the scientists who examined him with a history quite literally drawn by the natural world. In the scars covering his body, the scientists read the difficulties of the boy's solitary existence in the wild; their careful physical descriptions shade into a conjectural history of experiences that a mute, language-less subject could never convey. Numerous cuts, scrapes, and bruises "prove that he had no garments while he lived in the forest," notes Bonnaterre, "and that his body must have been that much more vulnerable to scarring since he was not at all protected against the attack of animals, the mordant points of thorns, the cutting edges of rocks, and the density of undergrowth" (G, 199; L, 34). Virey confirms the likelihood of this physical exposure, adding that Victor "has no more hair on his body than any other child of the same age" (an unexpected feature, as hirsutism was among the three characteristics of the Linnaean *Homo ferus*).[10] Itard also details the physical evidence of the boy's "isolated, precarious and wandering life."

> We reckoned four [scars] on the face, six along the left arm, three at some distance from the left shoulder, four at the circumference of the pubis,

one on his left thigh, three on one leg and two on the other; which together make twenty-three scars. Some of these appear to have come from the bites of animals, others from scratches and excoriations, more or less large and deep; numerous indelible testimonies of a long and total abandonment. (G, 287; M, 100)

Not all the scars on Victor's body were marks left by stones and thorns and brush, however; perhaps the most telling sign of the adversity he suffered was the visible trace of a wound that all three scientists agreed could only have been inflicted by a human hand. Measuring some forty-one millimeters in length, all who examined it concurred that only a knife could have caused the horizontal scar across the boy's throat. Bonnaterre melodramatically wonders whether "some barbaric hand, having led the child into the wilds, [struck] him with a death-dealing blade to render his loss more certain and more complete" (G, 199; L, 34). Itard speculates with more assurance: "It is to be presumed that a hand more disposed than adapted to acts of cruelty wished to make an attempt upon the life of this child; and that, left for dead in the woods, he owed, to the timely succor of nature, the speedy cure of his wound" (G, 304; M, 120).[11]

Whatever the boy might be imagined to have endured in the wild, however many hardships might be seen inscribed in the numerous abrasions on his body, this singular scar offers the most poignant testimony of the child's history, for it indelibly marks the violence, the mystery, the "barbaric" contrariness to nature of an abandonment or botched infanticide—indeed, it marks *abandonment* (rather than self-sufficiency) as the origin of the child's subsequent formation and points to a history *prior to* that of the "pure state of nature" to which he was consigned. When Virey invites his readers to imagine the animal-like state of the feral child, the early stage of the child's abandonment owes a debt to the scenario of infancy and childhood implicit in Rousseau's state of nature, but at the same time it illuminates its obvious aberrancy, the shocking curtailment of caretaking that effectively aborts the process of humanization. "What great difference" could there be, asks Virey, "between an infant suckled and nursed to the age of four or five years . . . in the midst of the woods, far from all instruction . . . and afterward abandoned to the bosom of the forest, to all the harshness of Nature, what difference [is there] say I, between such an individual, in the most profound ignorance, and a young monkey or any other animal left to itself?" (G, 227; my translation).[12]

While the evidence of a near fatal knife wound points backward—to the brutal origin of Victor's isolation—the precise position and depth of the scar on Victor's throat may be seen to point forward—to the most important immutable impairment consequent to that isolation. Its location "at the upper extremity of the trachea and on the middle of the glottis" prompted Virey to speculate that the boy's mutism might be the result of this injury (G, 236; L, 38). Suspecting that the wound would not have so successfully healed "if the muscular and cartilaginous parts belonging to the organ of the voice" had been severed, Itard reaches a different conclusion, that Victor's inability to make articulate sounds ought not be attributed to the wound itself but to the "total disuse" of that organ during his years of isolation (G, 304; M, 120). Indeed, the "cries and inarticulate sounds" that Victor could utter (and the few syllables Itard was later able to teach him to articulate) do suggest that the organ of speech was not damaged but that the wound is cruelly, appropriately well placed near the organ which would never be used to communicate. Bonnaterre had speculated that, "having remained for some time out of all communication with humans," Victor would have lost any speech he might have acquired prior to his abandonment, and Itard ventured that "the acquisition of speech, although very energetic and active during the first years of life, is rapidly enfeebled by the progress of age and insulation" (G, 202, 320; L, 38; M, 139).[13] Of course, at the time of his first report Itard did not suspect that the years of Victor's isolation would render him irremediably language-less, but, as it turns out, the scar that did not sever his vocal cords might nevertheless be seen as the source of his linguistic impairment, for insofar as it marks his abandonment to survive or perish in solitude, it also signifies the principal cause of the child's permanent isolation from human intercourse.

o o o

If Victor's scarred body may be read as a physical record of the traumatic form of his introduction to and existence in the wild, the scientific observations of his behavior make legible the legacy of those privations. The boy's "ever-present need of nourishment," for example, is remarked on by all who examined him as a likely indicator that hunger and the search for food must have been his principal preoccupations in the wild, as the clearest sign of the limitation of his intellect, and as an explanation for that limitation. "You might say his mind is in his stomach; it is his life center," writes Virey, the most evocative of the scientists in his observation of the child's obsession with food: "He seeks only to nourish himself; he desires only to eat; throughout the whole day, he has only this principal function in view; it entirely occupies his being; it is his only desire, his supreme happiness; it subjugates him entirely" (G, 241; my translation).[14]

Using Victor's obsession with food to demonstrate what he calls the "indivisible unity" and "pure egoism" of his character, Virey inadvertently presents evidence for severe impairment in the child's orientation toward other persons. Victor's apparent lack of responsiveness to the guardians who prepare and serve his meals indicates, to Virey, his "indifference" to affection and kindness. Victor sees and takes the proffered food with obvious eagerness and avidity but somehow, and disturbingly, neither sees the person who gives him food nor the personhood of that person nor the act of giving itself.

> Would you look after him? He does not concern himself with anyone in the world, not even he who feeds him. Show him kindness? He is perfectly indifferent. Give him something to eat? He grabs it greedily without indicating the slightest gratitude. He thinks of nothing or, rather, he feels nothing but his self alone, he is the indivisible unity, pure egoism; he attaches himself to no one, to no creature in the world; he recognizes his guardian because he gives him [food] to eat, because he attends to him, but he has no affection whatsoever for him. (G, 241; my translation)

Similarly Bonnaterre observes that Victor shows "no sense of gratitude toward the man who feeds him, but takes the food as he would take it from the ground" (G, 203; L, 39).[15] And Itard, in his 1807 report, recalls that Victor "showed no sign of paying any particular attention to the person who looked after him . . . he saw her only as a hand that fed him and in that hand he saw only what was held."[16] The child's obsession with food, it is suggested, must account for his marked indifference to other persons (of course his vision of others is atrophied, this line of reasoning suggests, for all he can think about is getting his next meal). However, while Victor's chronic hunger and preoccupation with food may have everything to do with the scarcity he must have experienced in the wild, the behavioral or affective symptoms attributed to that hunger and exhibited long after the conditions that produced it had been removed suggest that something else lies behind his "pure egoism." The behavior Virey describes indicates that Victor's perception of persons is impaired rather than pointing to a profound self-centeredness. "He seems insensitive to affection," writes Virey. "His heart is encircled by indifference as if by a hundred iron bars that isolate him perfectly" (G, 241; my translation). The limitations of the boy's interactions with other persons, as it is described in all three reports, has even led a recent commentator on the case to hypothesize that Victor might have been autistic, fueling a lively debate about whether prolonged isolation from human contact could *cause* a child to develop the "mind-blindness" characteristic of autism. Insofar as Victor's behavior indicates "an inability to understand states of mind . . . as if other minds did not exist," it begs the question of whether his cognitive and affective disabilities were caused by his years in the wild or were themselves the cause of his desertion by parents unwilling or unable to manage them.[17]

Victor's apparent indifference to other persons is not unrelated to his "deafness" to the sounds of human speech. Impassive and inattentive when addressed, the boy was initially assumed to be deaf but, as Virey later observed, he would respond to the sounds of "a walnut broken behind him, a dog that barks out of sight, a door that is opened in the dark" (G, 236; L, 39). His sense of hearing, according to Bonnaterre, "is almost entirely passive and without any link whatsoever to language," a finding Itard agreed with, explaining that "in the bosom of the forests, and far from the society of every rational being," Victor's ear was "not an organ which discriminates the various articulate modifications of the human voice: it was there simply an instrument of self preservation which informed him of the approach of a dangerous animal, or the fall of some wild fruit" (G, 200, 302; L, 36; M, 117). Certainly to respond to another person one would have to know that one is being addressed—and to know *that* one would already have to perceive a great deal that Victor obviously could not, including the communicating intent of speech.

Natural Man or Unfinished Statue? The Feral Child as Philosophical Subject

After five years during which Victor's instruction had been the doctor's exclusive occupation, Itard composed a second (and final) report on the boy's progress for the Ministry of the Interior (published in 1807) which, even as it argues for the continuation of his education, also chronicles the insuperable limits of the his charge's educability. Itard concludes that Victor's years in the wild would leave him forever unable to use language and only incompletely socialized. "Realizing that neither the passage of time nor the continuance of my endeavors could effect any change," writes Itard, "I resigned myself to giving up my experiments with speech and abandoned my pupil to a life of incurable dumbness" (M, 174).[18] Victor's "dumbness" does not refer to his ability to effectively reproduce articulate speech (for he could, after Itard's painstaking training, produce the requisite sounds) but to his inability to "get" language—to consistently use the limited vocabulary he had been taught, to form and understand sentences, to apprehend grammar and syntax. And while his language-lessness would necessarily impede his acculturation ("following on the almost total absence of speech, the young man's education is still and always will be incomplete"), it is not the only barrier to the boy's cognitive and affective development, according to Itard. The period of his isolation is deemed formative, its effects irreversible.

> Because of their long period of inactivity, his intellectual faculties can develop only slowly and with difficulty and . . . this development, which among children raised in civilized society is the natural outcome of time and circumstances, is here the slow and arduous result of an active education where the most forceful methods have been used to obtain the slightest results. . . . The emotions, emerging with equal slowness from their long torpor, are subordinated in their application to a deep feeling of selfishness. (M, 178)

The difference between Itard's conclusions of 1801 and those of 1807 cannot be overstated. In 1801, mere months after emerging from the forest, Victor's condition—"deprived of the characteristic faculties of his species . . . without intelligence and without affection"—could be seen as representative of "man in a pure state of nature." In 1807 he can no longer be seen as such, for he has been introduced to the society of others, ministered to, and educated—and yet he has also made no substantial *progress* beyond his initial condition. It is one thing to say that the man of nature is not yet fully human; it is quite another thing to say that the man of nature cannot *become* fully human.

Why is it that changes in the conditions and circumstances of Victor's life did not result in the efflorescence of the "characteristic faculties of his species"? Philippe Pinel, director of the Paris asylums for the mentally disturbed and another early consultant on Victor's case, would have seen, in Itard's final report, confirmation of his own earlier diagnosis of "idiocy," and support for his hypothesis that the boy was not impaired because he had been abandoned in the woods, but rather that he had been abandoned because of his impairments.[19] The question of whether the array of Victor's impairments are congenital in nature or are the result of prolonged, early, and extreme isolation from others recurs in modern discussion of Victor's case, as well as cases of other feral children whose development was similarly arrested. "The majority of these children," writes Claude Lévi-Strauss, "suffered from some congenital defect and their abandonment should therefore be treated as the consequence of the abnormality which almost all display and not, as often happens, as its cause." Maurice Merleau-Ponty, on the other hand, maintains that if a child "is not in an environment in which there are people who talk then he will never be able to talk with the same ease" as other children and that the linguistic impairments typical of "so-called wild children who have been brought up among animals or away from people" are the inevitable result of their isolation at a critical early period of language acquisition.[20] The conflict between these positions on the etiology of the cognitive and linguistic disabilities characteristic of feral children is more apparent than real, however, for both Lévi-Strauss and Merleau-Ponty would agree that feral children are fundamentally *anomalous* cases on which to reflect on human development: "They may be cultural monstrosities but in no way [do they provide] accurate evidence of an anterior state."[21]

Earlier in the eighteenth century, however, prior to Victor's discovery, the interest in feral children lay precisely in the possibility that they might provide evidence for an anterior human condition. The Scottish natural historian Lord Monboddo (James Burnett), for example, had cited the wild girl of Champagne, the wild boys of the Pyrenees, and Peter of Hanover as "facts establishing the existence of a state of nature" in his *Antient Metaphysics* (1784).[22] Speculation regarding the significance of wild children for the study of human nature involved not only natural historians but also, and more importantly with regard to the question of education, epistemologists for whom the mind of the wild child could be seen as a real instance of a purely hypothetical model of mental development. Hence, for example, Abbé Sicard's excited anticipation that Victor would offer those philosophers "who have long desired to raise a child cut off from all society" the opportunity to observe and trace the first sensations, ideas, and thoughts. Indeed, the starting point of much philosophical speculation about how the human being acquires knowledge of itself and its world has consistently provoked the imagination of isolation or separation. Whether the image is that of a "mind in a dark room" (as in Locke) or of a statue gradually made animate (as in Condillac), the philosopher's meditation begins with an abstraction and a setting apart that implicitly removes the subject from its social habitat.[23] The animal-like condition of feral children suggested that—as empiricists had theorized—knowledge is acquired through experience and there are no innate ideas. However, the extremely limited intellectual progress made by these children after their period in the wild presented a considerable philosophical puzzle. It was clear enough that, not having been taught, the feral child could not put two and two together, but it was not at all clear why efforts to teach the feral child to add two and two would fail.

One tentative solution to this puzzle, proposed by Condillac in his *Traité des sensations* (1754), involves an odd compromise whereby, on the one hand, the isolation of the subject is retained as the theoretical starting point for development, while, on the other hand, the feral child is judged too aberrant to serve as an example of such development. In a brief digressive chapter on the Lithuanian bear-child "who gave no sign of reason, walked on his hands and feet, had no language, and uttered sounds that in no way resembled human sounds," Condillac concludes that some insurmountable physical or physiological obstacle explains the arrested development of the wild child. The imaginary statue is a better model of development than the real child who emerged from the forests, because it is unconstrained by the exigencies of mere survival. If intelligence and reason are to awaken, Condillac argues, the need for food cannot be all-consuming; if his statue were "totally absorbed in the search for nourishment," he reasons, then it "would live a life that was purely animal" because "the need of nourishment [would] benumb its mental faculties." Such conditions, according to Condillac, must have shaped the Lithuanian child, whose "deadened faculties could only be provoked by the need to look for nourishment." The physical hardship of hunger, then, and the preoccupation with survival—rather than the state of isolation—explains why the feral child is without reason, curiosity, or self-awareness.[24]

Condillac's image of an existence consumed by hunger and the search for food provides an instructive contrast to the picture Rousseau presents in his *Discourse*, where natural man is carefully placed in a luxuriantly fertile world with food in abundance and readily available—and yet fails nonetheless to develop any intellectual faculties or to acquire any ideas. Having removed a preoccupation with nourishment and survival as *explanations* for limited mental development, solitary and self-sufficient existence emerges all the more starkly as the principal explanation for natural man's failure to evolve beyond what both Rousseau and Condillac identify as an "animal state." "It is inconceivable," writes Rousseau, "how a man could, by his own strength alone, without the help of communication," cross the great divide between "pure sensations and the simplest knowledge" (151, *144*). However, it is precisely such a possibility that Condillac would require us to conceive, for his own effort to trace the path from sensation to knowledge assumes an isolated mind (in the body of a statue no less) as the ideal starting point for theoretical reflection on intellectual development.[25]

If one of the most significant and long-lived insights of empiricist epistemologists such as Condillac is the primacy of experience in the acquisition of knowledge, then surely the most striking blind spot in these theories is their failure to incorporate and reflect on the most constant experience of all: the abiding presence of other persons. In its rigorous conception of the extremely limited existence of the creature that grows and develops in the absence of others, Rousseau's *Discourse* may be seen to illuminate (albeit in characteristically paradoxical form) the extent to which the human individual develops, and can only develop, in relation to other persons. "For want of communication with his fellow man," writes Rousseau, "all knowledge...seems to be altogether beyond the reach of Savage man" (204, *199*), underscoring the notion that communication with others is both necessary and *formative* of distinctly human faculties. Itard's conclusion that "in a pure state of nature," the human being is "confined to the bare functions of animal nature" is one that the *Discourse* itself should elicit insofar as it *leaves* natural man language-less and ignorant, in a solitude out of which he cannot evolve.

o o o

The two epigraphs at the start of this chapter evince an instance of unacknowledged, perhaps inadvertent, but nevertheless blatant borrowing. Bonnaterre appropriates Rousseau's formulation for his own use, perhaps in the way that words or expressions are introduced from one language into another—in this case, from the language of philosophical reflection on human nature to that of scientific analysis and observation. Words used to hypothesize the "simple, solitary, uniform existence" of human beings in a "state of nature" turn out to be particularly useful in describing a case of incomplete, and indeed impossible, human development. The challenge lies in evaluating the significance and implications of such an apparent "fit" between Rousseau's conjectures and the scientists' observations.

While the *Discourse* is the source of formulations detailing Victor's limitations and impairments, a superficial notion of Rousseau's natural man as a pure, original human form has often led to the conclusion that a case such as Victor's must definitively undermine that ideal. By isolating *isolation* itself—rather than the merely incidental "naturalness" of dwelling in a forest—as the essential element in both Rousseau's theoretical account and in the documents concerning Victor, it becomes possible to see the remarkable consistency between the philosopher's account and the records of the scientists. More precisely, the use of the *Discourse on Inequality* in this context illuminates the paradoxical procedure adopted in that text: an argument that association is the necessary matrix for the development of human forms of life is advanced by rigorously pursuing its counterhypothesis to dead ends. Rousseau's natural man is not an idol toppled by the wild child but a hypothesis designed to illustrate the impossibility of using solitary self-sufficiency as a theoretical starting point for reflection on human development. Bonnaterre's borrowing thus yields an unexpected return, making it possible to see natural man not as a model of the human being but as a model of all that the human being cannot be on his own.

CHAPTER 4

"Unfathered Vapour"

THE IMAGINATION OF ORIGINS IN *THE PRELUDE*

The readings of Rousseau's "natural man" and Locke's "isolated mind" undertaken in previous chapters suggest that these enlightenment fictions of original autonomy are fundamentally compromised even as they are constructed. The undermining of autonomy in these seminal texts is not accidental; the mind's subjection to influence is a generating tension in Locke's *Essay*, and the isolation of natural man is an explicit target of Rousseau's critique of other states of nature. What is at stake in these philosophical arguments becomes evident when the implicit narratives of human development underlying them are brought to the surface, along with their attendant anxieties, fears, and longings. Unfolding alongside and shaping Locke's arguments about how the mind comes to know the world is a story about childhood fears and anxieties and their haunting persistence long after the child attains independence. The impulse to erase, disown, and forget the condition of dependence in which one is subject to those fears gives rise to two powerful enlightenment myths of autonomy: the mind as autonomous knower of the world, and natural man as an originally free, independent, and asocial being. Rousseau appears to construct an original condition of human independence characterized by contentment, liberty, and metaphysical harmony, but the *Discourse on Inequality*, in fact, tells a powerful story about philosophical misconceptions of origins, about the impossibility of human development from a state in which individuals dwell in isolation from one another.

In turning now to literary texts—Wordsworth's *Prelude*, Mary Shelley's *Frankenstein*, and John Stuart Mill's *Autobiography*—it is no less the case that the challenge of understanding how these texts imagine autonomy lies in identifying the relation between their philosophical investments and the narratives they shape. To propose that the works of Shelley and Mill contain arguments is only to credit the clear presence of philosophical preoccupations in their writing, as well as the inheritance and influence of eighteenth-century philosophy, in particular, in the actual patrimony of both authors. Whether Wordsworth is seen to have been influenced by them or to be overturning them, his engagement with eighteenth-century theories of mind is well established in criticism.[1] In approaching Wordsworth's *Prelude*, I am primarily interested in how this important romantic work belongs to the history of critical thinking about human origins and autonomy traced in this study, a task best accomplished by staying close to the poem's own articulation of its storytelling and argumentative tasks. For this reason I will not trace direct lines of affiliation between Wordsworth and specific enlightenment philosophers, though I will point to the presence and persistence of problems framed by Locke and Rousseau in *The Prelude*'s vexed representation of its hero's seeming independence.

The philosophical ambitions of *The Prelude* are generally announced as coincident with its subject matter. The poem promises something apparently straightforward, to set down the "story of my life," "a tale of . . . the glory of my youth," its "theme . . . what passed within me," and in so doing to set forth a "heroic argument" about "how awful is the might of souls, / And what they do within themselves while yet / The yoke of earth is new to them, the world / Nothing but a wild field where they were sown" (3:168–180).[2] The ostensible clarity of subject and theme notwithstanding, to define the story and argument of the poem more precisely, and how they relate to each other, is to enter into a history of critical disagreements that commences with the poem's posthumous publication in 1850 and from which philosophy has never been absent. One line of argument (though itself plagued by disagreement) begins with the proposition that *The Prelude* has a "metaphysical more than a biographical purpose."[3] This assumption places the poem within a philosophical tradition of thinking about the development of the mind; as the reviewer for *Graham's Magazine* wrote, it "conveys more real available knowledge of the facts and laws of man's internal constitution than can be found in Hume or Kant."[4] In the twentieth century the "metaphysical" argument of the poem has generally been understood as a rejection of the "rationalist strain" of enlightenment thought (identified with Locke and the English associationists) and an articulation of a sensibility that is remarkably "consonant" or "parallel" to the German philosophy of Kant, Fichte, and Hegel with which the poem is considered to be contemporary.[5] Readings that associate it with German metaphysics typically understand the poem to tell the story of the evolving relationship between two "agencies"—"man and the world, mind and nature, the ego and the non-ego."[6] Though *The Prelude* has been seen to reach different conclusions, or perhaps steadily more egocentric versions of the same conclusion (for Bradley, "man's intelligence finds in nature, which may at first seem alien to it, its counterpart"; for Abrams, the "mind, confronting nature, discovers itself in its own perfected powers"; for Hartman, the discovery is "the autonomy of imagination . . . its independence from outward stimuli"), the protagonists of the poem are consistently identified as man (mind, imagination, spirit, intelligence) and nature.[7]

The narrative of a life and philosophical theorization are not self-evidently related projects, and certainly what might be called the "metaphysical" perspective on this autobiographical poem entails peculiar assumptions, not only of what the self is but also of what is relevant to a history of the self. When Jeffrey writes that the poem is not interested in the "mere circumstances" of life but in the "inner current of life itself," as when Abrams writes that the poem is the "first sustained history of an inner life," one in which the "people, actions, and events of Wordsworth's quotidian life" are merely "the clutter and contingency of ordinary experience," we are being asked to accept not only that *The Prelude* does not include many of the kinds of details and episodes that might be expected in an autobiography but also that daily life, ordinary experience, and the people with whom a life is lived are "details of outer life" irrelevant to what is "inside" the mind.[8] This notion of isolated individual development and experience (however implausible and strange) makes a strength of what a number of the poem's early readers found to be a puzzling weakness of the poem—its failure to give any sustained account of significant relationships in the life story. This absence is at the heart of a second, long-lived line of argument about the poem, one that finds in it matter worthy of moral censure or psychological scrutiny. In telling a life story in which he seems "equally and always alone," David Masson complained in the *British Quarterly*, Wordsworth betrays himself to be someone without "any interest in human beings."[9] More recently, psychoanalytically inflected interpretations of the absence of other persons in the poem find the focus on mind and nature to be symptomatic of repression or displacement. From this perspective, Wordsworth's attachment to the landscape attests to the traumatic early loss of both parents, and the story the poem tells is one of longing for and recovery of "lost objects of love." Alternately the very impersonality of the tale has been seen to betray unresolved Oedipal guilt, or shame at the abandonment of a lover and child in France, and the poem is read as an oblique self-indictment for failings of the poet's youth.[10]

These two main lines of argument—the metaphysical and the psychoanalytical—and the multiplicity and variety of interpretive possibilities they have generated have led, neither surprisingly nor unreasonably, to a sense of *The Prelude* as a poem in which the story of individual development is beset by the presence of numerous "counter-plots" and characterized by oscillation between "forces of resolution and forces of obstinate questioning."[11] Equally persuasive arguments that the poem culminates in the discovery of the "spirit's autonomy" and in the realization that the "individual mind . . . is unable to achieve more than the illusion of absolute autonomy" indicate not only that there are contradictory strains in the poem but also that the notion of autonomy itself is a central locus of contradiction.[12]

It is possible to go further toward defining the contradictions of the poem if it is placed in relation to the philosophical tradition that preceded it rather than that with which it happens to be contemporary. The self-consciously fictitious reconstruction of early childhood that is so important at the outset of the poem (its penchant for "days / Disowned by memory" and "hours that have the charm / Of visionary things") represents a powerful fusion of two enlightenment fictions of autonomous origin (1:642–643, 659–660). The poem recognizably brings together features of the sylvan, idyllic state of nature ("as if I had been born / On Indian plains . . . A naked savage") and elements of the empiricist narrative of the mind's gradual acquisition of knowledge from sensation and experience ("The earth and common face of Nature. . . . impress[es] / Collateral objects and appearances" which "impregnate" and "elevate the mind") (1:301–304, 614–625). It is able to effect this combination by identifying isolation itself, the "self-sufficing power of solitude," as the feature common to both fictions of origin, and by making aloneness the most consistent element of the experiences recollected in the early books. Even when terms denoting solitude do not appear—as in he "stood alone / Beneath the sky"; "Moon and stars / Were shining over my head; I was alone"; "on the perilous ridge I hung alone"—the solitariness of the child's experience is implicit in the context of the recollections (his plundering of birds' nests and theft of a boat are necessarily lone acts of stealth; skating among other children, he nevertheless "retire[s] / Into a silent bay... leaving the tumultuous crowd"). The poem joins the two philosophical fictions together inconsistently, however. Often, especially in book I, it naturalizes empiricist accounts of mental development by setting the mind in a natural environment (the "seasons on my mind had stamped / The faces of the moving year") (1:587–588), or by crediting abstractions with nurturing agency ("I grew up / Fostered alike by beauty and by fear") (1:305–306). But it also frequently exposes the artificial conceit behind its organic images of origin, and this tendency to de-naturalize its own natural figures runs as a countercurrent to the unfolding tale of childhood, disclosing the necessarily constructed or conjectural form of memories of "days disowned by memory." For example, the initial botanical image "fair seed-time had my soul" is aligned with the poem's "heroic argument" about the "might of souls, / And what they do within themselves while yet / The yoke of earth is new... the world / Nothing but a wild field where they were sown," and, as such, it is not so much a recollection as a thesis about the individual as self-originating, self-begot (1:305; 3:178–181). The figure of the self as seedling evokes (even as it complicates) that most implausible imagination (from Hobbes's *De Cive*) of "man sprung out of earth, fully grown, like a mushroom." The poem makes apparent and draws attention to the artifice of an ostensibly organic image, not so as to refute or reject it but to self-consciously indulge it, to explore the need or desire fulfilled by this mythic notion of the self as autonomously formed, to consider what such a conception of the self enables and disables.

Heroic Argument and the Moral of the Story

The history the poem presents as natural rests on an artificial groundwork that both shapes the early recollections and serves a broader argument about the moral education of the individual. To tell a story of origins is identified as a self-evident pleasure (an indulgence in the "weakness of human love for days / Disowned by memory"), but it is also introduced as something far more important, as a support and explanation of the thesis that is the title of book 8: "Love of Nature Leading to Love of Mankind." The solitary child of nature, protagonist of the "heroic argument" of the poem ("the might of souls... while yet / The yoke of earth is new") becomes a man who loves and reveres human nature. This man becomes the protagonist of a tale of loss and crisis, finding his love thrown into question during the years of the French Revolution but ultimately reaffirmed on his return to the environment that had originally fostered the emotion. However, the final three books of *The Prelude* (books 11–13)—in which the poet gives himself up to the ministrations of nature and reaffirms his reverence for its "power / To consecrate . . . and to breathe / Grandeur upon the very humblest face / Of human life" (12:282–286)—have struck many as overstrained in their confidence and optimism. And the almost Panglossian concluding pronouncement that "all" (sorrow) "is gratulant, if rightly understood" is an unconvincing resolution of concerns about human suffering raised within the poem itself, and increasingly so in its final books (13:385).

Those primarily interested in the "metaphysical" aspect of *The Prelude* identify the climax of the poem in the apotheosis of the imagination (as "amplitude of mind / And reason in her most exalted mood") (13:169–170) and so tend to slight the poem's preoccupation with human happiness, misery, and dignity. Few have been so bold as M. H. Abrams (and A. C. Bradley before him) as to insist that the poem coherently and systematically connects its revelations about the power of the imagination with a moral vision of how "love manifests that it abounds over pain and evil."[13] For many readers of Wordsworth, his contemporaries and our own, a central and defining paradox of the poetry is that the love it so often speaks of seems not love at all but what has been described as "an enmity to man which he mistook for love."[14] It is important to keep in mind, however, that such a misgiving about the authenticity of the love and sympathy professed in *The Prelude* is given voice in *The Prelude* itself—most notably at a climactic point in its account of how love of nature leads to love of mankind:

> Neither guilt nor vice,
> Debasement of the body or the mind,
> Nor all the misery forced upon my sight,
> Which was not lightly passed, but often scanned
> Most feelingly, could overthrow my trust
> In what we may become, induce belief
> That I was ignorant, had been falsely taught,
> A solitary, who with vain conceits
> Had been inspired, and walked about in dreams.
>   (8:802–810)

It would be difficult to imagine a more self-compromising affirmation of conviction. The positive testament of faith ("my trust / In what we may become") follows weakly from specification of all that must be overlooked, not ignored, but seen past in order to maintain that trust. And the conviction about mankind, so curt and vague (what exactly might we become?), is superseded by a second conviction (I am not ignorant, not falsely taught), the elaboration of which actually introduces the very doubt it would refute. The possibility admitted here, admitted in the form of a denial that leaves the doubt it denies more precise and articulated than the belief it professes, is that of being "falsely taught, a solitary" deluded by "vain conceits" to the point where one might mistake a dream world for reality. In the context of book 8, what might seem false, ignorant, and vain about the solitary's love of mankind is his vision of man as "a solitary object and sublime," his abstract perspective of man "purified / Removed, and at a distance that was fit," remote enough to inspire belief that man is good despite all evidence that men are wicked (8:407, 439–440). In other words, the protagonist of the poem may be "falsely taught, a solitary" for holding precisely the kind of optimistic yet objectifying idealism about human nature for which Wordsworth is still so often indicted. Insofar as this "love of mankind" is seen to flow from, and be the consequence of, the child's solitary tutelage by nature, it is an end that the poem's myth of self-origination is supposed to achieve, something the myth enables. It will be worth considering, then, whether the seeming denial of having been "falsely taught, a solitary" might, in fact, betray an anxiety and misgiving about that tutelage which runs as a strong countercurrent and counterargument to some of the poem's most enthusiastic strains.

Original Figures: Seedling / Savage / Babe / Building

I have suggested that one of *The Prelude*'s most organic figures of individual origins—"fair seed-time had my soul"—draws attention to its own artifice, to the fact that human beings are not borne, as a seed, by indifferent winds to some wild patch of earth but are conceived from intercourse and love. This is to say that even as the poem deploys natural imagery in its "recollections" of early childhood, the implicit contrast to the real conditions of human birth and upbringing is sharp enough to denaturalize the developmental process it describes. Consider, for example, this powerful image of nurture:

> even then,
> A child, I held unconscious intercourse
> With the eternal beauty, drinking in
> A pure organic pleasure from the lines
> Of curling mist, or from the level plain
> Of waters coloured by the steady clouds.
> (1:588–593)

It is not a matter of mere literalism to insist that the term *intercourse* introduces an expectation of the presence of a second person; that the other turns out to be "the eternal beauty" establishes a pattern wherein terms that imply or hint at an intersubjective relation are applied to the relation between the child and nature (be it in the abstract, as "eternal beauty," or as a material presence, as in the "lines of curling mist"). The principal relation evoked and displaced here is, of course, that between the child and nursing mother, and the question I would like to reopen is why the poem so explicitly conjures up this primary relation only to make it over into something else. In what sense are we to understand the relationship between this child of nature, who draws nourishment from mists and waters, and children whom we know to take in quite other nourishment from quite another source? To say that the comparison here is straightforward, that the "eternal beauty" of nature nourishes as the mother nourishes, is to assume that the force of this figure lies solely in its implied analogy (intercourse with an abstract entity / intercourse with another person; drinking in pleasure from mist / drinking in pleasure from mother's milk) and not also in the obvious contrast it draws.

Readers of the poem generally take one of two seemingly opposed but, in fact, complementary positions on the poem's assimilation of nature and maternal presence. For some, Nature itself is the only parent of the mind whose history the poem is telling. So, for example, Hartman explains that "nature drew him out, released the life in him, and gradually made him conscious," and Abrams specifies that "nature is endowed with the attributes and powers of a mother, father, nurse, teacher, lover." On this reading, the mother herself is a mere instance of the fostering activity of nature: "the babe in the security of his mother's arms" is "the crowning figure of [a] metaphoric complex" that Wordsworth constructs in order to show how "objects enter, flow, are received, and sink down into the mind."[15] For psychoanalytically inclined critics, nature is not the metaphysical parent but the surrogate for the lost parent; according to Onorato, the mother is "the essential reality of the world" for the child and, for Wordsworth, the "absent and traumatically introjected reality." It follows that representations of "the hearing or ingesting of primal lessons" depict the relationship between "the mother-substitute, Nature, and the growing child."[16] On either reading, nature retains a primacy in the developmental process described in the poem because no distinction is made between the child's relationship with or memory of a person and the child's experience of an environment devoid of other persons. Whether nature is viewed as a manifestation of the "mother or maternal mind," or whether the mother is viewed as an instantiation of nature's fostering presence, the difference between imagining a child, alone, drinking in pleasure from mist and imagining a child nursing in his mother's arms is altogether lost.[17]

I said at the outset that complications in the accounts of autonomy considered in previous chapters emerge when the arguments of philosophical texts are placed in relation to the broader, implied narratives of which they are a part. I now want to suggest that *The Prelude*'s most memorable account of human origins, its most primal recollection—the hymn to the blessed babe "who sleeps / Upon his mother's breast" (2:237–280)—is not a part of the life story or fictional tale of origins being told in the poem. It is, rather, an alternative story of origins, a story the poem does not tell, and the story that, by way of contrast, helps to bring into focus the artifice of its own tale of self-origination. Such a possibility evolves from attending to the odd position of the "blessed babe" passage in book 2 and from reexamining the long-standing, though recently challenged, assumption that the passage is a tribute preceding lines that obscurely allude to the mother's death ("now a trouble came into my mind / From unknown causes: I was left alone / Seeking the visible world, nor knowing why" [2:291–293]).

The Prelude is not, of course, a strictly chronological account, but nor is it radically achronological. Given that book 2 begins with recollections of a period following the death of Wordsworth's mother, it is puzzling that the poem's most sustained treatment of infancy would be placed in the middle of a book that dwells on teenage memories and adventures rather than among the earlier recollections of book 1, alongside memories of the boy left free to "run abroad in wantonness to sport." The "blessed babe" appears not only as a digression from the story of the child of nature, the naked savage sprung to life as a seed sown on the wild earth, but also an infelicitously placed one—if it is indeed part of the unfolding biographical narrative. The context of the passage suggests that it may be wrong to view it as such, however, for it is elicited or prompted by a pause in the narrative, a pause made up of a series of reflections on the task of attempting to reconstruct individual origins in the way that the poem has thus far been doing:

> But who shall parcel out
> His intellect by geometric rules,
> Split like a province into round and square?
> Who knows the individual hour in which
> His habits were first sown even as a seed,
> Who that shall point, as with a wand, and say
> 'This portion of the river of my mind
> Came from yon fountain'? Thou, my friend, art one
> More deeply read in thy own thoughts.
> (2:208–216)

> And thou wilt doubt with me, less aptly skilled
> Than many are to class the cabinet
> Of their sensations, and in voluble phrase
> Run through the history and birth of each
> As of a single independent thing.
> Hard task to analyse a soul, in which
> Not only general habits and desires,
> But each most obvious and particular thought—
> Not in a mystical and idle sense,
> But in the words of reason deeply weighed—
> Hath no beginning.
> (2:227–236)

The story of the self sprung up out of the earth like a sprouting seed is here associated with—and presented as no less implausible or abstract than—the effort to "parcel out the intellect by geometric rules" or "to class the cabinet of sensations" and tell the "history and birth of each / As of a single independent thing."[18] In the context of this argument about *not* knowing "the individual hour in which . . . habits were first sown," the celebration of the "blessed babe" cannot be assimilated to the story of origins which the poem has been telling. The hymn appears, rather, as a critical alternative to, and admonition of, that story—one to which the poem assigns philosophical value, introducing it with the admission that "in the words of reason deeply weighed," habits, desires, thoughts have no beginnings as single independent things.

The resumption of the first person narrative after its evocation of the infant "who sleeps / Upon his mother's breast" is most frequently understood to record the loss of the mother whose "belovèd presence" has been so powerfully conjured. However, the lines "Now a trouble came into mind / From unknown causes: I was left alone" (2:291–292) are so notoriously vague and oblique that even those readers most interested in revising the idea of *The Prelude* as the "story of a fundamentally unmothered life" concede the impossibility of proving that they refer to the death of the poet's mother.[19] And there is more of interest in the lines that follow the "blessed babe":

> From early days,
> Beginning not long after that first time
> In which, a babe, by intercourse of touch
> I held mute dialogues with my mother's heart
> I have endeavoured to display the means
> Whereby the infant sensibility,
> Great birthright of our being, was in me
> Augmented and sustained. Yet is a path
> More difficult before me, and I fear
> That in its broken windings we shall need
> The chamois' sinews and the eagle's wing.
> For now a trouble came into my mind
> From unknown causes: I was left alone
> Seeking the visible world nor knowing why.
> (2:281–293)

It is important to be precise about what the poet has "endeavored to display" thus far, now that he is returning to his own story. The tale of "early days" and "infant sensibility" begins "not long *after* that first time"—a first time, or original era, identified as the time of intimate proximity with his mother. Hence the early days recollected are not the earliest days of the nursing creature: its point of origin is necessarily other than that origin, the beginning of the story necessarily a second beginning. Moreover, attention to the context surrounding the "blessed babe" passage suggests that the "path more difficult" referred to here, the "trouble . . . from unknown causes," is a return or continuation of the narrative interrupted by the series of reflections about not being able to trace the "individual hour in which his habits were first sown":

> I was left alone
> Seeking the visible world nor knowing why.
> The props of my affections were removed,
> And yet the building stood, as if sustained
> By its own spirit. All that I beheld
> Was dear to me, and from this cause it came
> That now to Nature's finer influxes
> My mind lay open—
>
> (2:292–299)

"Now to nature's finer influxes my mind lay open" picks up the story where it had left off, at the point when the poet had begun to tell how Nature came to be "sought for her own sake":

> Those incidental charms which first attached
> My heart to rural objects, day by day
> Grew weaker, and I hasten on to tell
> How Nature, intervenient till this time
> And secondary, now at length was sought
> For her own sake. But who shall parcel out
> His intellect by geometric rules . . .
>
> (2:203–209)

The "props of my affections" removed through "unknown causes" refers back to these mysteriously weakened "incidental charms" of the rural scene, a loss more than amply compensated in the mind's new openness to "Nature's finer influxes." It is this story about mind and nature that the reflections on the impossibility of reconstructing one's origins and the expository homage to the "blessed babe" have interrupted, and it is to this story that the poet now returns.

I propose, then, that the "blessed babe" is unrelated to the "naked savage" of book 1, that the being imagined to "drink in pure organic pleasure" from "lines of curling mist" is essentially different, in conception, from the infant who "drinks in the feelings of his mother's eye"—

and that *The Prelude* is interested in the consequences and implications of conceiving or reconstructing the origins of the individual in one way rather than the other. Let us now look more closely at a principal difference between the naked savage and the blessed babe: the weakness and dependence of the infant, his subjection to attachment, as set against the robust, independent adventures of the child of nature. The recollections of book 1 almost all entail motion, speed, and exercises of liberty: the child "run[ning] abroad in wantonness to sport," "wander[ing] half the night among the cliffs," "hurrying on, still hurrying, hurrying onward," climbing "lonesome peaks," "wheel[ing] about proud and exulting like an untired horse." The nursing babe lies still, sleeping, limp, and "torpid" until he is awakened in relation to his mother and "subjected to the discipline of love." Even as his mind becomes quickened, vigorous, he remains a "frail creature . . . helpless as frail" (1850; 2:253). "Tenacious of the forms [his mind] receives in one beloved presence," the infant's world is both in flux and stable, and the infant is securely fixed within it as the passive denizen of an active universe:

> No outcast he, bewildered and depressed;
> Along his infant veins are interfused
> The gravitation and the filial bond
> Of Nature that connect him with the world.
> Emphatically such a being lives,
> An inmate of this *active* universe.
> (2:261–266)

This inmate—coinhabitant, indweller, one who shares his home with others—is to be contrasted with the child who, though left alone, is a free-standing being, the independent and sole occupant of his self: "The props of my affections were removed, / And yet the building stood, as if sustained / By its own spirit." The child free to wander along lofty heights alone is the one who is ultimately left alone to seek the visible world, because, presumably, he is the kind of outcast the infant is never at liberty to become.

Gravitation and the Filial Bond

The hero of this story of autonomous development, first a seed, now a building, is also, strangely enough, a fundamentally un-grounded being.

The terms of attachment the poem uses suggest one path along which *The Prelude* pursues the implications of conceiving of the self as essentially independent. The building that stands "as if sustained by its own spirit" is precisely not secured or held down by "the gravitation and the filial bond" interfused in the infant's veins. But what exactly is the implied relation between these terms? In a passage that so powerfully evokes the intersubjective environment of infant experience, the forging of a "filial bond" is suggestive of both the infant's unchosen dependence on and passionate attachment to the "beloved presence" that sustains him. "Gravitation" is a far less obvious transmission, and the term bears consideration for its literal sense, and for the particular meanings *The Prelude* attaches to it. Gravitation, the force impelling two bodies together, the irresistible movement of one body toward another, is clearly related to gravity itself, the force that keeps our feet reliably on the ground—the force that would hurl down a boy hanging alone on a perilous ridge were he not "almost, as it seemed, / Suspended by the blast which blew amain" (1:344–345). Weight, weightiness, ponderousness, must also be included among the range of ideas associated with gravity, and in *The Prelude* these are terms almost invariably associated with human misery, tragedy, and unhappiness, as in "life's mysterious weight of pain and fear," "the weight of meanness," "the weight of injustice," "the weight of many a weary day," the "deadly weight" of depressing thoughts. Comparable use of the term is also to be found in "Tintern Abbey" ("the heavy and weary weight of all this unintelligible world") and the "Ode: Intimations of Immortality" ("custom lies upon thee like a weight, heavy as frost, and deep almost as life"; "the soul shall have her earthly freight"). What "gravitation" adds to the "filial bond" is the sense of an ineluctable, unwilled force of natural law to which all are subject that is associated with unwonted and unavoidable perception of human subjection to meanness, pain, and fear—a perception that poses a profound moral challenge.[20]

If, "in the words of reason deeply weighed," the "blessed babe" is introduced into the poem as a creature originally, necessarily, and naturally subject to the heavy burden of human attachment ("gravitation and the filial bond"), then it becomes possible to see just what the solitary child of nature is spared. The mythic tale of the child as "naked savage" enables the imagination of (a) being unburdened by human attachment—a condition the poem consistently renders as a kind of defiance of gravity, as in the figure of the mind as an unsupported building "sustained by its own spirit." The "recollections" with all the "charm of visionary things" recounted in books 1 and 2, interrupted by the reflections on origins that culminate in the "blessed babe" passage and now resumed with the figure of the youthful mind "left alone," tell a story of liberation from the weight of human meanness. And yet, in subsequent books, such a conception of the self is implicated with idealism about human nature that is shown to be delusional or blindly indifferent to the actual circumstances of human lives. Moreover, this particular failing (of perception, attention, focus) in relation to other human beings is linked to a "visionary" experience of the natural world that is the special privilege of the poetically inclined solitary. The heroic tale of imagination "lifting up itself . . . Like an unfathered vapour" (6:525–527) unfolds along with and in relation to another tale of self-doubt and concern for the realties of human life that may be distorted or hidden by such intoxicating clouds. The "visible world" the youth discovers on his own is one in which he observes "affinities / In objects where no brotherhood exists."

Eminences, Heights, and "Elevating Thoughts of Human Nature"

The most valued moments in the story of the mind left alone to seek the visible world involve not only solitude but also strangely disembodied sensations, sights and sounds intensely experienced yet paradoxically invisible and inaudible. These are experiences of what the poem names "visionary power," as in this recollection of early morning wanderings:

> I sate
> Alone upon some jutting eminence
> At the first hour of morning, when the vale
> Lay quiet in an utter solitude.
> How shall I trace the history, where seek
> The origin of what I then have felt?
> Oft in those moments such a holy calm
> Did overspread my soul that I forgot
> That I had bodily eyes, and what I saw
> Appeared like something in myself, a dream,
> A prospect in my mind.
> (2:361–371)

The attenuation of "bodily" sense while nevertheless seeing or hearing—"one song . . . Most audible then when the fleshly ear . . . Forgot its functions and slept undisturbed" (3:431–434)—the yielding to visions that seem like dreams—"beauteous pictures now / Rose in harmonious imagery . . . As from some distant region of my soul / And came along like dreams" (4:392–395)—and absolute solitude are the constitutive elements of these experiences. These memorable moods of transport and tranquility have long been identified as central to a Wordsworthian metaphysics whereby the "inner eye" is gradually shown to be a powerful, shaping force on the "outer" world. They represent a stage in what Geoffrey Hartman calls the "movement of transcendence" in the poem, wherein nature (as an observable reality) eventually leads beyond nature to the revelation of a higher reality that, as the poet will ultimately realize, is independent of external phenomena. The obscurity of these moments of visionary power, the paradoxical sense of seeing the unseen is, in this argument, nature's "merciful, gradual" way of "vex[ing] the soul toward self-independence."[21]

The visionary experiences are indeed moments of metaphysical revelation, but they are also presented as instances of quasi-misanthropic withdrawal from experience among other human beings. This context is forgotten or overlooked in analyses that emphasize the access to a "transcendental" reality suggested in the visionary passages but might be recovered if considered in relation to two forms of highly influential philosophical reflection to which they are near kin: the Rousseauvian reverie, with its combination of utter solitude and absolute inner plenitude, and the Cartesian meditation, with its withdrawal to solitude and the drama of doubt that withdrawal enables.

The diminution of physical sensation that allows for the revelation of harmonious unity and a profound sense of contentment is characteristic of the Rousseauvian "sentiment of existence," famously elaborated in the fifth of the *Reveries of the Solitary Walker*: "a sufficient, perfect, and full happiness which leaves the soul no emptiness it might need to fill," a "precious sentiment of contentment and peace." "With bliss ineffable," writes Wordsworth, "I felt the sentiment of being spread / O'er all that moves, and all that seemeth still, / O'er all that . . . to the human eye / Invisible, yet liveth to the heart" (2:420–424). For Rousseau, this state, in which "we are sufficient unto ourselves like God," is the compensatory contentment available to a man "cut off from human society," the unique joy available to the outcast who dwells in a solitude that "still seems like a dream."[22] Isolation and exile from a life among others, the explicit context of the Rousseauvian reverie, is also the implicit condition for the possibility of the Wordsworthian vision.

In turning the possibility that the world I see may be a dream into a blessing, not an affliction, these "sentiments of being" are also both powerful revisions of Cartesian meditation. Descartes, in the grip of solitary reflections, cannot but doubt the reality of the visible world, and Wordsworth cannot but be convinced of the presence of an invisible reality. Descartes's hypothesis that "the heavens, the air, the earth, colors, shapes, sounds" are "nothing but illusions and dreams [*illusions et rêveries*]" inspired by an evil genius is countered by Wordsworth's sense that "all exterior forms, / Near or remote, minute or vast . . . a stone, a tree, a withered leaf . . . the broad ocean and the azure heavens," speaks "perpetual logic to [the] soul" (3:159–165).[23] Solipsistic panic is transformed into visionary conviction: "I had a world about me—'twas my own, / I made it; for it only lived to me, / And to the God who looked into my mind" (3:142–144). This is the "abyss of idealism" Wordsworth elsewhere describes as an inability "to think of external things as having an external existence."[24] Descartes knows that his denials might seem like the fancies of "certain lunatics whose brain is so troubled and befogged by the black vapors . . . that they continually affirm they are kings when they are paupers." The enthusiast is equally vulnerable to the charge of lunacy. Wordsworth's admission that his sense of "the one presence, and the life / Of the great whole" was "with me in my solitude / So often among multitudes of men" introduces the possibility that his experience is a type of madness (albeit in the guise of a denial):

> Some called it madness; such indeed it was,
> If childlike fruitfulness in passing joy,
> If steady moods of thoughtfulness matured
> To inspiration, sort with such a name;
> If prophecy be madness; if things viewed
> By poets of old time, and higher up
> By the first men, earth's first inhabitants,
> May in these tutored days no more be seen
> With undisordered sight. But leaving this,
> It was no madness; for I had an eye
> Which in my strongest workings evermore
> Was looking . . .
>
> (3:147–158)

These are not refutations of the charge of madness but analogies to unknowable or unrecoverable states of being. The child, the prophet, the poet, the "first inhabitants of the earth" who see as this eye does are quasi-mythical types within *The Prelude* itself (like the boy of Winander who makes "concourse wild and jocund din" with owls of the night, and the Arabian horseman of the poet's dream prophesying apocalypse). If the visionary experience is explicitly associated with exceptional and solitary figures, to say that one sees as they see is to say that one's vision may be difficult to credit because it is unshared or unshareable.

The revelation of "perpetual logic" and the "one life" constitutes one early climax in *The Prelude*, a point identified as the "eminence" of the life history recounted thus far. Here is the articulated juncture of the "tale" of the poem (the "glory of my youth"), its "theme" ("what passed within me"), and its "heroic argument" ("the might of souls and what they do within themselves while yet the yoke of earth is new to them, the world nothing but a wild field in which they were sown"). The "godlike hours," in which man feels the "majesty sway we have / As natural beings in the strength of Nature" (3:192–193), are proper to the self conceived as originally solitary—that is, they are linked or bound up with the fiction of autonomous development that the poem has been unfolding. Here, then, is also the juncture between "visionary power" and the tale of the solitary child of nature: the experience of such might and such glory is unique to a self-originating being, one whose origin is as that of a seed sown on a wild field.

Solitary origin is the condition for the possibility of visionary experience, but the "utter solitude" so essential to the achievement of "holy calm" also necessarily entails a willful retreat from social experience. Unlike Rousseau, for example, whose reveries are those of the outcast and exile, Wordsworth seeks out solitude, even when "among multitudes of men" ("Oft did I leave / My comrades" so as to be alone under "heaven's blue concave" [3:97–100]). Experience of underlying unity, harmony, and logic in the natural world is linked to the tale of the child of nature (as the "glory" and "eminence" the tale achieves), and happens only within a solitude that is the preferred state of the youth whom the child of nature has become. However, as a solitary and a visionary, this character is vulnerable to the charge of madness and knows it well enough to recollect, with gratitude, the faithful terrier who would give him fair warning of approaching strangers so that he might "shape [himself] / To give and take a greeting that might save / My name from piteous rumours such as wait / On men suspected to be crazed in brain" (4:117–120).

It is not only the pantheistic mysticism of the metaphysical visions that Wordsworth himself presents as vulnerable to the charge of delusion; the humanistic vision is equally and more troublingly vulnerable to the charge of being the vain conceit of one "falsely taught a solitary . . . who walks about in dreams." In the argument of book 8, that love of nature leads to love of mankind, the arousal of that love is explicitly associated with the visionary sense of the "one life" that is "joy":

> [At] the time in which
> The pulse of being everywhere was felt,
> When all the several frames of things, like stars
> Through every magnitude distinguishable,
> Were half confounded in each other's blaze,
> One galaxy of life and joy. Then rose
> Man, inwardly contemplated, and present
> In my own being, to a loftier height—
> (8: 626–633)

The "high thoughts of God and man" inspired by nature are concretely figured by the recollected sight of the single shepherd on a mountain top:

> Along a narrow valley and profound
> I journeyed, when aloft above my head,
> Emerging from the silvery vapours, lo,
> A shepherd and his dog, in open day.
> Girt round with mists they stood, and looked about
> From that enclosure small, inhabitants
> Of an aërial island floating on,
> As seemed, with that abode in which they were,
> A little pendant area of grey rocks,
> By the soft wind breathed forward.
> (8:93–101)

The solitude and remoteness of this figure remembered with "joy and love" are realized through a particularly appropriate optical illusion. It is no accident that the shepherd appears "aloft," fantastically afloat on a cloud of "grey rocks" as if in defiance of gravity. Not only distance but also elevation is a consistent element in the poem's figuration of man "glorified." "Him have I descried in distant sky, / A solitary object and sublime, / Above all height": thus Wordsworth sums up his recollections of one particular shepherd, glimpsed "ascending fast with his long pole in hand," or seen a "few steps off, / In size like a giant, stalking through the fog," leaving the youth to "feel" his presence in the mountains "As of a lord and master, or a power, / Or genius" (8:382–407). These visions are an essential piece of the logic inexorably leading to love of mankind: "A solitary object and sublime, / Above all height . . . Thus was man / Ennobled outwardly before mine eyes, / And thus my heart at first was introduced / To an unconscious love and reverence / Of human nature" (8:407–414). And, like the vision of the "one life" "invisible to the eye," this vision of human nature must also be defended against the charge of madness: "Call ye these appearances / Which I beheld of shepherds in my youth . . . A shadow, a delusion?" (8:429–431). The rhetorical question suggests possibilities present in the very form of the images chosen to embody the "elevating thoughts" of mankind advanced in book 8.

Indeed, a counterargument to the thesis of book 8 is intimated in the explicit opposition between its visions of man aloft and the sight of human beings "under the weight of meanness." The love of mankind inspired by the vision of man "purified, removed, and at a distance that was fit" appears to enable and to require a deliberate seeing past or seeing through human vice and misery and pain. As a "rambling schoolboy," the child of nature "little saw, cared less" that the solitary and sublime shepherd was a man who "suffered with the rest / From vice and folly," but as a youth, "temporal shapes / Of vice and folly [are] thrust upon [his] view," "guilt" "vice," "debasement" and "misery [are] forced upon [his] sight" (8:425–427, 643–644, 802–804). "High thoughts of God and man" can only be "triumphant over all those loathsome sights of wretchedness and vice" if pain and misery the eye cannot choose but see are willfully displaced by the idea of "Man, inwardly contemplated" (8:64–66, 633). The capacity to sustain "elevating thoughts" of human nature in spite of palpable evidence of human debasement is traced back to an early life during which distance from "the deformities of crowded life" provided a "sure safeguard and defence / Against the weight of meanness, selfish cares, / Coarse manners, vulgar passions" (8:453–455). The implication is that if forced to bear this weight, high thoughts of God and man would tumble to the ground: "Were it otherwise / And we found evil as fast as we find good / In our first years, or think that it is found, / How could the innocent heart bear up and live?" (8:443–446). The interpolation—"or think that it is found"—is the merest concession of the possibility that the "appearances" of man as "a solitary object and sublime, above all height," are indeed delusional. And it is this possibility that is more fully articulated later in book 8 in that compromising affirmation of conviction "in what we may become," discussed above, in the paradoxical and simultaneous denial and admission of the notion that "I was ignorant, had been falsely taught, / A solitary, who with vain conceits / Had been inspired, and walked about in dreams" (8:808–810). One who sees the world in which he is "brought more near . . . to guilt and wretchedness" as a place to which he has been "transported . . . as in a dream" may indeed be suspected of confounding weighty matters of human life and ungrounded ideals of human nature.

Unheroic Argument and the Moral of the Story

Those who read *The Prelude* as constructing a providential plot for the hero in which all experiences ultimately contribute to the telos of the discovery of his poetic vocation may see, in Wordsworth's expressions of defensiveness ("It was no madness"; "I was not ignorant"), the rhetorical mode of biblical parable, the prophetic communication of vision that will not signify to those hard of heart. It is a mode that Wordsworth himself evokes: the very notion that his vision of man as solitary and sublime might be shadow or delusion could only occur to "ye who are fed / By the dead letter, not the spirit of things" (8:431–432). However, the poem also makes available the terms of the retort to such a claim: one who sees a man afloat on an aerial island of rocks has perhaps drunk too deeply of the visionary power. The experience of admonishment and reproof, recurrently represented in Wordsworth's poetry, does not always take a clear, unmistakable form (such as the emblematic figure of the blind beggar in a London crowd, on whom the poet gazes "as if admonished from another world"). Subtle manipulations of narrative voice and temporal perspective in *The Prelude* also produce ironic self-reflection so that the intensity of a previously cherished conviction may be conveyed at one and the same time as retrospective awareness of error.[25] At the very least, the admission of the possibility of madness and delusion—even in the context of dismissing and rejecting such misgivings—conveys anxiety about the visions recorded with such confidence and endowed with such value. To credit this ambivalence and entertain the notion that the "love of mankind" articulated in book 8 is indeed unsubstantial, shadowy, and delusional would entail reconsidering not only whether the argument of book 8 is meant to stand but also whether the ensuing narrative of *The Prelude* is a story about the loss and recovery of that love or about a recovery from self-delusion.

If the early books of the poem introduce and develop a solitary character prone to visionary spells of madness, then a plot involving such a protagonist may lead to a crisis of disillusionment, and the underlying argument would concern the unsustainability of an abstract idealism about human nature. Insofar as that very idealism is associated with and shown to be a consequence of an initial conception of the human individual as a singular, self-originating being, the overturning of the thesis that love of nature leads to love of mankind would occur as a revolution in the hero's character, the seeds of which are planted in the poem's earliest representations of the child of nature. Of course, such a plot and such an argument are by no means straightforwardly presented; indeed, the later books of the poem appear to alternate between rueful recognition of disillusionment and willful reaffirmations of early convictions. *The Prelude* is sufficiently complex to record hesitations and reluctance to renounce an idealism about human nature, in spite of having shown that idealizing love to be ungrounded. Similarly the poem does not openly renounce its myth of autonomous selfhood, though, insofar as it identifies the beginning of its own tale as some time after "that first time" of infant dependence, it compromises the primacy of the origins it represents.

The mythic story of origins, of a child of nature not subject to "gravitation and the filial bond," is bound up with the story of a delusory idealism about human nature that is ambivalently overcome. To trace the interrelation between these stories is to understand that the crisis the hero undergoes is not only a reaction to historical events (in autobiographical terms, Wordsworth's record of response to the French Revolution) but is also presented as the consummation or inevitable consequence of conceiving of the self as fundamentally and originally autonomous (in the poem's own theoretical terms, the crisis represents the overturning of its initial "heroic argument" about the self being "sown even as a seed" upon the earth). The balance of this chapter considers the representation of the crisis the youth undergoes, the emerging role of other persons in the later books of the poem, and the remarkable change in the content of the childhood memories singled out for recollection in order to highlight the manner in which *The Prelude* avoids telling a straightforward tale of recovery or, rather, uses its narrative of recovery in order to revise its own starting point for reflection and recollection of individual origins.

"Heaviest sorrow," the "ground of moral obligation," and the "plain below"

If there is a turning point in the plot of *The Prelude*, it is surely the trial of belief, the "shock / Given to my moral nature," which Wordsworth calls a "revolution" (10:233–237). But what is this disturbance that arrests the poet's "progress on the self-same path," and forces his "likings and loves [to run] in new channels" (10:238, 770)? The convictions shaken by the revolution are usually understood to be those expressed in the book on the "love of mankind" and are also usually differentiated from the abstract optimism about human nature frequently identified as the "Godwinian rationalism" that the poet briefly adopts. But there is certainly more to the story of this disillusionment. The faith in human nature so shaken at this time is not recovered after the philosophy that displaces it comes to crisis, because the philosophy itself is not a deviation from earlier belief but a last effort to sustain it. Approaching books 9 and 10 with a sense of the underlying ambivalence about the substance of the "love of mankind" espoused in book 8 makes it possible to see the essential similarity between the tendency of the child of nature to view "human nature from the golden side" and a philosophy that would "look through all the frailties of the world" and thus "abstract the hopes of man / Out of his feelings" thenceforth to fix them "in a purer element" (10:663, 820, 807–808).

The sentiments of childhood and youth are explicitly associated with the sense of joy and love at first affirmed and later shaken during the time of the French Revolution:

> I moved among mankind
> With genial feelings still predominant,
> With erring, erring on the better side,
> And in the kinder spirit—
>
> . . . .
>
> In brief, a child of Nature, as at first,
> Diffusing only those affections wider
> That from the cradle had grown up with me.
> (10:738–741, 752–754)

The catalyst of the crisis is not any one of the tragic convulsions in revolutionary France (the massacres, the terror, the fall of Robespierre, the coronation of Napoleon, all of which are recorded in *The Prelude*) but is England's entry into the war against the new republic. Convictions about human nature ("trust in what we may become") are not initially affected; rather, vital "sensations near the heart" undergo revolution. Love, suddenly and involuntarily, turns to loathing. "Love of mankind" (as espoused in book 8) can only be sustained by seeing past all evidence of guilt, vice, and debasement, but it cannot withstand the experience of guilt and vice within the self, the "sense / Of treachery and desertion in the place / The holiest that I knew—of my own soul" (10:378–380).

> I felt
> The ravage of this most unnatural strife
> In my own heart; there lay it like a weight,
> At enmity with all the tenderest springs
> Of my enjoyments.
> (10:249–253)

Weighing and bearing down on the heart are irresistible emotions of joy in others' grief ("I rejoiced ... truth painful to record, / Exulted" in English defeats) and bitter alienation from countrymen ("I only, like an uninvited guest, / Whom no one owned, sate silent" during prayers for English victory and "Fed on the day of vengeance yet to come!") (10:258–274). Affections hitherto untried by the complications of such inner conflict do not outlast it. The poet is "thrown out of the pale of love," his genial sentiments "soured and corrupted upwards to the source" (10:760–761). It is in this context that the poet embraces "wild theories" of human nature. Since "sentiments / Could ... No longer justify themselves through faith / Of inward consciousness," more secure "evidence" for belief is sought elsewhere (10:784–787). The philosophy of the moment to which Wordsworth turns is merely the latest version of the solitary's visionary abstraction and elevation of human nature, a "tempting region ... For zeal to enter and refresh herself" (10:810–811):

> ... the dream
> Was flattering to the young ingenuous mind
> Pleased with extremes, and not the least with that
> Which makes the human reason's naked self

> The object of its fervour. What delight!—
> How glorious!—in self-knowledge and self-rule
> To look through all the frailties of the world,
> And, with a resolute mastery shaking off
> The accidents of nature, time, and place,
> That make up the weak being of the past,
> Build social freedom on its only basis:
> The freedom of the individual mind.
>
> (10:814–825)

As articulated here, this dream hardly differs from the earlier dream of human nature, solitary and sublime, elevated above vice, folly, and meanness. "Frailties of the world," like miseries forced upon the sight, may be looked through and seen past; instead of bending under the "weight of pain and fear," the contingencies of human life and history that impose that weight are to be shaken off. The "weak being of the past" is both historical man, the victim of tyranny and oppression, and man as he is (born), weak precisely because subject to "accidents of nature, time, and place." To say that social freedom can only be built on the basis of the "freedom of the individual mind" is to say that certain philosophical dreams of justice (like certain poetic visions of mankind "glorified") rest on a conception of the human being as self-transparent and self-governing ("in self-knowledge and self-rule") and thus require not seeing the human being as weak, and all that he may become as vulnerable to accident and circumstance. The espousal of this kind of philosophy is not a falling off from the love of mankind professed in book 8 but a last effort to sustain it, to never "[think] ill of human-kind," to still "pursu[e] / A higher nature" (10:831, 835).

In the self-probing analysis to which Wordsworth is driven, the culmination of his crisis in the "yield[ing] up of moral questions in despair" (10:900), what is rejected is only most superficially Godwinian rationalism. The "heart which had been turned aside / From nature" is able, reflectively, to consider not only the unsustainability of its latest beliefs but also of "reasonings false from the beginning" (10:884–886). Moreover, the effects of the dissecting analysis are not entirely negative or destructive. In seeking "the ground / Of moral obligation," Wordsworth recalls, "I pushed without remorse / My speculations forward, yea, set foot / On Nature's holiest places" (10:894–895, 876–878). In terms the poem itself has established, the downward thrust of these thoughts suggests a descent from implausible heights. To set the foot down on sites once sanctified and seek solid ground is to renounce "elevating thoughts" of human nature, to recognize that "feeble men / Walk on this earth" (11:147–148). This renunciation and recognition may be traced, in later books, through the resolve to seek "the dignity of individual man" not by shaking off but by taking full measure of "all the weight / Of that injustice" under which he labors, not by looking up and away but by going down among "lowly men" (12:83–105). Dignity turns out to be fragile and contingent, dependent (as his own love of mankind proved to be) on "accidents of nature, time, and place." "Where oppression worse than death / Salutes the being at his birth, where grace / Of culture hath been utterly unknown, / And labour in excess and poverty / From day to day pre-occupy the ground / Of the affections" there indeed a "deeper nature" prevails over "Nature's self" and "Love cannot be" (12:194–201): these conditions of life are no longer to be looked through.

The wanderings on Salisbury Plain among the "lowly" and "obscure" culminate in a visionary experience that is also a distinct revision of earlier revelations: a reverie of the distant past in which primitive man is not seen alone, in a state of nature, but among "multitudes" and as a social and historical creature of "barbaric majesty." As with the earlier visionary experiences, the senses are superseded by dream images ("A midnight darkness seemed to come and take / All objects from my sight"), but instead of seeing the human being "purified, removed, at a distance," the poet is near enough to feel the "rattling spear / Shaken by arms of mighty bone," to see the "dismal flames" of the "sacrificial altar, fed / With living men," and to hear the cries of the victims, "how deep the groans!" (12:320–332). Even as another, enchanting dream of druids on the plain with "white wands / Uplifted, pointing to the starry sky" follows the dark reverie, violence, superstition, and pain remain integral to the vision. The poet, like the druids of this dream, now points "alternately"—to the sky above and to the "plain below" (12:349–351). And unlike the early visions of invisible unities and silent harmonies, this is not the kind of revelation given only to an exceptional being who sees as a prophet or as "poets of old time" or "earth's first inhabitants." Lost is a conviction in the singularity of vision that by virtue of its singularity cannot be shared: the "Points have we all . . . Where all stand single; this I feel and make / Breathings for incommunicable powers" (3:186–188). Confidence arises in its stead that what the poet sees, others, too, can see: "I seemed about this period to have sight / Of a new world—a world, too, that was fit / To be transmitted and made visible / To other eyes" (12:370–373).

"Strength to thyself" but "by human love assisted"

The "metaphysical" plot of the poem culminates, not surprisingly, at a height: the ascent of Mount Snowdon, and the "meditation that rose in me... / Upon the lonely mountain" of a "higher love" (12:66–67, 161). Higher than what is "human merely," what Wordsworth terms "intellectual love," is made possible by "imagination"—a power that, in the final book of *The Prelude*, is literally identified as the locus of autonomy:

> Imagination having been our theme,
> So also hath that intellectual love,
> For they are each in each, and cannot stand
> Dividually. Here must thou be, O man,
> Strength to thyself—no helper hast thou here—
> Here keepest thou thy individual state:
> No other can divide with thee this work.
> (13:185–191)

There is, however, work that can and must be divided with others. If the heroic narrative comes to a climax in this definition of a space in which the individual must be "strength to thyself," then the counterplot culminates in the lines that immediately follow, in the admission that friendship and love "complete the man... made imperfect in himself" (13:203–204).

Autonomous, yet incomplete, perfected by others and thus not whole in itself—these irreconcilable contradictions in *The Prelude*'s construction of the individual are conveyed by a figure that uncomfortably incorporates both sexes:

> And he whose soul hath risen
> Up to the height of feeling intellect
> Shall want no humbler tenderness, his heart
> Be tender as a nursing mother's heart;
> Of female softness shall his life be full.
> (13:204–208)

Tensions that run throughout *The Prelude* are arrested yet unresolved in this implausible combination (the erection of "feeling intellect" and the "softness" of the "nursing mother's heart"). "That pair, the lamb / And the lamb's mother" illustrates the notion that "From love . . . / Do we begin and end . . . from pervading love— / That gone, we are as dust" (13:149–152). But this image and idea of life's beginnings exists alongside that of the soul sowing itself as a seed:

> The prime and vital principle is thine
> In the recesses of thy nature, far
> From any reach of outward fellowship
> Else 'tis not thine at all. But joy to him
> O, joy to him who here hath sown—hath laid
> Here the foundations of his future years.
>   (13:194–199)

The figures of the dependent babe and the free-growing seedling are ultimately irreconcilable insofar as each is designated as the origin of the individual. Wordsworth proposes that the "foundation" for future years is laid on the autonomous basis of imagination and intellectual love, but *The Prelude* also offers such recurrent and consistent evocations of dependence as to effectively reverse its own priorities.

The admission that friendship and love "complete the man . . . made imperfect in himself" introduces the acknowledgments and thanks that draw *The Prelude* to a close. Wordsworth pays tribute to Dorothy, the "sister of my soul" and the "sister of my heart" ("who ought to have been / Conspicuous through this biographic verse") (13:211–246, 339–342), to Coleridge, the "beloved friend" addressed throughout the poem and here recalled particularly as "associate in [the] labour" of poetry (13:247–268 and 386–427), and also to Calvert, whose brief friendship, early death, and generous bequest to Wordsworth are the accidental combination of circumstances that provide the poet with "necessary maintenance" and thus make possible his vocation (13:350–366). "He cleared a passage for me," writes Wordsworth, "and the stream / Flowed in the bent of Nature": in so strong an affirmation of the irresistible inclination to be a poet it is easy to overlook the recognition of assistance, but it is nonetheless clear that without the passage cleared, no stream can flow, that natural inclination itself is subject to accident and circumstance. This sense that the support of others is not incidental but essential to what the individual may become runs as a deep countercurrent to the tracking of "imagination up her way sublime" through the final books of *The Prelude*, suggesting that "higher love" rests on and arises from the human love that grounds it and without which all foundations and buildings the imagination may erect "are as dust."

The final movements of the poem—the avowal of incompleteness, and the warm introduction of those on whom the poet depends—recapitulate, and thus illuminate, the highly condensed account of recovery from the despair—philosophical and personal at once—of ever finding the "ground of moral obligation." Having lost "all feeling of conviction," the poet is restored to himself, spared, and "preserved still a poet" in and by the presence of others:

> Ah, then it was
> That thou, most precious friend, about this time
> First known to me, didst lend a living help
> To regulate my soul. And then it was
> That the belovèd woman in whose sight
> Those days were passed . . .
> Maintained for me a saving intercourse
> With my true self.
>
> (10:904–915)

While this recovery seems an abrupt break from the impasse at which the poet had presented himself, it is worth pausing to consider what the apostrophic turn introduces into the poem. "Ah"—an exclamation of surprise, of discovery, of recognition? Prosaically (and with the supplement of biography) the lines allude to Coleridge and to Dorothy, but the spareness of the diction and omission of proper names invite consideration of something more generally and elementally "first known" at this time. "Ah . . . thou" registers sudden awareness of another presence, simultaneous with the appreciation of that presence as a friend, and of the friend as one who provides "living help." Perhaps no more and no less than admission of need for others is registered by the sudden exhalation or cry, but, if so, then the admission itself is essential to the poet's becoming his "true self." As others have not failed to notice, the recovery of the later books is figured as rebirth ("Nature's self, by human love

/ Assisted" together "Revived the feelings of my earlier life") (10:921–924). It may also be a vital reconception, a kind of metamorphosis. The "true self" maintained now by intercourse with others is perhaps no longer a falsely taught solitary; the "living help" of the friend, the "saving intercourse" of a "belovèd woman," "uphold" a soul no longer self-sustaining. The self that is recovered here is reconceived as a weak being, not a free-standing structure (a building "sustained by its own spirit") but one subject to accidents of nature, time, and place. And in being upheld and supported by others, this self recognizes the gravity and weight thus far defied by the elevating thoughts reared on myths of its autonomy.

The child of nature, the son "bowed low," and the gravity of memory

The weight that, I suggest, falls on the central character of *The Prelude* also pervades the childhood recollections singled out in the concluding books. Many readers have noted the seeming disjunction between the purpose Wordsworth assigns to the "spots of time"—the power to lift the "deadly weight" of oppressive thoughts or numbing routine on the mind—and the content of the memories chosen as illustration (11:257–268). The two "affecting incidents" recalled are indeed the bleakest episodes of the poem. In the first, the five-year-old child loses his guide on a desolate moor and, lost and alone, stumbles on a stone monument to an execution carried out on the spot long ago; still lost and alone, the child ascends to a "lonely eminence," seeking the lost guide who is nowhere to be seen (11:278–315). In the second incident, the thirteen-year-old boy restlessly watches on the "highest summit" for the horses that will take him home from school for Christmas, his "anxiety of hope" as he sits only half-sheltered from the "stormy, and rough, and wild" weather destined to be linked, in memory, with the funeral procession to the father's grave days later, the son "bowed low" with an irrational but irresistible sense of being punished for his impatience (11:344–385). These childhood memories are radically different from those recollected hours with the "charm of visionary things" in book 1. Indeed, the adventurous boy roaming and wandering on his own deep into the night seems an altogether different character from the child who "through fear" dismounts his horse when he finds himself alone, who "stumbles" and "falters" through the landscape. Unlike the boy who would walk alone on "starlight nights" and "drink the visionary power," this child's solitude is darkly colored by the feeling of being lost: "visionary dreariness" falls upon the natural scene "while I looked all around for my lost guide" (who, in memory at least, is never found) (11:310–311).

Recollected in the spots of time, as nowhere in the earliest books, is the child's subjection not to fear but to loss and to the dread of loss. It is no accident that these are memories of being in high places—a "lonely eminence" and the "highest summit" of "a crag, an eminence" commanding a view of the highways. But there is no transport, no "fits of vulgar joy" or "giddy bliss" or thrill of solitude at these heights (1:610–612). There is, rather, a solemnity to these scenes, gravity in the sense that the poem has given the term—a weighty sense of human history, tragedy, and subjection to loss. Ghosts of human tragedy darken the natural world that the child inhabits; crime, punishment, and death are literally "engraven" on the rough stone of the moor. The "storm and tempest" that inspire the child of nature with a feeling of "whate'er there is of power in sound / To breathe an elevated mood" are antagonistic forces for the lost boy (2:322–325). The blast of wind that sustains the boy hanging perilously on a high ridge in book 1 blows, too, on the lonely eminence of book 11, as the force that vexes and tosses a woman's garments, a force against which she has to "force her way" (11:306). Instead of "drinking in / A pure organic pleasure from the lines / Of curling mist" (as the child of nature does), the boy who "would drink / As at a fountain" at the sight of advancing lines of mist is also drinking in the painful recollection of the imminence of his loss, of all that followed the day that he sat "straining [his] eyes intensely" to see through the fog to the road below, waiting and "look[ing] in such anxiety of hope" (1:590–592; 11:383–384, 361, 371). The young boy here is not a naked savage and intrepid climber, not a child of nature, but the son of a father who will die, a child inevitably "bowed low" under the weight of loss and grief.

The Startling Sound of an Acorn Falling

I have argued that *The Prelude* engages two powerful enlightenment myths of autonomy—the originary autonomy of natural man and the autonomous development of the isolated mind. The "child of nature" conceived in the poem is imagined to be free from "gravitation and the filial bond," terms that in this poem evoke both the unchosen burden of human attachment and the unavoidable perception of human subjection to pain, fear, misery, and injustice. My argument is not that Wordsworth renounces the myth of autonomous being, or the imagination of the "freedom of the individual mind," but that *The Prelude* incorporates an ambivalent and critical perspective on that myth, an awareness, in particular, of a moral vacuity at the heart of the idealism about human nature which such myths of autonomy enable. It is worth recalling, in this context, why Rousseau insists on the impossibility of "returning" to the state of nature. Those "whose passions have forever destroyed their original simplicity," he writes in the *Second Discourse*, and who "can no longer subsist on grass and acorns" are also endowed with a moral sense that cannot be sloughed off.

> Those who were honored in their first father with supernatural lessons; those who will see the intention of giving to human actions from the first a morality which they would not have acquired for a long time ... will respect the sacred bonds of the societies of which they are members; they will love their kind and serve them with all their power. (203, 217)

These supernatural lessons (as discussed in chapter 2) entail the moral possibilities of human relations, the challenges of which are both a blessing and an unwilled inheritance. The "passions" and the "sacred bonds" constitutive of the human being born into dependence and association with others in Rousseau are echoed in Wordsworth's depiction of the "blessed babe" who "doth gather passion from his mother's eye" and thus becomes subject to the "filial bond"—a coincidence suggestive of an underlying coherence or agreement about human birthright.[26] The polyvalence of the term *bond* itself bears consideration here, ranging as it does from the neutrality of an unspecified link or connection to the negative inflections of bondage and restraint to the active sense of a willed obligation, agreement, or covenant. All extenuate, if not altogether obviate, independence. To be bound is precisely not to be "free, enfranchised and at large," as Wordsworth presents himself at the outset of *The Prelude*. The glad preamble may be seen as a splendid indulgence in the fantasy of returning to a mythic state of nature, "To drink wild water, and to pluck green herbs, / And gather fruits fresh from their native bough," and to think oneself at liberty. Here is how Rousseau presents the impossible drive to break free of unchosen bonds in the *Second Discourse*:

> O you, to whom the celestial voice has not made itself heard, and who recognize no other destination for your species than to end this short life in peace; you who are able to leave behind in the cities your fatal acquisitions, your restless minds, your corrupted hearts, your unbridled desires . . . go into the woods to lose the sight and the memories of your contemporaries' crimes. (203, 217)

It is as such a one that Wordsworth first presents himself:

> A captive . . . coming from a house
> Of bondage, from yon city's walls set free,
> A prison where he hath long been immured.
> Now I am free, enfranchised and at large,
> May fix my habitation where I will.
> (1:6–10)

This liberation of the self is designated as extraordinary, supernatural, marked by ascension, and figured as the putting down of a weight:

> Trances of thought and mountings of the mind
> Come fast upon me. It is shaken off,
> As by miraculous gift 'tis shaken off,
> That burthen of my own unnatural self,
> The heavy weight of many a weary day . . .
> (1:20–24)

The poem's initial broad vistas of "open fields" and of "the earth . . . all before me" evoke flight and freedom so absolute that will is become whim ("Shall a twig or any floating thing / Upon the river point me out my course?") (1:31–32). But this incredible lightness of being is arrested in the sheltered grove in which the poet lingers, gratuitously, it seems, pausing between making the "choice / Of one sweet vale whither my steps should turn" and actually "journey[ing] towards the vale which I had chosen" (1:81–82, 100). Why does the poem mark the time between resolution and onward movement? Or, rather, what is marked in this moment of apparent quiescence?

> Thus long I lay
> Cheared by the genial pillow of the earth
> Beneath my head, soothed by a sense of touch
> From the warm ground, that balanced me, else lost
> Entirely, seeing nought, nought hearing, save
> When here and there about the grove of oaks
> Where was my bed, an acorn from the trees
> Fell audibly, and with a startling sound.
> (1:88–95)

The poetry virtually conjures up the double meaning of repose—that of a body lying at rest and a body lying dead. Thus prone, the poet is spared from utter senselessness not by any exertion of thought but by the purely passive reassurance of the persistent presence of the ground beneath him: "soothed by a sense of touch / From the warm ground, that balanced me." Head resting on the earth, the poet is not at risk of losing his balance in the sense of falling down, and thus the poem invites consideration of just what is balanced or in need of balancing. The syntactical ambiguity of "else lost" in this context allows for two readings. The first literally depicts the "action" of the scene, the poet's semi-slumber and the sound that interrupts it: "I lay soothed by a sense of touch from the warm ground, apart from which I sensed nothing, saw nothing and heard nothing except the occasional sound of an acorn falling." In this case, the "balance" furnished by the warm ground is merely physical equipoise. A second reading would exploit the obviously maternal figuration of the earth cradling the poet: "I lay soothed by a sense of touch from the warm ground, without which I would be lost entirely, would see and hear nothing." Such a reading also makes it possible to account for the affective content of the scene: for the poet's "chear," for the "geniality" with which the earth pillows the poet's head, for its "soothing" sense of touch, its warmth. But it is possible to be more specific still about the mothering enacted here.

The earth does not only cradle and soothe. The primacy of touch among the senses emphasizes the physical presence of a body that is balanced, in the sense of being weighed, of a self that would otherwise be naught. The suggestive correspondence between this repose on the "genial pillow of the earth" and that of the infant Wordsworth imagines sleeping "upon his mother's breast," all of whose sensations are "derived from this beloved presence," brings to the fore the sense in which to ground something is to make it possible. I would suggest that the counterplot to *The Prelude*'s tale about an autonomous mind in relation to nature has its roots in this sheltering grove of oaks. The poet's repose is not a moment of suspended activity but of settling—not mountings of the mind but grounding of the body and of the flight of a fantastically liberated self. Not by accident, but by necessity, is this reverie of being lost entirely to sense (yet not dead, at peace in "perfect stillness" and tangibly soothed by the warmth of touch) interrupted by the startling sound of an acorn falling. The fruit thrust to the earth by the force of gravity that also keeps the poet reassuringly balanced on solid ground is also a reminder of the natural law to which all are subject, a reminder of the soul's earthly freight.

CHAPTER 5

Fantastic Form

FRANKENSTEIN AND PHILOSOPHY

ON DEVELOPMENT AND DEFORMATION: THE MONSTER'S FANTASTIC SIZE

It is as a giant that the creature makes his first appearance in *Frankenstein*. He is the "strange sight" that attracts the attention of the explorer whose ambition and curiosity have driven him toward the polar region of the North Sea. The "being which had the shape of a man but apparently of gigantic stature" strikes Walton as clearly of a different kind than Frankenstein, the wretched, emaciated stranger that the ship's crew later pulls aboard the vessel.[1] The creature's giantism is both a fantastic element in the fiction (mysteriously, inexplicably, magically, the human limbs Frankenstein selects are extra-human in proportion) and exemplary of Mary Shelley's use of the fantastic both to further the narrative of the imaginary being's development and to mount a critique of philosophical theories that would render his development in any way plausible.

That the creature is born as a full-grown body enables his physical survival, but the extraordinary size of that "miserable frame" embodies the omission of infancy and childhood from Frankenstein's conception. He does not come to life as a small, helpless infant in need of the care of others for survival; his height and his vigor are exaggerated inversions of the tininess and weakness of newborns. The long shaping period that follows birth and entails varied and prolonged dependence on others is precluded by the mature form he has at birth. The creature himself associates the absence of a formative history of dependence and relation with his anomalous physical form as he describes his developing sense of being "similar, yet strangely unlike," human beings:

"I was unformed in mind; I was dependent on none, and related to none.... My person was hideous and my stature gigantic" (128). *Frankenstein* contends with ideals of autonomy and self-sufficiency not only by narrating the unnatural *birth* of a creature in an act of solitary conception but also, and perhaps more important, by narrating the impossible development of the creature after it is abandoned to its solitary fate.

The Promethean arrogance of Frankenstein's project, the ambition to create life without the other, and the inescapable erasure of the feminine and the maternal which that ambition and project entail—all these have been the *foci* of varied feminist interpretations of the novel. As an evident sign of the occlusion of an unavoidably female act, the creature's non-birth, the lack of gestation in his coming into being, has also been a common point of emphasis. Shelley's "early and chaotic experience, at the very time she became an author, with motherhood," informs Ellen Moers's reading of *Frankenstein* as a "*woman's* mythmaking on the subject of birth." In its invocation of extratextual notions of "female experience," such an approach risks reducing the text to a "monstrous symptom" of the author's psyche, according to Mary Jacobus. Drawing on the psycholinguistic theories of Lacan, Cixous, and Irigaray, she herself resists an emphasis on "female experience" and instead reads *Frankenstein* as an intertextual "drama of Oedipal rivalry." Subsequently Margaret Homans's synthetic analysis moves to combine a historical account of female experience with a theoretical emphasis on the discursive construction of the feminine. Her reading of the novel as a critique of "the gendered myth of language that is part of [androcentric] ontology" accommodates the relevant, well-known biographical details, psychobiographical conjecture, and analysis of Shelley's appropriation of literary precedents such as *Paradise Lost* and *Alastor*.[2] Homans's interpretation is exemplary of the persistence of psychoanalytic models within feminist criticism and their inevitable focus on maternity, reproduction, and the female body. Although compelling and valuable, such interpretations represent only one dimension of what might be understood as the novel's feminism. While its critique of autonomy is remarkably consistent with contemporary feminist thought, its core lies not in the creature's inception—and therefore not in the psychoanalytic depths of the narrative—but in the intellectual history so evident on the narrative surface. Shifting the focus requires not only an engagement with recent developments in philosophy but a return to Shelley's own philosophical sources for *Frankenstein*, for each illuminates the other.

In its engagement with enlightenment theories of education, human nature, and sociality, the novel displays Shelley's depth as a reader and thinker working both within and against a philosophical tradition into which she was quite literally born. Its account of the creature's education responds directly to eighteenth-century philosophical conceptions of human nature that have themselves lately been the objects of feminist revaluation within philosophy. As I indicated in the introduction to this book, critique of the autonomous individual is one point of focus shared by feminists whose specific interests range from moral and political theory to analytic philosophy and epistemology. The *locus classicus* of modern philosophical inquiry—the mind in isolation, meditating on its origins, abstracted from the physical and social body—has been repeatedly identified as an unworkable starting point for the effort to think through the development of cognition, the acquisition of language, and the capacity for ethical judgment.[3] Strikingly absent from traditional philosophical narratives of development—the tradition on which Mary Shelley herself drew—are accounts of infancy, childhood, the network of relationships within which the individual is necessarily embedded from his first moments of life, and the role of dependence and relation generally in the formation of individuals. Condillac's imagination of a statue gradually brought to life (to choose an example of particular relevance for *Frankenstein*) is only the most obvious illustration of a deliberate and yet undermotivated turning away from the easily observable conditions of infancy to the artifice of social isolation in philosophical reconstruction of "the first sensations that we experience," our "first mental operations," the "origin of our ideas."[4] Animating the fully formed but unconscious statue one sensation at a time, Condillac presents the mind's progress from emptiness to plenitude, from crude feeling to idea, as the achievement of an autonomous individual. Shelley's creature follows in this tradition by acquiring the full array of human faculties without parents or associates. The novel anticipates contemporary feminist reinterpretation of the philosophical canon, however, in its engagement with the theoretical and ethical implications of this forgetting or disowning of the dependence and vulnerability at the origin of human forms of life.

o o o

While it has long been understood that Shelley draws on Godwin (to whom the novel is dedicated), Locke, Rousseau, and Condillac for the narrative of the creature's development and education, there has been a tendency to assume that Shelley's selection of details from philosophical works is designed to lend plausibility to the tale.[5] Yet the novel is no less strange, no less fantastic, in its handling of the creature's growing up (not that he ever does grow, of course) as it is in its handling of the creature's birth. The tale of the creature's *Bildung* is designed to expose the implausibility, the fantastic fictionality, of accounts of development widely taken to describe real processes of individual formation and intellectual development. I focus on how closely and carefully the novel alludes to the two philosophical texts central to this study—Locke's *Essay concerning Human Understanding* (1689/1706) and Rousseau's *Discourse on the Origins of Inequality* (1755)—in order to demonstrate the powerful critical revision to which these sources are subjected. Shelley's appropriations from these influential eighteenth-century works define the original position from which the creature's incredible development proceeds as one of social privation. His strange isolation both characterizes and exposes the constraints of the prior philosophical imagination of the developing human subject.

Lockean Child, Rousseauvian Man: The Monster as Philosophical Subject

Locke's inquiry into how human beings acquire knowledge begins (as we saw in chapter 1) with an isolated mind upon which the world and others in it almost aggressively intrude. In Locke's *Essay*, a text Shelley was studying as she worked on *Frankenstein*, the mind first awakens to a multitude of sense impressions: "*Light*, and *Colours*, are busie at hand every where, when the Eye is but open; *Sounds*, and some *tangible Qualities* fail not to solicite their proper Senses, and force an entrance to the Mind."[6] At the outset of the core narrative of *Frankenstein*, Shelley adopts this empiricist idiom, presenting the monster at the birth of his first sensations. "It is with considerable difficulty that I remember the original era of my being," he begins,

> A strange multiplicity of sensations seized me, and I saw, felt, heard, and smelt at the same time; and it was, indeed, a long time before I learned to distinguish between the operations of my various senses. By degrees, I remember, a stronger light pressed upon my nerves, so that I was obliged to shut my eyes. Darkness then came over me, and troubled me;

but hardly had I felt this, when, by opening my eyes, as I now suppose, the light poured in upon me again. (102)

The violence of such an awakening, in both Locke and Shelley, should not be overlooked: the world "forces an entrance to the mind," "presses" itself upon nascent consciousness; the mind is "seized" by sensations and "impressed" in the sense of being forcibly affected and constrained to pay attention. The multiplicity of sensations is itself almost threatening, a chaos of stimuli the simultaneity of which seems unendurable: "No distinct ideas occupied my mind," recalls the creature, "all was confused; I felt light, and hunger, and thirst, and darkness; innumerable sounds rung in my ears" (103). The origin of ideas in empiricist psychology entails overcoming this confusion of sensation, drawing distinctions between the stimuli of lightness, darkness, heat, cold, hunger, and so forth. This effort "to class the cabinet of . . . sensations," as Wordsworth puts it in *The Prelude*, and "run through the history and birth of each / As of a single, independent thing"[7] is both essential to the project of understanding *how* all knowledge derives from the senses and an artificial reconstruction of the early life of the individual. Condillac's imaginary statue, for example, animated one sense at a time, is an analytic device designed to compensate for the fact that "we are unable to observe our first thoughts and our first movements." The person is thus reduced to a "sequence of conscious experiences or doings," "disembodied and disembedded" from the social context.[8] In Locke, figures for the mind such as the "empty cabinet" to be furnished by sensation (1.2.15) or the "white paper void of all characters" (2.1.2) are not only designed "to set [the understanding] at a distance and make it its own object," they are also assumed to shed light on the obscure first era of understanding. It is especially striking that accounts of development enabled by such fantastically artificial figures consistently metamorphose into descriptions of experiences undergone by actual infants and children.

The experience of light, in the *Essay* and in the creature's account, is the first distinct sensation, the first pleasure, and hence the first idea. According to Locke, "Children new-born . . . always turn their Eyes to that part, from whence the Light comes," thus exhibiting "how covetous the Mind is, to be furnished with all such *Ideas*, as have no pain accompanying them" (2.9.7). So Shelley's creature, reawakening in darkness, notices a "gentle light stole over the heavens [which] gave me a sensation of pleasure" and singles it out from the clutter of indistinct sensations: "the only object that I could distinguish was the bright moon, and I fixed my eyes on that with pleasure" (103). Pain is, of course, the other primary stimulus commanding the attention of the newborn mind. Locke's infant is "seldom awake, but when either Hunger calls for the Teat, or some Pain . . . or some other violent Impression on the Body, forces the mind to perceive, and attend to it" (2.1.21). A similar oscillation from dormancy to pain-induced wakefulness is marked in *Frankenstein*. Shelley's creature lies "resting from . . . fatigue, until tormented by hunger and thirst" and is "overcome by sleep" once satiated only to be roused by "feeling pain invade [him] on all sides" (103). To these elemental physical sensations, however, Shelley adds one not to be found in Locke, the feeling of aloneness: "I felt cold, and half-frightened, as it were, instinctively, finding myself so desolate" (103).

The extrasensory perception of isolation is an unmistakable deviation from the foundational Lockean hypothesis that there are no innate ideas. It suggests that the presence of others may be as natural and pressing a need for one newly born as food and warmth, while also begging the question of how a creature who comes to consciousness on its own would be in a position to sense that it *is* alone—to sense, say, that the natural forms and sounds surrounding it are not company. Recall, for example, that hunger drives Locke's infant to call for the breast, a metonymy for the human caretaker that elides the distinction between the perception of persons and things and between affective and physical need.[9] Left out of the *Essay*'s reconstruction of the origins of ideas and knowledge in the individual mind is any sense that the experience of other persons would be significantly different from the experience of inanimate objects in the environment. It is precisely such an omission that the "as it were instinctive" experience of aloneness as pain in *Frankenstein* brings to light. Given that the narrative is working within the framework of empiricist theory, the creature's natural sense of desolation is a kind of super-natural endowment, one Shelley adds on to the cluster of empiricist sensations, and one that presents the condition of isolation from which the empiricist account of development begins as one of lack and privation.

o o o

While the creature's recollection of his first sensations of pain, pleasure, light and dark, hunger and cold educes the Lockean narrative of individual formation, the wilderness that is his first home and the wanderings of his first days evoke enlightenment genealogies of the species, especially and most notoriously Rousseau's account of the state of nature in the *Discourse on the Origins of Inequality among Men*. The creature "gaz[ing] with a kind of wonder" on the moon recalls Rousseau's man "as he must have issued from the hands on Nature," who is first seen walking upright "with his eyes surveying the vast expanse of heaven." Just as natural man is imagined "sating his hunger beneath an oak, slaking his thirst at the first stream, finding his bed at the foot of the same tree that supplied his meal," so does Shelley's creature eat the berries that he "found hanging on the trees, or lying on the ground . . . slak[e his] thirst at the brook; and then li[e] down . . . overcome by sleep" (103).[10] Yet the direct evocation of Rousseau at these moments should not be mistaken for uncritical appropriation.

Shelley's use of the state of nature in *Frankenstein* is actually consistent with criticisms she would explicitly articulate in her 1839 biographical essay on Rousseau for Lardner's *Cabinet Cyclopedia*. Her assertion that "nothing can be more unnatural than Rousseau's natural man" is itself based on Mary Wollstonecraft's forceful argument (in the *Vindication of the Rights of Woman*) against Rousseau's "false hypothesis" of a "naturally . . . solitary animal." "He disputes whether man be a gregarious animal," writes Wollstonecraft, "though the long and helpless state of infancy seems to point him out as particularly impelled to pair."[11] Having come to life fully grown and thus not helpless, Shelley's creature is fantastically exempt from this state of infant dependency; his gigantic proportions and extraordinarily robust constitution draw exaggerated attention to his unnatural liberation from the need for caretaking. If he is a version of Rousseau's natural man, then he is reconceptualized as a monstrous deviation from the human.

For Shelley, "the cares required by children," like the "helpless state of infancy" invoked by her mother, are evidence that the solitary state is unnatural to human beings, and autonomy an artificial theoretical starting point for human development.[12] These very arguments return in recent critiques of traditional states of nature for "expung[ing] human reproduction and early nurturance from [the] account of basic human nature."[13] The force of this insight, however, draws on strains and tendencies inherent in the very theory it opposes. The challenge to the state of nature made by Wollstonecraft, Shelley, and more recently by contemporary feminists grappling with the same philosophical canon is all the more powerful for being consistent with the *Discourse* itself, for allowing the relentlessly critical and paradoxical movements of that work's conjectural history to become legible as the substance of its argument rather than as points of inconsistency for exegesis to resolve or rebuke. Rousseau's work is commonly associated with a nostalgic yearning for the untroubled contentment of the autonomous beast he imagines in the state of nature, but (as discussed in chapters 2 and 3) the text is clear that solitude and autonomy are the absolute and unbreachable barriers to his evolution beyond an animal state. "What progress could mankind make, scattered in the Woods among the Animals?" asks Rousseau. "And how much could men perfect and enlighten one another who . . . might meet no more than twice in their life, without knowing and speaking with one another?" (152). "None" and "not at all" are the answers to these questions, for both Rousseau and Shelley.

"It is inconceivable how a man could, by his own strength alone," traverse the "distance between pure sensations and the simplest knowledge," according to Rousseau. A series of unanswerable questions about the origin of fire illustrates the impossibility of intellectual progress for creatures living apart from one another:

> How many centuries perhaps elapsed before men were in a position to see any other fire than that of Heaven? How many different chance occurrences must they have needed before they learned the most common uses of this element? How many times must they have let it go out before they mastered the art of reproducing it? And how many times did each one of these secrets perhaps die together with its discoverer? (151)

Shelley follows Rousseau here. Having learned to distinguish between his sensations "and to perceive objects in their right forms," the creature comes across the remains of a fire in the forest. He discovers, by experience and observation, that it is painful to touch, that the addition of wood will sustain it, and that it gives off light as well as heat, but the art of reproducing it is necessarily beyond his ken (104–105). Rousseau's natural man is not a modern Prometheus nor, the subtitle aside, is Shelley's creature.[14]

In Rousseau, "centuries [go] by in all the crudeness of the first ages" in a state of nature from which there is no clear exit. Shelley's creature remains in the forest for mere days precisely to allow the narrative of his development to proceed beyond this initial point of awakened consciousness. He is compelled to abandon the fire he comes upon by accident, because (in contrast to the fertile world of the *Discourse*) food is scarce in his environment. Hunger drives him out of the forest and into contact with human communities, and it is his search for food that leads to his first encounters with other human beings. Driven from the first village he comes upon, the creature takes refuge in the hovel that will thereafter become his home and the site of his education. This shift from the forest to the structure adjacent to the DeLacey cottage, and hence from nature to culture, corresponds to a definite movement away from an engagement with one kind of account of origins—the Rousseauvian phylogenetic narrative—and back to the Lockean account of ontogeny with which the creature's story began.

Enlightenment in a Dark Room

Locke consistently represents the mind as a delimited interior space, enclosed, distinct, and separated from an outside world that penetrates it with impressions. His well-known image of the mind as a dark room (discussed in chapter 1) is worth recalling here: "External and internal Sensation, are the only passages that I can find, of Knowledge, to the Understanding," writes Locke. "These alone, as far as I can discover, are the Windows by which light is let into this *dark Room*. For, methinks, the *Understanding* is not much unlike a Closet wholly shut from light, with only some little opening left, to let in external visible Resemblances, or *Ideas* of things without" (2.11.17). Compare this imaginary space to the small hovel in which the creature takes refuge. Built adjacent to the DeLacey cottage, it is separated from that structure by a wall and window; the "panes had been filled up with wood," but some little opening remains—"a small and almost imperceptible chink, through which the eye could just penetrate," thus allowing the creature to observe the human world on the other side (108). The creature's tale recommences here, his hovel becoming a kind of empiricist crib from which he looks abroad, acquaints himself with the world without, and acquires an array of human faculties. However, whereas Locke's account is intended to be a "true *History of the first beginnings of Humane Knowledge*" (2.11.15), Shelley's narrative presents the creature's development as only plausible in a fantastic fiction that requires repeated suspensions of disbelief.

The creature's first glimpse of the cottagers from his dark hovel is not that of one unacquainted with human manners but the informed gaze of a sensitive observer.

> An old man [sat], leaning his head on his hands in a disconsolate attitude . . . presently [the young girl] took something out of a drawer, which employed her hands, and she sat down beside the old man, who, taking up an instrument, began to play, and to produce sounds sweeter than the voice of the thrush or the nightingale. It was a lovely sight, even to me, poor wretch! Who had never beheld aught beautiful before. . . . He played a sweet mournful air, which I perceived drew tears from the eyes of his amiable companion . . . she sobbed audibly; he then pronounced a few sounds, and the fair creature, leaving her work, knelt at his feet. He raised her, and smiled with such kindness and affection, that I felt sensations of a peculiar and overpowering nature; they were a mixture of pain and pleasure, such as I had never before experienced, either from hunger or cold, warmth or food; and I withdrew from the window, unable to bear these emotions. (108)

How can one who has "never beheld aught beautiful," or ugly or sweet or bitter, appreciate such a "lovely sight"? How much would one already have to know in order to be able to see and make sense of this human scene? The cultured setting of the emotional exchange between father and daughter should not escape notice: tools are employed, music is played, and a fire warms the room. One must be taught to play an instrument, and surely one also learns how to hear mourning or joy in a series of musical notes; no less true, the logic of this scene suggests, would one have to learn that a smile and an embrace can bring comfort to another. Identifying this episode as "the origin of the monster's sympathy," David Marshall argues that Shelley here "adopt[s] the theatrical model of sympathy she inherited from eighteenth-century aesthetics and moral philosophy by placing the monster as an unseen, sympathetic spectator to the *tableau de famille* of the DeLacey's"[15]—an evocative reading that nevertheless ignores the novel's paradoxical use of an acquired aesthetic sensibility to represent a first moment of untutored responsiveness. The domestic sentimentality of the DeLacey interactions may indeed be seen as a tableau from a *drame bourgeois*, but its very artifice draws attention to the acculturation necessary to appreciate such scenes. How is the creature able to read these affective expressions—the tears that fall at this moment and elicit response, the movement closer to the other, the smile which, at this moment, bespeaks kindness—to read them correctly, to read them as signifying anything at all? What could possibly be the content of the "peculiar and overpowering sensation" of mingled pleasure and pain inspired by the old man and young girl? The creature's response has no precedent in his limited experiences of physical need and satiety ("such as I had never before experienced, either from hunger or cold, or warmth or food") and, as such, begs the question of its genesis, particularly because his feeling is not the spontaneous reaction of a passive observer but the result of active interpretation of behavior. The affections themselves, or at least their modes of expression, belong to the realm of culture and tutelage in human forms of life.

The narrative, having granted him the capacity to perceive the signs of human misery, now turns to his efforts to resolve the mysterious conditions of that unhappiness. The creature decides, at the end of his first day in the hovel, to remain there "watching and endeavoring to discover the motives" for the cottagers' actions. His "discoveries" build on, without dispelling, the mystery of how the isolated creature could acquire ever more precise and insightful ways of reading human behavior. His understanding is at first limited to one of the few conditions he shares with the cottagers: hunger. Observing that "their nourishment consisted entirely of the vegetables of their garden, and the milk of one cow," he concludes that the young man and woman "suffered the pangs of hunger very poignantly for several times they placed food before the old man, when they reserved none for themselves" (111). This first insight into the cottagers' unhappiness involves identification between the creature and the objects of his attention that is based on, but also restricted to, his own experience of hunger. But the belief that they endured this condition "poignantly"—intensely and touchingly—has no basis. What does, or can, the creature mean by the term? Perhaps no more than the enigma of their behavior: they place before another food they might themselves consume; they remain hungry when they might eat. His recognition of poignancy in human action, even as it seems carefully constructed to develop from observations of an experience he indeed might understand, is nevertheless as implausible an empathic insight as his reading of pain and succor in those first tears and smile he observes.

The creature's ability to read human actions and affect goes unexplained in the narrative and leads to another mystery, his inspiration to act on his sympathy. Why does the recognition of the cottagers' need move the creature to generosity? What, in such a discovery, constitutes a motive? Is it a natural inclination or a learned behavior? The laconic narrative raises unresolvable questions about the origins of moral motivation and good will. To understand Shelley's brevity as functional is to see its result—a creature that possesses not only ideas but moral sense—as a mystery. One cannot find the creature "too good," as at least one recent critic has,[16] without also finding him to be too knowledgeable, for the narrative hardly elucidates the epistemological underpinnings of moral sense, the array of perceptions over time that inform and inspire his response. As we saw in chapter 1, Locke's *Essay* presents "matter," "objects," and "persons" as equivalent cognitive stimuli in the child's environment:

> Follow a *Child* from its Birth, and observe the alterations that time makes, and you shall find, as the Mind by the Senses . . . comes to be more and more awake, [it] thinks more, the more it has matter to think on. After some time, it begins to know the Objects, which being most familiar with it, have made lasting Impressions. Thus it comes, by degrees, to know the Persons it daily converses with, and distinguish them from Strangers. (2.1.22)

This passage is typical not only in its blurring of any distinction between persons and things but also in its rendering of development as the effect of time and the mind's activities.

Insofar as he is constrained to learn what he can from the isolation of a dark room that abuts, but does not admit entry to, the world of human interaction, the creature occupies a position analogous to Locke's mind-in-formation, and yet he becomes acquainted with the persons he observes in a way undreamed of in Locke's *Essay*, and unexplained in Shelley's fiction. Such lacunae in the narrative led a contemporary reviewer of the novel to complain that in "the account which the creature gives of his instruction by means of watching the polished cottagers, the hastiness of the composition is most apparent," that Shelley was careless with the very material she ought to have been most careful about: "a correct representation of the mind of one who had, (from whatever circumstances) reached maturity without any acquired knowledge." *Frankenstein*, the anonymous critic complains, presents the reader with an account so suggestive of "how much more it might be wrought out, that it brings strongly into view its own imperfectness."[17] However, the "hastiness" and "imperfectness" of the creature's narrative consistently have the effect of exposing the impossibility of a mind reaching maturity under conditions drawn from empiricist accounts of development. Stages in the creature's development are imperfectly, or incompletely, presented, not because the novel fails to provide a "correct representation" of such development, but because it successfully illuminates imperfections and incompleteness in the well-known and widely accepted philosophical theories it incorporates.

The narrative at the center of *Frankenstein* thus moves in two contradictory directions at once. At each stage conceptual difficulties and complications arise and are then magically, fantastically, overcome. The creature's emotional response to the first cottage scene he observes raises questions about the origin of his understanding of expression and behavior, but one might reach further back in the narrative and ask how he could know how to relieve the pangs caused by hunger, how he might know to eat, let alone what to eat. To rely on a notion of instinct as an explanation for such conundrums—to say that he must instinctively know how to ensure his physical survival, that his sympathy and benevolence are natural endowments—is to resolve the very questions about the role of nurture and tutelage in human development that the narrative insistently puts forward and, in so doing, to ignore this other supernatural dimension of the novel.

"Godlike Science" and Supernatural Study: The Creature's Fantastic Fluency

Of all the faculties the creature implausibly develops by looking out from the chink in the wall of his dark hovel, language is perhaps his most fantastic acquisition. Discovering, somehow, the communicative purpose of the sounds the cottagers uttered, the creature sets himself to learn this "godlike science":

> Their pronunciation was quick; and the words they uttered, not having any apparent connection to visible objects, I was unable to discover any clue by which I could unravel the mystery of their reference. . . . During the space of several revolutions of the moon in my hovel, I discovered the names that were given to some of the most familiar objects of discourse; I learned and applied the words, *fire, milk, bread,* and *wood.* I learned also the names of the cottagers themselves . . . the old man had only one, which was *father.* The girl was called *sister,* or *Agatha;* and the youth *Felix, brother,* or *son.* . . . I distinguished several other words,

without being able as yet to understand or apply them; such as *good, dearest, unhappy*. (112)

The creature's apprehension of nouns like *fire, milk,* and *bread* occurs in much the way Locke imagines the learning of names in the *Essay*. "If we will observe how Children learn Languages," he writes, "we shall find, that to make them understand what the names of simple *Ideas*, or Substances, stand for, People ordinarily shew them the thing . . . and then repeat to them the name that stands for it, as *White, Sweet, Milk, Sugar, Cat, Dog*" (3.9.9). What does it mean to think of language as a "mystery of reference," of sounds bound to objects? What can it mean to learn the word *father* in the same way as one learns the word *wood*? How would the use of words be understood, the mysteries of grammar, the elaborate syntax and vocabulary displayed in the telling of this very tale?[18] From names to thoughts is a huge leap. Wittgenstein analyzes this very issue in the opening pages of *Philosophical Investigations*. Commenting on a remarkably similar recollection of instruction from Augustine's *Confessions* (when "my elders named some object, and accordingly moved towards something, I saw this and I grasped that the thing was called by the sound they uttered when they meant to point it out"), Wittgenstein remarks: "These words give us a particular picture of the essence of human language. It is this: the individual words in language name objects—sentences are combinations of such names. . . . If you describe the learning of language in this way you are, I believe, thinking primarily of nouns like 'table,' 'chair,' 'bread,' and of people's names . . . and of the remaining kinds of words as something that will take care of itself."[19] The rest of language does not, of course, "take care of itself"— except perhaps in a world where a man can create a living being out of dead body parts.

The narrative presentation exacerbates the paradox, for it requires a kind of concrete detail and individual elaboration left out of generic philosophical exposition. The mere fact that an artificially created being occupies the position of Locke's "mind" in Shelley's fiction invites questions about the realism of the philosopher's subject; beyond that provocative premise, the contextual specificity, significance of detail, and narrative unfolding that are the building blocks of a novel are also tools for the dismantling of philosophical hypotheses that rely on abstract constructions of experience.[20] For example, the isolated situation of the cottagers, the fact that the creature sees and hears only these three persons, impresses on us that his apprehension of these few words and their signification is limited to a single place and context. Moreover, the contrasting situations of the cottagers on one side of the wall and the creature on the other invites a reckoning of the difference between experiencing language as communicative interaction and observing it from outside the interactions of which it is a part. So it is not only the "remaining kinds of words" (verbs, prepositions, and so forth) that an account such as Locke's or Augustine's omits, but far vaster realms of learning. "In 'learning language' you learn not merely what the names of things are," writes Stanley Cavell, "but also what a name is . . . not merely what the word for 'father' is, but what a father is. . . . [Y]ou do not merely learn the pronunciation of sounds, and their grammatical orders, but the 'forms of life' which make those sounds the words they are, do what they do—e.g., name, call, point, express a wish or affection."[21]

The fundamental impossibility of the language-learning scenario in *Frankenstein* is not overcome simply because time passes and, after a winter of applied study, the creature is said to have "improved sensibly" in the science of language. Rather, the fantastic dimension of this part of the novel is precisely the inexplicable progress past obstacles to the creature's development that are theoretically insuperable. The pace of the creature's education accelerates; questions about how the creature could grasp anything beyond the names of a few things and persons are left behind as focus shifts to the tale of how the creature comes to be fluent, literate, and ultimately eloquent by eavesdropping on the language lessons Felix gives to Safie, his Arabian fiancée. His progress is extraordinarily swift: "In two months I began to comprehend most of the words uttered by my protectors"; "I improved more rapidly than the Arabian. . . . I comprehended and could imitate almost every word that was spoken." The movement from oral fluency to literacy is marked by a mere conjunction: "While I improved in speech, I *also* learned the science of letters . . . and this opened for me a wide field for wonder and delight" (118–119). Observing that the monster's acquisition of language "appears to require that he behave as though he already functions within language," Christian Bok nevertheless shies away from his own conclusion that *Frankenstein* "deconstructs the possibility of such an origin" for language acquisition when he identifies the creature and Safie as comparable figures of alterity, each being equally "perfectly other."[22] On the contrary, the novel's insistence on the difference of their origins actually underscores the absolute otherness of the monster.

Safie arrives among the cottagers with another language, another culture, a history of familial ties—with all the ordinary forms of relation that the monster has never had to lose or to enjoy, to long for or to replace. It is she who learns a *second* language, and whose introduction into the narrative serves as a reminder that the creature is essentially unlike the human, stranger than the foreign. Wittgenstein submits that Augustine (and we may now add Locke and Shelley) "describes the learning of human language as if the child came into a strange country and did not understand the language of the country; that is, as if it already had a language, only not this one"—precisely the "as if" that the novel adopts in order to complete the creature's linguistic education.[23] The introduction of Safie invites an imagination of the creature as strange in the same way as the stranger from a foreign land, but it is an invitation withdrawn by all that the creature learns in following her lessons.

Stranger and Stranger: "I Have no Relation or Friend on Earth"

The more the creature comes to know about human forms of life, the more conscious he becomes of his difference. His acquisition of language enables him to follow the cottagers' readings of history and discourses on the "strange system of human society," but this new cultural literacy leads him to understand that he has no such history and belongs to no society. His education culminates in the discovery that his past is a "blot," a "vacancy," because he has no memory of having been raised in the way that all human beings are raised.

> I heard of the difference of sexes; and the birth and growth of children; how the father doated on the smiles of the infant, and the lively sallies of the older child; how all the life and cares of the mother were wrapped up in the precious charge; how the mind of youth expanded and gained knowledge; of brother, and sister, and all the various relationships that bind one human being to another in mutual bonds. But where were my friends and relations? No father had watched my infant days, no mother had blessed me with smiles and caresses; or if they had, all my past life was now a blot, a blind vacancy, in which I distinguished nothing. From my earliest remembrance I had been as I then was in height and proportion. I had never yet seen a being resembling me, or who claimed any intercourse with me. What was I? (121)

At this climactic point in the development of the creature's self-awareness, the question of *what* he is arises from the realization that he has no relations and that human selves are born and formed in relation to others. "I am brother, cousin and grandson, member of this household, that village, this tribe: these are not characteristics that belong to human beings accidentally," writes Alasdair MacIntyre, describing the "interlocking set of social relationships" within which individual identities are constituted.[24] Radical autonomy is the essence of the creature's difference, that which makes him unlike the human, and also that which marks him as belonging to the "strange world," as Benhabib describes it, of much modern moral and political theory—a world "in which individuals are grown up before they are born; in which boys are men before they have been children; a world where neither mother, nor sister, nor wife exist."[25] The history the creature lacks is figured by his sudden realization that it is unnatural to have always been the same "height and proportion," to have come to life fully formed—the most explicit affiliation of the creature's giantism with the occlusion of infancy and childhood.

Having discovered the difference between himself and human beings in the vacancy of a past that includes no friends and relations, the creature struggles to understand what he is but cannot proceed much further than the idea of being absolutely unique. "I had never yet seen a being resembling me," he observes. "I saw and heard of none like me"; "I was dependent on none and related to none." Such expressions have tempted readers to associate the creature with a specifically Rousseauvian sense of singularity. "The monster acts out and at times seems to translate the striking first words of [the *Reveries*]: 'Here I am then, alone on earth, without brother, neighbor, friend, or any society but myself'" (according to Marshall); "the boast that opens the *Confessions*—'I am made unlike anyone I have ever met; I will even venture to say that I am like no one in the whole world'—applies quite literally to the creature" (according to Lipking).[26] Yet such identifications ignore a distinction that the novel insistently draws. The creature's *Bildung* culminates in the discovery that he is "like no one in the whole world," and the fantastical quality of his existence consists in the *literal* truth of that statement, in the fact that it is true of the creature in a way that it cannot be true of any other character in the novel—in a way that it cannot be true of Rousseau either. After all, the self-evident gambit and characteristic paradox of Rousseau's claim to uniqueness is that it is so easily comprehended, seems a sentiment that anyone might utter in a moment of pride or awkwardness or self-pity. It matters that we know, or can imagine, what Rousseau means by "I am like no one in the whole world."

When I say that *Frankenstein* does not confound but rather sharply differentiates between the literal truth of the creature's lonely singularity and the condition of all the other characters, I mean to draw attention to the manner in which the novel meditates on the ordinary usage of words such as *alone, lonely, solitary,* and even *monster.* Elizabeth's exclamation (after Justine's trial) that "men appear to me as monsters" exemplifies a typical figurative use of the term *monster,* and insofar as the monster never appears "as the figure of a man," the creature may be seen (according to David Marshall) as a victim of the failure of figurative imagination and the novel as a "story of failed sympathy and misreading."[27] But such a straightforward opposition between literal and figurative meanings does not capture the contextual complexity of Shelley's deployment of notions such as solitude, isolation, and abandonment. When, for example, Walton writes, "I have no friend," the categories of the literal and the figurative are of limited use in understanding just how he understands himself as friendless, or in capturing the exquisite fact that the statement is made in what can only be called an exchange of intimacy with his sister.

Walton's confessions of loneliness are always also the utterances of a subject embedded in a social context, his words bound to be understood, or misunderstood, but, in any event, *taken* by another. Alone as he may feel himself to be, his sister will (perhaps) sympathize with or (perhaps) find self-indulgent, but in any case make sense of his "desire [for] the company of a man who could sympathise with me." The creature's desire for someone "with whom I can live in the interchange of those sympathies necessary for my being" (144) is necessarily of a different order than Walton's. Whatever the brother may mean when he says, "I have no friend," it cannot be what the creature means when he says, "I have no friend and relation." Likewise, neither Safie nor any of the other characters who have lost or become estranged from their immediate relations share the creature's condition, although analogies between these "orphans" and the creature are frequently ventured.[28] The plight of being abandoned or neglected is mitigated by adoption and inclusion—Elizabeth, Justine, and Safie are all taken in and cared for by other families. Even when the creature is seen as being unlike these others, his utter exclusion from community is still rendered all too human, "touch[ing] on the profound anxiety that the self inexplicably may not be worthy of others."[29] But this point of possible identification is also complicated by the novel because it is Frankenstein, not the creature, who most frequently expresses worries about belonging. He recalls that he "shunned [his] fellow creatures as if guilty of a crime" (during the creative process [56]), that he was "seized by remorse and guilt . . . [and thus] shunned the face of man" (after the execution of Justine [90]), that he had "no right to claim [his family's] sympathies" (after making his pledge to the creature [149]), that he "saw an insurmountable barrier placed between me and my fellow men" (ruining the pleasures of his journey to England with Clerval [158]), that he looked on the North Sea as "an insuperable barrier between me and my fellow-creatures" (after destroying the second creature [169]), that he "had no right to share intercourse" with others (after the death of Clerval and his own return to Geneva [185]). However, insofar as these fears chronically plague Frankenstein, they are also subdued by the loyalty, attention, and care of family, friends, and even of those strangers in remotest Scotland who believe him to be a murderer but nurse him nevertheless.[30] The story Shelley gives Frankenstein to tell oscillates between the series of deaths and losses he suffers, and the care and ministration that sustain him after each blow.

It has often been remarked that the creature's course of revenge against Frankenstein is designed to bring him to share the creature's miserable isolation. But no matter how desolate, how fully stripped of attachments, companions, and intimates Frankenstein becomes, he necessarily remains included among, attended to, and taken in by other human beings. He is at first, finally, and throughout the novel the object of human sympathies from which the creature, first, finally, and throughout, is excluded. Frankenstein's feelings of alienation and isolation are embedded within the context of attentions from father, friend, fiancée, and finally Walton—the stranger who comes to "love him like a brother."

o o o

An important paradox that readers of *Frankenstein* confront is that a physical monstrosity that the novel cannot and does not even try very hard to illustrate is central to the narrative.[31] In arguing for a more precise sense of what the novel allegorizes as monstrous, given its scant physical description of the creature, I have suggested that the creature's giantism exposes the monstrosity of leaving out the role of infancy, childhood, and the network of dependence and relation in the formation of human persons. I cannot offer so straightforward a reading of the "yellow skin," "lustrous black" hair, "teeth of pearly whiteness," "watery eyes . . . almost of the same color as the dun white sockets," and "straight black lips," which are the only, and only once mentioned, details describing the creature's face (57). I will venture to suggest that the monstrosity of his visage lies in the horror of its being unrecognizable as human. *Frankenstein* does not present us with a monstrous body, only with testimonies to its monstrosity so unvaried and unrelenting as to amount to the proposition that this is a creature that cannot be *seen as* a human being.

The creature is not, however, a figure for the failure of sympathy, for insofar as the novel insists that he can never be looked on without horror, it equally insists that the human form and countenance (however miserable, shattered, wrecked) will never excite such horror.[32] It is not a matter of choice or avoidance in the imagination of this novel that the human attitude toward the human face will be an "attitude towards a soul," that the "human body is the best picture of the human soul."[33] Is this to say that appearance and outer form guide human response to others? *Frankenstein* uses, but does not abide by, so straightforward an opposition between soul and body, being and appearance; indeed, in many ways the novel inverts the familiar figuration of the body as masking or obscuring the person within. The creature's fantasy and his initial hope (as he tells Walton) is precisely that of being seen through, of vision keen enough to perceive his inner essence: "to meet with beings, who pardoning my outward form, would love me for the excellent qualities I was capable of unfolding" (221). But the demand he makes of Frankenstein arises from his final realization that the "human senses are insurmountable barriers to our union" (144). This is the case not because the creature is cursed with a hideous body veiling a non-monstrous person but because to wear the human form in this novel is to bear a human history.

In closing I want to suggest that the relation of personal histories, the fact that each character has a story that must be told, is but one way that the novel deploys formal exigencies for theoretical or philosophical purposes. There is no reason why Walton's correspondence with his sister should include (what can only be an old story to her) a review of the origins of the desire that has driven him on his journey, but it is important that the desire is traced back to his "early years" and is determined in relation to a dead father's will. There is no reason why the admonitory tale Frankenstein decides to relate must begin at the beginning ("I am by birth a Genevese") instead of, for example, with his passion for alchemy and natural philosophy, but it is important that even the story of his birth requires backward digression into the history of individual relations and passions that ultimately united the man and woman who became his parents. There is no reason why Elizabeth's first get-well letter to Victor should include the biography of Justine ("I will relate her history"), but it is important that the central "events" of that biography are consequences of strong affections and disaffections (the favor of a father, the envy and guilt of a mother, the "great attachment" Elizabeth's aunt conceives for the unfortunate girl). These (and other) short histories of minor characters in the novel function not only as contrasting elements that define the creature's difference from others as a lack of such a history; they also draw attention to the philosophical implications of this fundamental element of narrative.[34] "The circumstances of his marriage illustrate his character," says Victor of his father—an observation that this novel, and indeed many novels, turn into a general rule: character is composed from the circumstances of relationship and engagement with others. The philosophical "mind," by contrast, is generally composed by abstraction from such "circumstances."

It would be a mistake, however, to say that the novel is in any simple sense a rejection of empiricism. The formative power of experience is not a premise that the novel challenges but one that it, in fact, enriches and elaborates. What the novel brings to light is the narrowness of experience imagined in texts such as Locke's *Essay*, particularly their vision of the course of human development. If *Frankenstein* successfully exposes certain constraints in philosophical representations of individual formation, it effects this exposure by embedding a conventional philosophical "narrative" of the mind's self-education within a form that relies on careful elaboration of context and specificity of detail and circumstance for its construction and for the successful unfolding of a tale that (however plausible) is unforgettably fictional. Shelley makes use of empirical theory in this novel, but it is a use that redounds on the source, exhibiting what it leaves out (the essential circumstances that make character, the omissions that result in a monster) and reminding us that theoretical constructions are not only partial in what they describe but are sometimes more limited in their representational force than forms we recognize as fictions.

CHAPTER 6

Mill Alone

> The social state is at once so natural, so necessary, and so habitual to man, that except in some unusual circumstances, or by an effort of voluntary abstraction, he never conceives himself otherwise than as a member of a body.
>
> JOHN STUART MILL, *Utilitarianism*

> Without knowing or believing that I was reserved, I grew up with an instinct of closeness. I had no one to whom I desired to express everything which I felt. . . . my circumstances tended to produce a character, close and reserved from habit and want of impulse . . . destitute of the frank communicativeness which wins and deserves sympathy.
>
> *The Early Draft of John Stuart Mill's Autobiography*

How can the profoundly solitary child of John Stuart Mill's *Autobiography* become father to the man who would insist that no individual can conceive of himself, and hence no philosophy ought to conceive of the individual, apart from a social life? No moral theory, Mill argues in *Utilitarianism* (1863), can exclude from its conception of human motives, interests, and ends "the deeply rooted conception which every individual even now has of himself as a social being." And yet this conception appears to be missing in the *Autobiography* (composed in 1853–1854; first published in 1873).

As the record of an "unusual educational experiment" remarkably successful in making Mill a thinker, yet chilling in its neglect of the passions and affections, the nineteenth-century philosopher's life story is at once a poignant transmission and radical revision of the Lockean psychology with which this study began. In the effort to develop a "science of morality" from psychological and sociological principles, utilitarian thinkers openly built on empiricist models for which Locke's *Essay* was a basis.[1] James Mill's 1829 *Analysis of the Phenomena of the Human Mind* (reissued with notes by John Stuart Mill in 1869) offers a theory of mind firmly embedded in an empiricist paradigm associated with, but clearly not confined to, the eighteenth century. Condillac, Hartley, and Locke are among the authorities the elder Mill draws on, and Locke's *Essay* provides the epigraphs of several chapters, including "Names," "Sensations," and "Consciousness."[2] Even a thinker steeped, as George Henry Lewes was, in German transcendentalism identified Locke as the "founder of modern psychology" (*Biographical History of Philosophy*, 1851), effectively agreeing with John Stuart Mill's assessment of the *Essay* as a work that "changed the face of science," furnishing the "beginning and foundation of the modern analytic psychology."[3] It is within the context of this inheritance of Lockean ideas of mind that I want to approach John Stuart Mill's strange *Autobiography*.

Mill's case presents a particular and complex transmission of the *anxieties* I have described as characteristic of Lockean psychology, but it bears remarking at the outset that his inheritance of Lockean *principles* is itself vexed. Mill is generally credited for offering a richer account of moral psychology than the overly constrained "empiricism of one who has had little experience," which he found in Jeremy Bentham's *Principles of Morals and Legislation* (1789). "Man, that most complex being, is a very simple one in [Bentham's] eyes," Mill writes in the famous essay "Bentham" (1838). "Even under the head of *sympathy*, his recognition does not extend to the more complex forms of the feeling—the love of *loving*." "A moralist on Bentham's principles may get as far as this, that he ought not to slay, burn, or steal," by which Mill means, in part, that his recognition of what belongs to a moral life will extend no further than his imagination of what he shares with others (property in this case, the body and the territory it inhabits). "What will be his qualifications for regulating the nicer shades of human behaviour," Mill wonders,

> for laying down even the greater moralities as to those facts in human life which tend to influence the depths of the character quite independently of any influence on worldly circumstances—such, for instance, as the sexual relations, or those of family in general, or any other social and sympathetic connexions of an intimate kind?[4]

That the philosophical affirmation of such "facts in human life" can be traced back to eighteenth-century responses to Hobbes should not be surprising, as it is precisely against the charge of Hobbesian psychological egoism that Mill attempts to defend utilitarianism. The admission of benevolent impulse "as a matter of psychological fact" will substantially alter a moral philosophy based on the theory that all human action may be reduced to a form of self-interest.[5] Further, and perhaps even more important within the context of this study, is the difference in kind, rather than degree, between Mill's "complex being" composed from "complex forms of feeling" and the "simple one" conceived by Bentham.

Mill credits the individual with wider sympathies and greater kindness than Bentham does because he admits the formative role of sociality on the individual psyche. This "view of the individual as fundamentally constituted in and by interpersonal relationships" has been described as Mill's most "important contribution to the liberal understanding of individual autonomy," but it is not clear how that key insight can be coherently integrated within an empiricist framework.[6] Mill's recognition "of altruistic or other-regarding feelings of sympathy and compassion" entails an understanding of the individual as originally and constitutively embedded in relationships but does not substantively alter the utilitarian analysis of society as a "system of independent centers of consciousness."[7] This tension between the psychology implicit in Mill's ethics and the Lockean psychological principles informing the work of Bentham and James Mill—and to which the younger Mill remained committed—has been widely recognized.[8] And while one question frequently asked about Mill is why his critical revision of Benthamite "simplicity" did not lead to more radical theoretical innovations, my interest lies precisely in the limited impact of Mill's seemingly profound valuation of sociality.

Although his recognition of "social and sympathetic connexions" as elemental *"facts"* of human life must be seen as a rejection of the possibility of taking the human being in isolation as a starting point for philosophical reflection, a form of psychic seclusion traceable to Locke persists in Mill's works. Solitariness and privacy remain existentially fundamental to Mill's conception of the individual, particularly in his principal "literary" writings—the *Autobiography* and the essays on poetry. The self-representation of the *Autobiography* powerfully demonstrates the deficiencies of the philosophical principles on which his education was based. Much as Shelley did in *Frankenstein*, Mill represents the uniqueness and aberrancy of the person made according to a theory of mind offered as a normative model. Still, a powerful articulation of the fundamental privacy of thought and feeling lies at the center of the *Autobiography*—the discovery of which, paradoxically enough, both provokes the crisis that is the dramatic climax of the work and forms the basis of its resolution.

The *Autobiography* as Anomalous Case

If, according to Mill, only as a result of "unusual circumstances" or by a willful effort at "abstraction" does a human being conceive of himself apart from the "social state," then the philosopher's autobiography certainly presents evidence of both conditions for that exceptional conception. The extraordinary educational experiment conducted on the young Mill together with the consistently impersonal expository style in which it is described tell a story of an individual for whom the forms of sociality—from familial intimacy to childhood companionship to friendly confidence—only come to be recognized as natural and necessary from a limited retrospective reckoning of their absence.

"Impersonality" is a way of naming what seems deficient in the self presented in Mill's *Autobiography*, as well as a name for the style or tone of the narrative: each confirms, without elucidating, the unsatisfactory character of this work that identifies itself as "autobiography." The remarkable disclaimer with which Mill begins is a deliberate disavowal of what ought to be the content of a life story. Deeming it "proper" to make "some mention of the reasons which have made me think it desirable that I should leave behind me such a memorial of so uneventful a life as mine," Mill offers not only a renunciation of confessional and expressive motivations for autobiography but also instructive definition of the kind of self whose history this work will reconstruct.

> I do not for a moment imagine that any part of what I have to relate, can be interesting to the public as a narrative, or as being connected to myself. But I have thought that . . . it may be useful that there should be some record of an education which was unusual and remarkable, and which, whatever else it may have done, has proved how much more than is commonly supposed may be taught, and well taught.[9]

To begin by saying that no "part of what I have to relate can be interesting to the public as a narrative, or as connected with myself" is already revealing of "whatever else" his education has done, for what can it mean to conceive an autobiography as a work without interest as a "narrative" and, even more peculiar, without interest "as connected with myself"? Who (or what) is the subject of this autobiography if Mill's focus is not "connected" with his "self"? A partial answer is given in the term *mind*, the "successive phases" of which Mill proposes to trace. The story he tells is that of "mental progress" and "mental changes," as opposed to "so uneventful a life as mine." Implicit here is not the exclusion of "whatever else" belongs to a life story but a sense of its being unnarratable, unrecordable. Not only does Mill conceive the subject of this autobiography as being disconnected from that other person he calls "*my*self," but there seems to be nothing to tell of that other self. In *Frankenstein*, the monster's autobiographical account of his own education can be read, paradoxically, as defining impossible conditions of development. Given his isolation from others, the emotional, intellectual, and moral experiences recounted and the very narration of those experiences belong to the realm of the fantastic, are as fantastic as the experiment of creation itself. Mill's *Autobiography* entails a related suspension of disbelief in asking its readers to imagine a life so constrained or misshapen in its formation as to leave its subject without a language for (and implicitly without awareness of) what, apart from that which it terms "mental," is constitutive, eventful, important. This is to suggest that Mill's *Autobiography* is not itself symptomatic but makes compelling aesthetic use of a "symptom" to represent a deformation of the individual. The affections, longings, and fears that Locke leaves out of his account of the mind's early acquisition of ideas are also left out of Mill's story of his life, but as a matter of design and in the effort to represent appropriately the aberrant aspiration, even the errors, of the Lockean-inspired theories on which his upbringing was based.

No commentator on the *Autobiography*, from the time of its publication in 1873 up to the present day, has failed to be struck by the distancing abstraction of Mill's style and the thin content of the story he tells. The utter peculiarity of the text is most frequently assessed in terms of lack, defined by what seems most obviously to be missing. Early reviews agreed in finding Mill's account "largely devoid of human emotion, a bloodless analysis," and even the most cursory glance at later scholarship reveals a persistent fascination with what Mill's insistently "public voice" withholds.[10] "The *Autobiography* is as remarkable for what it leaves out as for what it discusses," writes F. A. Hayek; "of what in the ordinary sense of the word we should call his life, of his human interests and personal relations, we learn practically nothing."[11] Many scholars, including Hayek himself, have attempted to make up for the deficiencies of the *Autobiography*, filling in its reticence through careful biographical study. From correspondence and from the testimony of contemporaries we learn of the intense depression Mill suffered after the death of his father, for example, a grief that never finds utterance in the *Autobiography*. Such research is a useful measure of the distance Mill apparently placed between his life and the "life" he composed. Most recently critical interest has focused on the presumed workings of repression in the text, drawing attention to persons and things powerfully present in spite of their cursory treatment in the narrative. Mill's mother, for example, has been seen to haunt the work by the "sheer excess of her absence," and Mill's bitter disappointment at the career his father chose for him is perceived to find voice in the very brevity with which he records his placement and advancement at the East India Company.[12] In identifying omissions of particular and poignant significance, such interpretations follow Hayek's suggestion that the *Autobiography* is most remarkable for what it leaves out. While my own reading of the *Autobiography* is also attuned to the loud silences in Mill's prose, I do not aim to uncover or diagnose traces of a more recognizably personal life within the structure of this most impersonal document; rather, I attempt to understand the specific shape of the subject constructed by the hauntingly impersonal prose on its surface.

When Hayek suggests that "in the ordinary sense of the word" Mill's *Autobiography* contains little of what "we should call his life," he not only makes a generic claim that a life record is something that should include "human interests" and "personal relations"; more important, he also takes for granted an *ordinary* sense of the word *life*—that such interests and relations constitute its events. These very definitions are suggested by the *Autobiography* itself, however, for it is, above all, the absence of such an "ordinary life" that the *Autobiography* thematizes—and not only in its bluntly self-conscious announcement that the author's personal life has been uneventful. In what follows I devote considerable attention to Mill's way of speaking in the *Autobiography*, because his deliberate, at times flagrant, substitution of impersonal or circumlocutious formulations for more common forms of speech most expressively defines the subject of the work as a self who has developed without the ordinary kinds of relation for which human beings have an ordinary language.

"How much more . . . may be Taught": Reading the Reserve of Mill's *Autobiography*

Every reader of the *Autobiography* will recall a childhood almost entirely limited to acts of reading, writing, and thinking. Page after page of Mill's first chapter, "Childhood and Early Education," resembles nothing more closely than bibliography.[13] A few digressions from this material offer the slightest glimpses into the Mill household and the scenes of Mill's instruction, but even these remarks serve to complete the general account of his mental development rather than to add a different dimension to the life. We learn, for example, that the eight-year-old was assigned the duty of instructing his siblings, "deriv[ing] from this discipline the great advantage of learning more thoroughly and retaining more lastingly the things which I was set to teach" (8). But for that "advantage," the mere existence of those brothers and sisters might have gone unmentioned. About his mother Mill is notoriously silent.[14] And of his father, of the innumerable hours spent in his presence, Mill offers no recollection unconnected to his own tuition.

Readers have not failed to notice how the record of books read, languages mastered, and compositions attempted is punctuated now and again by the memory of impatience on the part of the teacher and failure on the part of the student. Each of these recollections of "anger," "indignation," "reproach," and being taken "severely to task" is followed by an assertion of the value of the educational technique (6, 16, 19, 20). As a teacher, James Mill "was often, and much beyond reason, provoked by my failures in cases where success could not have been expected," Mill writes, "but in the main, his method was right, and it succeeded" (19). What exactly does that "but" imply? In what way does it follow that "his method was right" although he was "beyond reason, provoked by my failures"—or, rather, how does it not follow? Mill is not proposing that ends justify means in this case, nor is he suggesting an unintended causal relation between his father's irritability and the success of his educational regime. Insofar as "beyond reason provoked" does not serve as an alternative description for any sort of "method," a subtle differentiation is marked between painful personal memory and the "unusual and remarkable" education it records, and consequently between two possible autobiographical subjects: one recalling "my failures" and being taken "severely to task" and the other emphasizing what really matters in the recollection, the success of the "method" in "[making] me a thinker."

The logic of Mill's presentation in this early chapter is that, in this childhood, evidently, it was only the teacher's unjustified anger at the student's failures that was "beyond reason." Nothing else, not the relentlessness and extraordinary rigor of the schedule or the monomaniacal devotion to intellectual life or the father's role as sole teacher, authority, and disciplinarian, is recalled, or named, as unreasonable. Angry rebuke itself is evidently a reasonable response to son and pupil in cases where "success" could be expected—although one wonders what a reasonable definition of success could be in this context. Before returning to this topic, I want to turn briefly to Mill's most sustained criticism of this father who was so successful an educator and to one of the few places one might look in the *Autobiography* for the pupil's judgment of James Mill as father rather than teacher. In the second chapter, devoted to "Moral Influences in Early Youth," Mill writes,

> The element which was chiefly deficient in his moral relation to his children, was that of tenderness. I do not believe that this deficiency lay in his own nature. I believe him to have had much more feeling than he habitually shewed, and much greater capacities of feeling than were ever developed. He resembled most Englishmen in being ashamed of the signs of feeling, and, by the absence of demonstration, starving the feelings themselves. If we consider further that he was in the trying position of sole teacher, and add to this that his temper was constitutionally irritable, it is impossible not to feel true pity for a father who did, and strove to do, so much for his children, who would have so valued their affection, yet who must have been constantly feeling that fear of him was drying it up at its source. This was no longer the case, later in life and with his younger children. They loved him tenderly: and if I cannot say so much of myself, I was always loyally devoted to him. (32)

These remarks appear within a lengthy account of the ethical principles and philosophy Mill's father "inculcated" in his son, as if the absence of tenderness and emotional candor between father and son could be construed as a mere oversight in the scheme of moral instruction. That "as if" is tacitly rebuked by a voice that refuses to take personally what is so obviously personal an injury, maintaining an abstraction and distance at the very moment it wishes to condemn these qualities. To write, "*I believe* him to have had much more feeling than he habitually shewed" (my emphasis) is to suggest that the son neither knows nor dares assume such feeling in his father. To speak of one's father in this context as merely one among "most Englishmen" is not only to quell a particular disappointment (in the undemonstrativeness of the man who was my father, and not just, not only, another Englishman) but also to forego acknowledging *this* man as *my* father.[15] Surely it is only within a relation of particular intimacy that "signs of feeling" may be so palpably missed, and surely only intimacy is betrayed by such keen knowledge of the other as one who is ashamed of emotional display. To generalize here is also to occlude the particularity of this relationship and, in so doing, to refrain from any expression of forbearance. If "it is impossible not to feel true pity for a father" who inspired fear rather than affection in his children, then why does Mill use the passive voice and an impersonal pronoun? Why does he not speak of the pity *he* feels for *his* father? And, finally, the conspicuously circuitous locution Mill chooses in order to say "I did not love my father" is typical of the revealingly reticent tone sustained throughout the work. Even in the less restrained, canceled passages of the *Early Draft*, Mill's admission that "my father's children neither loved him, nor, with any warmth of affection, anyone else" (183) is similarly evasive in its candor (not "I," nor even "I and my brothers and sisters," but "my father's children" did not love him), and, as in the final version, this quietly devastating revelation is presented simply and passively as the "most baneful" of the "moral agencies that acted on myself."

The very impersonality of Mill's style in the *Autobiography*, as in this instance, is deliberately, paradoxically expressive—but of what? What is Mill saying, in addition to "I did not love my father," when he says, instead: "They loved him tenderly: and if I cannot say so much of myself . . ."? I want to suggest that part of what Mill evokes here is a form of life, a set of conditions and circumstances, in which the most obvious or direct expressions are unavailable, unused, unpracticed.[16] The phrase "I do not love you" will not fall from the lips of a person who has received no instruction in the use of the phrase "I love you": call these words "signs of feeling" and take Mill's conspicuous circumlocution as an invitation to imagine what it might mean to learn a language in which the use of such phrases has been "undemonstrated."

The discovery that "high feelings" might be "demonstrated" is reserved, in the *Autobiography*, to the fourteenth year of the pupil's life and his first prolonged absence from his father's house. What Mill calls his "knowledge" of the commonplace communication of sentiments is attributed to his experience in a foreign country, where, by implication, he also learned the expressive deficiencies of his native tongue. Note the emphatic negations that frame this appraisal of the great "advantage" Mill owed to his year's residence in France.

> This advantage was not the less real though *I could not then estimate*, or even consciously feel it . . . *I could not then know* the difference between [the English] manner of existence, and that of a people like the French . . . among whom sentiments, which by comparison at least may be called elevated, are the current coin of human intercourse, both in books and in private life . . . kept alive in the nation at large by constant exercise, and stimulated by sympathy, so as to form a living and active part of the existence of great numbers of persons, and to be recognized and understood by all. . . . *I did not know* the way in which, among the ordinary English . . . the habit of not speaking to others, nor much even to themselves, about the things in which they do feel an interest, causes both their feelings and their intellectual faculties to remain undeveloped . . . reducing them, considered as spiritual beings, to a kind of negative existence. All these things *I did not perceive* till long afterwards. (38; emphases added)

The difference between "not speaking to others" (the "English mode of existence") and engaging in "personal intercourse" (French "sociability") is at once more abstract and more vital than the stereotypical contrast of national character implies. "Manner" of existence here implies substance as well as surface, a way of being, a possibility of living that no culture could possibly claim to itself. What Mill attributes to the French in this passage, which concludes the chapter "Moral Influences in Early Youth," is the presence of precisely that which he identifies as having been so remarkably absent from his father's household: not simply the idea that sentiment, feeling, and even personal interests are "kept alive" in conversation but also the knowledge that there are such things to be kept alive, feelings that starve (to recall Mill's phrase) in the absence of demonstration and articulation. Silence neither keeps the affective life discreetly hidden nor deliberately reserves it but actively negates it. If the words that serve as (that *are*) "signs of feeling" are unused and unpracticed in the household Mill describes, then what kind of language does Mill learn? What makes up (for) personal intercourse? Let us return to "Childhood and Early Education" for the scenes of language learning and acquisition it presents as well as for a sense of what could be "recognize[d] and understood" as English conversation.

Recall that Mill makes it sound as though the first language he learned was a dead one: "I have no remembrance of the time when I began to learn Greek. I have been told that it was when I was three years old" (5). This is the first fact about himself the autobiographer offers; it is followed, in the space of the same paragraph, by a list of Greek works that he read by the age of eight and a record of the awkward scene in which such instruction was received.

> What [James Mill] was himself willing to undergo for the sake of my instruction, may be judged from the fact, that I went through the whole process of preparing my Greek lessons in the same room and at the same table at which he was writing: and as in those days Greek and English lexicons were not [available] . . . I was forced to have recourse to him for the meaning of every word which I did not know. This incessant interruption he, one of the most impatient of men, submitted to, and wrote under that interruption several volumes of his History and all else that he had to write during those years. (6)

Willingness to undergo, submission, forced recourse—this rhetoric of compulsion and sacrifice, indeed of compulsive sacrifice on the part of pupil and teacher—is particularly disturbing if one keeps in mind that the child is acquiring English as well as ancient Greek in this room. The young Mill learns many words as translations of the Greek, but also, apparently, he learns the significance of words such as *interruption* and *impatience*, the uncomfortable feeling of being "forced to have recourse," and a great deal else one might only imagine as passing between a young child and his father in such a context. More typical of this first chapter is the bibliographic exposition of what and how much Mill read; these prodigious lists may be read, following Mill's suggestion, as a record of "how much more than is commonly supposed may be taught" (3), but they also need to be understood as the record of a life restricted to reading—the absence of "stimulus," as Mill puts it, "to any other kind of activity than that which was already called forth by my studies" (23).[17] The solitude, silence, and monotony of private reading are interrupted only for daily "talks about the books" with a father who was also "the only person I was in communication with"; with the youth's "earliest recollections of green fields and wild flowers" is mingled that of "the account I gave [my father] daily of what I had read the day before" (6).

The mind thus shaped and filled remains strangely unselfconscious in Mill's representation. "I never thought of saying to myself, I am, or I can do, so and so," Mill recalls (21)—a self-effacing assessment but also an observation about possibilities created by the very grammar of personal agency, as yet unavailable to this youth who has learned so much else. Indeed the valuation of intellectual achievement in these pages is explicitly connected with the absence of a (sense of) self to be effaced.

> I have a distinct remembrance, that the suggestion thus for the first time made to me, that I knew more than other youths ... was to me a piece of information, to which, as to all other things which my father told me, I gave implicit credence, but which did not at all impress me as a personal matter. (22)

Such an impression is only possible for a being who lives in ignorance of "personal matters," one for whom nothing could count or signify or matter in a personal sense. What follows from this odd recollection, as if in explanation of it, are remarks on that feature of Mill's upbringing that has been implied throughout but never yet made explicit, namely, the child's extreme isolation.

"My father's scheme of education could not have been accomplished," observes Mill, "if he had not carefully kept me from having any great amount of intercourse with other boys. He was earnestly bent upon my escaping not only the ordinary corrupting influence which boys exercise over boys, but the contagion of vulgar modes of thought and feeling" (22). This particular deprivation is, to say the least, extraordinary: not merely an "unusual circumstance" but the definitive and formative context of this education, the very condition of its possibility. Implicit here is that Mill's father understood "intercourse with other boys" to be synonymous with "corrupting influence" and "contagion." The sexual suggestion is undeniable, particularly since the passage proceeds to comment on the "animal need for physical activity" Mill had to satisfy on his own and also because this is one of the rare places in the *Autobiography* where the reader is made aware of the boy as a body as well as a mind. But given Mill's use of an abstract and impersonal idiom to define and *symptomatically* represent the kind of person formed under these conditions, the passage literally points to a kind of language left unlearned, to the grammar of "intercourse" itself.

Having been kept from conversation with others, it is only logical that little sense can be made of what might have been missed:

> The deficiencies in my education were principally in the things which boys learn from being turned out to shift for themselves, and from being brought together in large numbers. From temperance and much walking, I grew up healthy and hardy, though not muscular; but I could do no feats of skill or physical strength, and knew none of the ordinary bodily exercises. (22)

What is remarkable here is all that Mill does not count among the "things which boys learn . . . from being brought together." Sport and game and physical play are by no means trivial features of a child's life, but Mill's is a trivializing presentation, reducing all that the child acquires from these activities to "feats of skill" and "physical strength." To have been kept from "intercourse with other boys" is to have been kept from immeasurably more than this, and the philosopher, who would, in *Utilitarianism,* imagine conscience to be "all encrusted over with collateral associations, derived from sympathy, from love, and still more from fear . . . from self-esteem, desire for the esteem of others, and occasionally even self-abasement," has taken qualitative measure of this deprivation.[18] In the *Autobiography,* however, the story of a person abstracted from the "natural . . . necessary . . . habitual" social state, Mill's account of lacking companions is so impoverished and spare as to effectively describe an isolation complete enough to admit no (sense of) loneliness. The principal "deficiencies" of this upbringing are not those enumerated above but those implied by the very poverty of this imagination of the kinds of "things" to be had from regular intercourse with others. Call this poverty of the child's imagination a further specification of the "negative existence" Mill describes as a consequence of "not speaking to others."

The inability to say "I am" or "I can," the inability to take anything about oneself as a "personal matter," is inextricably bound up with the unfelt absence of any other person "to whom I desired to express everything which I felt" in a life which includes no one who might inspire such a desire. The well-known crisis at the center of Mill's *Autobiography* involves the awakening of "an irrepressible self-consciousness" simultaneous with, and inseparable from, a first sensation of this extreme form of loneliness. "'Suppose that all your objects in life were realized,'" Mill famously asks himself, "'would this be a great joy and happiness to you?' And an irrepressible self-consciousness distinctly answered, 'No!' At this my heart sank within me . . . I seemed to have nothing left to live for" (81). The "I" speaking so self-searchingly here is also, for the first time, irrepressibly conscious of its alone-ness:

> I sought no comfort by speaking to others of what I felt. If I had loved any one sufficiently to make confiding my griefs a necessity, I should not have been in the condition I was. I felt, too, that mine was not an interesting, or in any way respectable distress. There was nothing in it to attract sympathy. Advice, if I had known where to seek it, would have been most precious. The words of Macbeth to his physician often occurred to my thoughts. (81–82)

The lines from *Macbeth* which occur to his "thoughts" (as if only touching him as thought) plead for the healing of a mind diseased: "Canst thou not minister to a mind diseas'd . . . Raze out the written troubles of the brain . . . Cleanse the stuff'd bosom of that perilous stuff which weighs upon the heart?" (5.3.40–45). In the context of the *Autobiography*, that "perilous stuff which weighs upon the heart" is the stuff of the mind—the mind itself as disease. ("My heart sank within me," Mill says; under what if not the weight of the mind?) His father could not serve as his "physician" because "everything convinced me that he had no knowledge of any such mental state as I was suffering from." The grounds of this conviction are given in its very expression: the only way that this suffering could be known to his father is as a "mental state," but such language cannot touch the pain Shakespeare names a "stuff'd bosom." James Mill, it is worth recalling, was "never . . . a great admirer of Shakespeare" (11), according to his son.

"A Crisis in My Mental History" is almost always understood as the central chapter of the *Autobiography*, the self-proclaimed importance of its content reinforced by its formal placement in the center of the narrative. There has been less critical agreement about the meaning of Mill's crisis, and the matter is further complicated because Mill appears to have compressed into a single episode what was, in fact, a recurrent mood of crisis that would come and go without clear resolution.[19] The most suggestive interpretations are those that marshal textual clues around this central chapter to recover the repressed substance of the episode, generally taken to involve displaced mourning and guilt following the death of his father.[20] Again, my aim is not to look elsewhere for what Mill omits from his account but, rather, to look closely at what the text makes manifest. In this case—and the very history of critical dispute underscores the point—what is obvious about the crisis Mill describes is that it escapes his powers of description. He understands himself as without the words with which to make himself understood.

Relief—as Mill imagines it in these few pages of the *Autobiography*—is conditional on the prospect of finding an adequate language: "I had none to whom I had any hope of making my condition intelligible" (82). While Mill might insist that "it was abundantly intelligible to myself," all that is intelligible is the condition of incommunicability itself: "If I had loved any one sufficiently to make confiding my griefs a necessity, I should not have been in the condition I was." Reading this episode in Lacanian terms, Linda Zerilli has suggested that Mill's crisis registers a pre-Oedipal trauma that leaves him longing for an impossible form of "unmediated communication." The recourse to poetry, according to Zerilli, is an effort to recapture a "world in which language offered the (illusory) possibility of crossing the abyss between subject and object, a world without difference and separation."[21] But this is to assimilate the extraordinary subject of the *Autobiography* within an interpretive framework in which despair at communicability is always representative of a longing for some original, irrecuperable intimacy. Lost is the contextual particularity of this expression of sad incommunicability, the constrained aspiration of the desire to do no more and no less than engage in the kind of successful, intersubjective exchange one might call intimate conversation or confidence. There is nothing illusory about the capacity for communication of this kind, but there may be something quite illusory, painfully and damagingly so, about imagining oneself (as Carlyle described Mill) "imprisoned as in the thick ribbed ice, voiceless, uncommunicating."[22] The subject constructed in this *Autobiography* would seem to be invulnerable to the illusion of perfect, unmediated communication, convinced as he appears to be that no one could possibly understand his condition, that he is essentially incommunicado.[23]

The inarticulate intelligibility rendered throughout the text by the reserved impersonality of the autobiographical voice may be precisely what is "irremediable" in the "failure" of his father's plan of education. Mill famously finds relief in the language of poetry, though it is more the dubious comfort of finding one's self-diagnosis confirmed than it is the relief of cure, for the feeling communicated in poetry is nothing other than, nothing more precise than, the feeling of incommunicability itself. Poetry is a comfort for Mill not because it "expresses feelings" but because it affirms their inexpressibility, articulating the fact that certain parts of the self cannot be articulated. I return to this topic below, but it bears remarking here that insofar as poetry offers Mill a kind of confirmation, or proof, that ineffability of feelings is not a condition (or disease) uniquely his own, an idea of individuals as profoundly solitary lodges itself at the heart of the *Autobiography*.

○ ○ ○

Although what Mill calls his "mental progress" proceeds after the chapter "A Crisis in My Mental History," his self-presentation as a subject vulnerable to the kind of crisis he has described recedes. The names on Mill's reading list change (Carlyle, Coleridge, Goethe, Schiller, and Fichte replace Bentham, Locke, Hartley, Berkeley, and Hume), but they also signify a return to the activities (as well as the implied limitations) described in the chapters devoted to childhood. The voice of "irrepressible self-consciousness" falls silent, and the "I" speaking in the *Autobiography* again becomes a being whose years are recorded as lists and series of acts of reading, writing, and thinking. That "I" famously becomes a "we" in Mill's account of his collaboration with the friend who eventually becomes his wife in the chapter entitled "My Most Valuable Friendship." In turning to the one intimate relationship celebrated as such in the *Autobiography*, it may seem as though the illusion of ineffability dissipates, that the extraordinary loneliness and affective isolation Mill has described is ultimately alleviated by an equally extraordinary, ideal form of closeness. But when Mill describes his union with Harriet Taylor as a "conjunction of her mind and mine" (150), he is using language appropriate for the extraordinary subject constructed by this *Autobiography* in order to name something as ordinary as sustained and unreserved conversation with a loved one. Insofar as Mill has deployed the impersonality and reticence of this text to offer subtle revelations, then it is in the story of Harriet Taylor that the subject of this narrative presents the possibility of sharing "ordinary" life. The oddly unpoetic yet seemingly exaggerated romance brings no more and no less than the mundane "facts in human life" Mill so clearly identified in his philosophical writing—sexual and social relations, sympathy, and intimacy—into the life recorded in the *Autobiography*.

MILL'S EFFUSION: SEX AND THE SINGULAR MAN

To be puzzled or disturbed by the role that Harriet Taylor is given in the *Autobiography*—the honor Mill pays to her intellect, the work and ideas he attributes to her—is, in part, to register a kind of embarrassment at a display so out of keeping with the restrained sensibility of the work as a whole.[24] And yet the pages devoted to Taylor cannot justly be described as outpourings of feeling; indeed, Mill's account of the relationship is remarkable precisely because it so dispassionately conveys its passion. There is simply nothing like the following passage in Mill's *Autobiography*:

> We met with new pleasure, and, I may add, with a more decisive preference for each other. It was however three weeks longer, before the sentiment which trembled upon the tongue, burst from the lips of either. There was, as I have already said, no period of throes and resolute explanation attendant on the tale. It was friendship melting into love. . . . Mary rested her head upon the shoulder of her lover, hoping to find a heart with which she might safely treasure her world of affection. . . . I had never loved till now; or, at least, never nourished a passion to the same growth, or met with an object so consummately worthy.

The account belongs to Godwin's life of Mary Wollstonecraft, and is predictably awkward or rhetorically clumsy in its effort to convey how a relationship of intimacy is formed.[25] The final set of appositions ("I had never loved . . . never nourished a passion . . . [never] met with an object") exhibits a telling deterioration of ordinary sense—as if "I had never loved" requires a kind of gloss, as if "[I had never] met with an object so consummately worthy" could serve as a way of saying (more lucidly) that "I had never loved." That impulse to explain and elaborate, however, derives from an ordinary misgiving about the meanings that simple words can convey: "I had never loved" does not say enough for Godwin here, and yet his use of the words, his need to qualify and supplement them, is meaningful enough.

Mill never uses the simple words, at least not in the *Autobiography*, and the strangeness of his devotion to Taylor, as it is expressed in this text, may involve no more than the avoidance of those simple words. I suggested above that the deliberateness with which Mill chooses not to say "I did not love my father" (and yet to say it unmistakably) evokes a form of life in which such expressions are unused and unavailable. Here the apparent reluctance to say, simply, that "I loved her" suggests a failure to imagine a form of life in which those words are vital and irreplaceable. The stylistic consistency of the *Autobiography* suggests a logical coherence as well: How would a mind formed in the way Mill has described render the fact and the achievement of association? The excesses of Mill's account of this "great friendship" are those of one who wants to find the right words but is not in possession of precisely those words that would make this feature of his life intelligible. Compare Godwin's awkwardly ordinary romanticism to what Mill says of one of the "most important events of my private life":

> My marriage, in April 1851, to the lady whose incomparable worth had made her friendship the greatest source to me both of happiness and improvement, during many years in which we never expected to be in closer relation to one another. . . . It was granted to me to derive from that evil [the death, in July 1849, of Taylor's husband] my own greatest good, by adding to the partnership of thought, feeling and writing which had long existed, a partnership of our entire existence. (143)

The "partnership of our entire existence" adds less than it might to the distinctly nonphysical partnership of "thought, feeling and writing." Godwin's "friendship melting into love," whatever else it may mean, euphemistically signifies, or honors the significance of, a sexual consummation that Mill's words imply but fail to make palpable or intelligible. Instead of the lips and head and shoulder Godwin connects to the hope of his lover's heart, Mill offers the words "entire existence" as an explanation of what he and Taylor are freed to share in marriage. However suggestive the phrase may be, the consummately philosophical term *existence* reiterates, without distinguishing between, the premarital union of the pair's "mental progress" and the union of their lives in marriage.

While the kind of intimacy implied and licensed by marriage is not altogether unmarked by Mill, it should not be surprising to find no common suggestion of that intimacy in an autobiography limited to the terms of mental development. What, after all, does sex have to do with the life of the mind? "For passionate emotions of all sorts," Mill recalls, "[my father] professed the greatest contempt" (31). The free and egalitarian society the elder Mill envisioned as utopian is also one in which sexual passion becomes vestigial: "He anticipated . . . that the imagination would no longer dwell upon the physical relation [between the sexes] ... and swell this into one of the principal objects of life." This "perversion of the imagination and feeling," Mill adds, was regarded by his father as "one of the deepest seated and most pervading evils in the human mind" (65). Note that the "mind" is not conceived as inherently separate from or opposed to the desires commonly associated with the body, but, rather, it is merely closed to those desires; the "imagination" is not permitted there to transform the "physical relations" into anything worthy of becoming one of the "principal objects" of a life.

Godwin can intimate the mingling of bodies with words like head and shoulder, but what I mean by his marking of sexual consummation is connected with, not reducible to, the way the lovers are named as bodies. Recall that before there can be a head on a shoulder in Godwin, "sentiment" has to find expression on the tongue and the lips: this might be imagined as an exchange of words, or the exchange of a kiss—but, in either case, we are being asked to imagine something more through the meeting of lovers' bodies. The possibilities of relation suggested here (call them passions or affections) can only appear, in Mill's *Autobiography*, as material belonging to the story of the mind, that is, they can only be accounted for in terms of mental life.

> Alike in the highest regions of speculation and in the smallest practical concerns of daily life, her mind was the same perfect instrument piercing to the very heart and marrow of the matter; always seizing the essential idea or principle. (113)

> To be admitted into any degree of mental intercourse with a being of these qualities, could not but have the most beneficial influence on my development; though the effect was only gradual, and many years elapsed before her mental progress and mine went forward in the complete companionship they at last attained. (114)

These claims are no more incredible than, or perhaps incredible in the same way as, Mill's account of the "things" he missed in being kept from regular intercourse with other children—that is, they will sound odd or extravagant only if attributed to a subject significantly different from the one Mill has all along been speaking of, speaking as. "Mind" is the only form that the lover of the being described in this autobiography could assume; "mental intercourse" is the most intimate and gratifying form of relation such a being could enter. The "complete companionship" of "her mental progress and mine" is what a marriage of minds sounds like. It is on and through these terms that the imagination this work contains can be understood to "dwell on the physical relation" and to "swell this into one of the principal objects of life" (65).

What more familiar, banal expression of love than that which speaks of the lover as the better half of one's self? Something like the ordinariness of that sentiment underlies the seemingly extraordinary claims Mill makes about Taylor's contribution to the works and to the workings of his mind: "not the work of one mind, but the fusion of two," he says. It cannot be surprising to find that a relationship established on these terms, in a life story restricted to acts of reading, writing, and thinking, takes the form of a book. Here is what Mill says of his work, *On Liberty*:

> The "Liberty" was more directly and literally our joint production than anything else which bears my name. . . . With regard to the thoughts, it is difficult to identify any particular part or element as being more hers than all the rest. The whole mode of thinking of which the book was the expression, was emphatically hers. But I also was so thoroughly imbued with it that the same thoughts naturally occurred to us both. . . .
>
> The "Liberty" is likely to survive longer than anything else that I have written because the conjunction of her mind with mine has rendered it a kind of philosophic text-book of a single truth. (150)
>
> After my irreparable loss one of my earliest cares was to print and publish the treatise, so much of which was the work of her whom I had lost, and consecrate it to her memory. I have made no alteration or addition to it, nor shall I ever. Though it wants the last touch of her hand, no substitute for that touch shall ever be attempted by mine. (152)

The effect, and the affections, of these lines are lost on the reader who takes them to be about a collaboration on a book and not (also) as an expression of the collaboration of lives that is a marriage. "The 'Liberty'" is Mill's way of speaking about both the grace of human intimacy (that gradual coincidence of minds in the "thoughts naturally occurr[ing] to us both") and the labor of loving which alone cultivates intimacy (so that a "joint production" can appear a "single truth"). "It wants the last touch of her hand": the phrase swells with meaning, yet its expressiveness is queerly sudden, inadvertent. What, after all, is "It" that "wants the last touch of her hand" (not the illumination of her thoughts but the touch of her hand) if not the whole of the man who has been telling but a part of his life—that part not "connected to myself"?

Socializing Philosophy, Privatizing Poetry:
A Paradox of Mill's Individualism

I began this chapter with two epigraphs from writings by John Stuart Mill, juxtaposed in order to underscore the paradoxical relationship between his philosophical position that the "social state" is both "natural" and "necessary" and the largely solitary existence he records in his *Autobiography*. I have been arguing that the remarkably sustained tone of impersonality and reserve that has impressed all readers of this text is itself a way of revealing or making known a form of life bereft of ordinary relations, of access to ordinary language and practice in the most ordinary forms of intimacy and exchange. The work is, as promised, a portrait of the kind of subjectivity shaped by an educational experiment narrowly focused on the intellectual cultivation of the mind alone, suggesting by its exclusions and oversights the crucial role of the mundane in shaping individual experience—the commonplace exchange of sentiments the youth only discovers in France, for example, and the unimaginable multitude of things boys learn from being brought together.

The implications of the rigorous and subtle distortions of ordinary language in the *Autobiography* are explicitly articulated in Mill's philosophical essays. The formative everyday engagement with others so absent from the childhood recorded in the life story is precisely the element Mill would identify as a crucial deficiency within Benthamite moral philosophy in his important essay on that philosopher. "The faculty by which one mind understands a mind different from itself and throws itself into the feelings of that other mind, was denied him by the deficiency of his Imagination," writes Mill. He goes on to define "imagination" as "the power by which one human being enters into the mind and circumstances of another"—words a philosopher of the preceding century might have used to define "sympathy" in order to name the spring for un-self-interested human action, as well as (for Hume and for Mill) the faculty that makes individuals epistemically available to one another.[26] It is worth noting that Mill had defended the *Essay concerning Human Understanding* against the very charge he levels against Bentham, arguing that the limits Locke set himself rightly excluded examination of the imagination (a subject that, in any case, was "ill-suited to the character of [Locke's] mind").[27] Whatever the reason for Mill's generous assessment of Locke's limitations, the constraints of Bentham's approach are to be found in the *Essay* as well. Bentham is neither the first nor the only thinker who, attempting "to create a philosophy wholly out of the materials furnished by his own mind," produced a conception of the human being that derives nothing from what Mill calls the "light of other minds."[28]

As I indicated at the outset, admission of the essential relations and dependencies that shape individual lives is the radical innovation Mill brings to utilitarian philosophy and to the empirical tradition within which it belongs. What, after all, could be more revisionary of Locke's image of the mind as a dark room than Mill's affirmation of the "light of other minds"? And yet the idea of the mind as a dark room, with its implications of hidden-ness, inwardness, and privacy, still exerts a powerful influence on Mill's conception of the individual. Among literary historians Mill is best known for his theorization of poetry as pure soliloquy, composed of words the self speaks only to itself in the serenity and security of solitude. Underlying the well-known distinction between eloquence and poetry in Mill's "Thoughts on Poetry and Its Varieties" (1833) is the presupposition of an irreducibly private realm in which the mind—paradoxically—communicates with itself alone.

> Eloquence is *heard*; poetry is *over*heard. Eloquence supposes an audience; the peculiarity of poetry appears to us to lie in the poet's utter unconsciousness of a listener. Poetry is feeling confessing itself to itself in moments of solitude. . . . Eloquence is feeling pouring itself out to other minds, courting their sympathy . . .
>
> All poetry is of the nature of soliloquy. . . . What we have said to ourselves we may tell to others afterwards; what we have said or done in solitude we may voluntarily reproduce when we know that other eyes are upon us. But no trace of consciousness that any eyes are upon us must be visible in the work itself. . . . When he turns round and addresses himself to another person . . . when the expression of his emotions . . . is tinged also by that desire of making an impression on another mind, then it ceases to be poetry and becomes eloquence.[29]

Poetry, on this view, is a public expression of the truth of privacy, of the idea that feeling and thought exist in their purest form in an invisible mental interior. What appears to be at stake for Mill in distinguishing poetry from all other forms of linguistic utterance is not the identification of a public form for private feeling but, rather, the affirmation of an immaculately solitary state of mind. To imagine that only within such a space is feeling authentic (not tinged by desire, bearing no trace of address to another) is to indulge in an ideal of lonely singularity. A Lockean conception of the individual mind as separate from and opaque to others underlies the idea of consciousness implicit in Mill's conception of the poetic subject enclosed "in a private cell of subjectivity."[30] It is to poetry, then, that Mill simultaneously banishes and preserves the existential features of Lockean psychology.

o o o

The conceptual split in Mill's writing between one account of the sociality of the self and another account of the self as essentially solitary should not be seen as neatly contained by a division between the philosophical and the aesthetic. Each account is consummately philosophical, each drawn from the intellectual tradition in which Mill was educated. Mill's effort to pull them apart—using one as the basis for an ultimately optimistic view of individuals as moral beings (for whom the "good of others becomes . . . a thing naturally and necessarily to be attended to, like any of the physical conditions of our existence")[31] and the other as the basis for a view of the self as potentially independent of others, capable of thoughts and feelings that bear no trace of other minds—only reduplicates a profound split within English eighteenth-century philosophy. As a moral agent, Mill's individual possesses the mind Hume described as a "mirror" to other minds; as a person of feeling, Mill's individual is opaque to others, irreducibly himself alone. The separation of these two views in Mill's writings—his evident interest in retaining the idea of isolation—offers another opportunity to think about the appeal of the philosophical invitation to think of the individual "come to full maturity without all kinds of engagement" to others.

From the Dark Room to the Moated Grange

The textual cases presented in this book can be seen as points in a trajectory along which an ideal of human independence deteriorates. By this I mean that the ideal loses power and authority, as elements associated with it fall off under the force of criticism and re-imagination. This theoretical and creative revision is most evidently at work on the imperative to think of the individual, first and foremost—*originally*—as an independent being. When given full imaginative realization (as in

Rousseau's *Discourse on Inequality* and Shelley's *Frankenstein*) the originally isolated and independent individual fails to become fully human, is left at a "primitive" stage. If development—linguistic, intellectual, and affective—ever more obviously entails dependence and relation, then independence not only seems an ever more implausible basis on which to conceive human formation, but it also seems an undesirable condition, characterized by privation, lack. Aloneness and isolation negatively inflect and ultimately subvert the ideal of self-sufficiency. But even when the imagination of an independent formation is indulged (as in Locke's *Essay concerning Human Understanding* and Wordsworth's *Prelude*), weakness, fear, and vulnerability disturb the secure equanimity of autonomy. Wordsworth's "falsely taught solitary" finds the love of others achieved in solitude and experienced abstractly, distantly, to be catastrophically insubstantial, initiating a crisis within the solitary self. In Locke, the consistent compromising of the conditions of epistemic autonomy is, to be sure, an implication rather than an aim of the theory. The problem of knowing and being known by other persons repeatedly arises as an unintended effect and affect within the epistemological argument: the privacy and impenetrability of minds leave the philosophical investigator feeling anxiously alone even when surrounded by others—wondering what (monstrous) beings might be hidden "inside" familiar human shapes, ruminating over a thousand ways a friend can cease to be once out of sight, certain that however clearly he understands another's words, he never really knows the other's thoughts. The "dark room" of the mind, Locke's famous figure of the secure, immured space from which the individual looks out on the world and others in it ultimately becomes a haunted scene of constraint in the *Essay*.

Seen in the context of the other isolated cases presented in this study, John Stuart Mill's emphasis on the "deeply rooted conception . . . every individual even now has of himself as a social being" would seem to mark a definitive shift: the most influential nineteenth-century transmission of a line of philosophical thinking that extends back to Locke radically overturns the central premise of original independence. Within the English empiricist tradition, Mill's reconception of the individual as socially and sympathetically connected to others, his embedding of the individual in sexual and familial relations, may be seen to represent a revision as profound as Rousseau's denaturing and dehumanizing of "natural man" among natural law philosophies. But to conclude with so straightforward a repudiation of autonomy would be to lose sight of the ambivalence and uneasiness entailed in the admission of the human being's constitutive dependence on and relation with others—the complex mixed feelings, as it were, attending that realization. In Mill's case, the use of the idea of poetry to sustain an ideal of privacy suggests the persistence of a longing to escape or deny the extent of dependence and relation, to conceive of the self as painfully but securely alone rather than unavoidably but vulnerably connected to others. Affirming the essentially social and related nature of the individual and yet, irresistibly, it seems, insisting on an essentially private, incommunicable core of the self—it is precisely this paradoxical tendency that makes Mill a fitting figure with which to close a study of writings that renounce a fantastic ideal of autonomy without substituting for it a heartening vision of human association.

o o o

Attempting to demystify and explain the urgings of "conscience" (the fact that each person "is conscious of himself as a being who *of course* pays regard to others"), Mill's sources of moral insight become the stuff of what came to be known as psychoanalysis. The "complex phenomenon" of conscience, he writes in *Utilitarianism*, is "derived from sympathy, from love, and still more from fear; from all the forms of religious feeling; from the recollections of childhood, and of all our past life; from self-esteem, desire of the esteem of others, and occasionally even self-abasement."[32] What would it mean to consider these very influences informing thought and feeling even when, especially when, the dutiful regard of others is not at issue? Might hatred or jealousy, to recall Rousseau, arise together with love? What feelings, other than conscience, might be derived from recollection of all our past life? Or, rather, what feelings could possibly arise free of such influence? Mill's theory of poetry avoids these questions and instead imagines the possibility of being liberated from the engagements and entanglements of life among others to a realm of purely self-determined experience. The feeling of poetry, the feeling that is poetry, is as if uninformed by the stuff of conscience.[33]

I said above that Mill's theory of poetry is an *indulgence* in the ideal of lonely singularity, but to appreciate it as such one must find the pleasure taken in a certain kind of pain—in this case the pang of absolute solitude, the pained recognition of an isolated, unreachable core of privacy. Wordsworth identifies this as the feeling that "points have we all within our souls where all stand single"; Winnicott calls this idea of a "permanently non-communicating, permanently unknown" center the "true self"; Wittgenstein identifies this sense of something "inner" and "private" as the irresistible temptation of a "surrender . . . to philosophical thought."[34] These characterizations themselves speak to the persistence of a deeply paradoxical and ambivalent reckoning with the profound sociality of the self. If psychoanalysis is, in some sense, all about the individual's coming into being in relation to others, then how odd to find, in some of the most sophisticated contemporary writing on the process, that a goal of the analytic encounter is to allow for the "capacity to be with one's self, unintruded upon by the need to relate" to the other, so as to arrive at "an area of essential aloneness."[35] A conceptual alignment of privacy, authenticity, and freedom survives in this particular aspiration formulated within the very center, as it were, of the alternative ontology of the individual that psychoanalysis stands for. The idea of a privately inexpressible core of the self persists as well in Wittgenstein. As much as the *Philosophical Investigations* urges acknowledgment of the deeply shared practices and conventions within which the very idea of privacy itself takes shape, it is also a work haunted by the hard fact of intersubjective disagreement and misunderstanding. Indeed, for Wittgenstein, the philosophical impulse to explain failures of understanding (by, for example, producing theories of language) is itself characteristic of an all-too-ordinary turn away from the ethical and existential challenge posed by human exchange ("the inevitable moment" when "my power comes to an end in the face of the other's separateness from me").[36] The works in *Isolated Cases* represent ambivalent, unmystified recognitions of the self's formation through, and ongoing need for, relation to other persons. Their complexity inheres as much in the acknowledgment that a certain feeling of privacy is inescapable as it does in the admission that the intimacies we have no choice in forming expose us to peril, risk, and disappointment. What sets Mill's work apart from the revisions of autonomy in Rousseau, Wordsworth, and Shelley is not the mere commitment to an idea of the self's privacy that seems to run counter to a theoretical affirmation of the individual's embeddedness in society but, rather, the persistence of a longing for safety in isolation— the imagination of privacy as a secure refuge for the self.

Though Mill resists the idea of the isolated individual in his philosophical work, it is affirmation of this very idea that Mill believes he finds in poetry; from it he draws personal consolation in the *Autobiography* and through it he allows the possibility of a unique liberation in his essays on poetry. Consigned to poetry, the idea of the irreducible privacy of the individual tantalizes with its offer of deliverance and relief. To "look within," to be "unconscious of being seen," to express thought or feeling unshaped by (the desire to express to) another—these are fantasies (from the 1833 essays) about the content of solitude to which Mill adds revealing substance in his 1835 review of Tennyson's poetry. Illustrating the poet's power to "summon up the state of feeling itself," Mill singles out "Mariana," the longing lament of the abandoned Shakespearean lover, "living deserted and in solitude in the 'moated grange.'"[37] Mill is impressed that the "love story is secondary in [Tennyson's] mind" to the static scene of solitude. The "right point of view" on the poem, he insists, excludes all but the "'moated grange,' and a solitary dweller within it, forgotten by mankind." Inhabiting this perspective, the reader will be impressed by the "intense conception" of the place and its "inmate," will find the scene "impregnated with the feelings of the supposed inhabitant." The site gives birth to the character imagined within it, engenders the emotions that determine the character. Made "vivid" in the poem is the "dreariness which speaks not merely of being far from human converse and sympathy, but of being *deserted* by it." It is a peculiarity of the poem that, although its subject is ostensibly defined by longing, "Mariana" does not move from or even between anticipation and disappointment: in that sense the poem is removed from the temporality of the love story. The repeated refrain "He cometh not" suggests the still *aftermath* of fear and misgiving, so that its single variation, at the end of the poem—"He will not come"—seems less a realization than a determined affirmation to keep certain, to keep the certainty, that he does not come.[38]

Much can be said about Mill's attention to "Mariana" in his review of Tennyson. It is intriguing, for example, that the "Palace of Art," with its remarkable dramatization of the soul "cursed with deep dread and loathing of her solitude," failed to forcibly impress Mill. Certainly that poem's chastening representation of a solitude enervated and finally broken down by guilt disturbs the ideal of a private refuge, of a space serene precisely insofar as it is private. It is easy enough to see how Mill might have read Mariana's words—uttered in solitude, addressed to no one—as consummately poetic according to his own definition, uninflected by hope or desire to move some other "to passion or to action"—but, at the same time, that very reading may be seen as symptomatic of Mill's misreading of poetry in general as soliloquy. The notion of expressive utterance emptied of communicative aim verges on incoherence, after all; Mariana's unaddressed words only make sense as contained in and contextualized by the poem's objectification of the subjective state it represents.[39]

Rich in oversights as Mill's preference for "Mariana" may be, however, the "state of feeling" the philosopher finds in the poem is perhaps most suggestive of its irresistible appeal. Mariana's state of isolation is relatively secure, the character relatively settled as a *"being deserted."* Precisely unlike Locke's dark room, Mariana's moated grange is uncompromised by anxious longing. "Impregnated," as Mill puts it, with the feelings of the lover certain of her desertion, the grange is impregnable, invulnerable to further loss. The pleasure to be found in this particular rendering of pain has to do with the fantasy of a permanent arresting of engagement, of an abandonment that places the lover safely out of reach, spared from further risk, removed from the scene of stories of love and hate, reborn a solitary.

Notes

INTRODUCTION

1. For a classic study of enlightenment concepts of mind, psychology, and society as critical to that "whole intellectual development through which modern philosophic thought gained its characteristic self-confidence and self-consciousness," see, for example, Ernst Cassirer, *The Philosophy of the Enlightenment*, trans. Fritz Koelln and James Pettegrove (1932; Princeton, N.J.: Princeton University Press, 1951), vi. Touchstones for the critical perspective on enlightenment constructions of the individual include Theodor Adorno and Max Horkheimer, *Dialectic of Enlightenment*, trans. John Cumming (1944; New York: Continuum, 1994); Michel Foucault, *The Order of Things: An Archaeology of the Human Sciences* (1966; New York: Vintage, 1973); and idem, "What Is Enlightenment?" in *The Foucault Reader*, ed. Paul Rabinow (New York: Pantheon, 1984), 32–50.

2. Thomas Hobbes, *De Cive* (1642), in *Man and Citizen (De Homine and De Cive)*, ed. Bernard Gert (Indianapolis: Hackett, 1991), 111–118.

3. Hobbes, *De Cive*, 110.

4. Charles Taylor, *Sources of the Self* (Cambridge, Mass.: Harvard University Press, 1989), 193. It is from this new starting point that we inherit "a conception that puts the autonomous individual at the center of our system of law" (195). See also Charles Taylor, "Atomism," in idem, *Philosophy and the Human Sciences* (Cambridge: Cambridge University Press, 1985), 187–210.

5. John Locke, *Second Treatise of Government*, in *Two Treatises of Government*, ed. Peter Laslett (Cambridge: Cambridge University Press, 1960), §§ 108 and 4, respectively.

6. Locke, *Second Treatise*, §§ 55–56.

7. René Descartes, *Discourse on Method and Meditations on First Philosophy*, trans. Donald A. Cress (Indianapolis: Hackett, 1980), 17, 57. On Descartes, see *Essays on Descartes' "Meditations,"* ed. Amélie Oksenberg Rorty (Berkeley: University of California Press, 1986), and Susan Bordo, *The Flight to Objectivity: Essays*

on Cartesianism and Culture (Albany: State University of New York Press, 1987).

8. Denis Diderot, "Chaldéens," *Encyclopédie* II (B–C), in *Oeuvres complètes*, ed. John Lough and Jacques Proust (1751–1772; Paris: Hermann, 1976), 6:331. (The remark occurs in the context of a defense of the liberty of thought against the shackles of religious authority.) Etienne Bonnot de Condillac, *La Logique, ou Les premiers développemens de l'art de penser* in *Oeuvres complètes de Condillac* (1780; Paris: Ch. Houel, 1798), 22:143 ("'Principe' est synonyme de 'commencement,' et c'est dans cette signification qu'on l'a d'abord employé").

Cassirer locates the "entire intellectual structure of the eighteenth century" in the transition from Cartesian to post-Cartesian enlightenment, which he defines as a movement from "the logic of 'clear and distinct ideas' " to the "logic of 'origin' " (35, 99). See also Hans Aarsleff's argument that origin "was the best mode of explanation and analysis [the eighteenth century] knew, just as understanding in terms of structure is perhaps the dominant and most natural mode in our time" (*From Locke to Saussure* [Minneapolis: University of Minnesota Press, 1982], 158).

9. Locke claims to adopt a "historical plain method" in the *Essay concerning Human Understanding*, ed. Peter H. Nidditch (Oxford: Oxford University Press, 1975), 1.1.2. Voltaire: "Tant de raisonneurs ayant fait le roman de l'âme, un sage est venu, qui en a fait modestement l'histoire," "*Sur M. Locke*," *Lettres philosophiques* (1733; Paris: Garnier, 1964), 83–84.

10. Locke, *Essay*, 2.1.2; Etienne Bonnot de Condillac, *Traité des sensations* (1754; Paris: Fayard, 1984); Julien Offray de La Mettrie, *L'Homme Machine* (1748) in *Oeuvres philosophiques* (Paris: Fayard, 1987).

11. Annette Baier, *Moral Prejudices: Essays on Ethics* (Cambridge, Mass.: Harvard University Press, 1994), 319.

12. J. B. Schneewind, *The Invention of Autonomy: A History of Modern Moral Philosophy* (Cambridge: Cambridge University Press, 1998), 81; Tzvetan Todorov, "Living Alone Together," *New Literary History* 27 (1996): 1; Seyla Benhabib, *Situating the Self: Gender, Community, and Postmodernism in Contemporary Ethics* (New York: Routledge, 1992), 5.

Todorov's questions, "Did not the [individuals of political theory] have to be children before they were adults? Did they not have to come from a mother's womb rather than a philosopher's brain?" are versions of Seyla Benhabib's earlier description of the "strange world" constituted by enlightenment political theories: "one in which individuals are grown up before they are born; in which boys are men before they have been children" ("The Generalized and the Concrete Other," in *Women and Moral Theory*, ed. E. Kittay and D. Meyers [Totowa, N.J.: Rowman and Littlefield, 1987], 162). The crux of Todorov's argument also has important precedents in feminist critiques of enlightenment social theory by Jennifer Nedelsky, "Reconceiving Autonomy: Sources, Thoughts and Possibilities," *Yale Journal of Law and Feminism* 1 (1989): 7–36; and Christine Di Stefano, *Configurations of Masculinity: A Feminist Perspective on Modern Political Theory* (Ithaca, N.Y.: Cornell University Press, 1991).

13. The remarkable number of books and essay collections with titles such as *Rewriting the Self* (ed. Roy Porter [New York: Routledge, 1997]), *Changing Subjects*

(ed. Gayle Greene and Coppélia Kahn [New York: Routledge, 1993]), *Constructions of the Self* (ed. George Levine [New Brunswick, N.J.: Rutgers University Press, 1992]), and *Reconstructing Individualism* (ed. Thomas Heller, Morton Sosna, and David Wellbery [Stanford: Stanford University Press, 1986]) evince (and date to the late 1980s and early 1990s) the consolidation of constructionist accounts of the history of thinking about the individual across a range of disciplines.

14. It is perhaps impossible, especially in literary critical circles, to speak of the constitutive role of others in the formation of subjectivity without reference to Freudian and post-Freudian psychoanalytic theories. There are rich disagreements about whether Freud decisively undermines or seeks to retain an understanding of individuals as whole and autonomous individuals. Lacanian and object-relations theories both clearly emphasize the primacy of relation in formation of the self. Still, it is a question whether, and from what perspective, acknowledgment of dependence and relation in individual formation must be understood as the "discovery" or even "invention" of psychoanalysis. "The idea that the individual cannot be understood in isolation" also has "a long and distinguished philosophical career," notes Jonathan Lear—himself both an analytic philosopher and a practicing psychoanalyst (*Love and Its Place in Nature: A Philosophical Interpretation of Freudian Psychoanalysis* [New Haven: Yale University Press, 1990], 157). Inevitably, at several points in its argument, *Isolated Cases* explores some of the same territory as Freud, Klein, Lacan, Winnicott, and other psychoanalytic theorists. While I acknowledge the relation at specific junctures (especially in chapters 1, 5, and 6), the aim of this project is not to offer an account of intersections between contemporary psychoanalytic theories and the investigations of individual origins and development that are in fact my focus. For the most part, I do not employ psychoanalytic concepts and terminology to define approaches to the question of individual origination for which the texts themselves have their own language. That they *do* have such a language—one that a psychoanalytic vocabulary would at best anachronistically (if sometimes helpfully) paraphrase—is, I think, demonstrated throughout the book.

15. Study of romanticism in the past half century offers a salient example of the manner in which accounts of the self in a particular period will tend to be shaped as much by response to dominant critical views as by new approaches to historical material. In the early 1980s, critics such as Jerome McGann and Marjorie Levinson transformed the study of romanticism while retaining—and, indeed, necessarily assuming—the very romantic subject that an earlier generation of critics had defined. The difference between Levinson's reading of Wordsworth's "Tintern Abbey" as a poem asserting the "freedom of thought" and "assum[ing] the autonomy of the subject" and Bloom's reading of the triumphally unmoored imagination in the same poem is ultimately not substantive but evaluative. In censuring the transcendental tendencies of romantic lyric personae, their detachment from social and historical contingencies, Levinson deplores what Bloom celebrates, but both are looking at the same kind of subjectivity (Marjorie Levinson, *Wordsworth's Great Period Poems* [New York: Cambridge University Press, 1986], 40, 48; Harold Bloom, *The Visionary Company* [New York: Anchor/Doubleday, 1961], 139–149). The subject

in question for both generations of critics might have always been more "modern" than romantic according to David Simpson, who has recently argued that a distinctly modernist interest in "problematical self-consciousness" unites critics as diverse as Lionel Trilling, Harold Bloom, Geoffrey Hartman, and Paul de Man ("Romanticism, Criticism, Theory," in *Cambridge Companion to British Romanticism*, ed. Stuart Curran [Cambridge: Cambridge University Press, 1993], 15–16). On the convergence between deconstructive and cultural materialist approaches to romanticism, see Frances Ferguson, "On the Numbers of Romanticisms," *ELH* 58 (1991): 471–498. For a recent effort to go beyond the "binary structure of the subjectivity debate" within romantic studies by attending instead to the "diversity of models for understanding subjectivity generated in the period," see Andrea Henderson, *Romantic Identities: Varieties of Subjectivity, 1774–1830* (Cambridge: Cambridge University Press, 1996), 3.

16. For literary critics, Jacques Derrida's groundbreaking study of nature, culture, and language in Rousseau remains the most well known analysis of the paradoxical movements of Rousseau's arguments (*Of Grammatology*, trans. Gayatri Spivak (Baltimore: Johns Hopkins University Press, 1974), 95–316. Methodologically different, but as radical, are the interpretations of N. J. H. Dent in *Rousseau* (Oxford: Basil Blackwell, 1988); and Victor Gourevitch, "Rousseau's 'Pure' State of Nature," *Interpretation* 16 (1988): 23–59. Revisionary readings of the state of nature, deconstructionist and otherwise, owe a debt to Emile Durkheim, "La Determination du fait moral," *Bulletin de la Société française de Philosophie* 6 (1906): 130–134.

17. Marshall Brown, "Romanticism and Enlightenment," in *Cambridge Companion to British Romanticism*, 29, 31, 44. Important literary studies that extend from the eighteenth to the nineteenth century tend to follow particular threads through each period rather than attempt a comprehensive history. Precise focus nevertheless can yield interpretations with wide implications; exemplary in this regard are David Bromwich, *Hazlitt: The Mind of a Critic* (New York: Oxford University Press, 1983); Frances Ferguson, *Solitude and the Sublime* (New York: Routledge, 1992); and David Marshall, *The Surprising Effects of Sympathy* (Chicago: University of Chicago Press, 1988).

18. On the challenge Rousseau, in particular, poses to the historian of English literature, see W. J. T. Mitchell, "Influence, Autobiography, and Literary History: Rousseau's *Confessions* and Wordsworth's *Prelude*," *ELH* 57 (1990): 643–664. Remarkably Irving Babbitt's early, ideologically inflected *Rousseau and Romanticism* (New York, 1919) has yet to be superseded by a major, contemporary account of the same topic. Jacques Voisine's *Rousseau en angleterre à l'époque romantique* (Paris: Didier, 1956) remains useful but stands in need of updating.

19. Many literary studies of the philosophy of the period nevertheless begin with reminders that the term *literature* encompassed not only poetry, plays, and novels but also histories, biographies, and moral and scientific treatises. Arguing that nonfiction was the dominant late-eighteenth-century literary form, Leo Damrosch suggests that the narrow definition of "literature" as work of the imagination was a later, romantic development (*Fictions of Reality in the Age of Hume and Johnson* [Madison: University of Wisconsin Press, 1989], 7). The need to defend the

inclusion of philosophical writing among literary forms suggests a lingering disciplinary discomfort with attending to (philosophical) ideas as well as (rhetorical) structure. Defending the selection of Shaftesbury and Smith alongside Defoe and George Eliot for his study of theatrical discourse, David Marshall asserts that "fiction, aesthetics, moral philosophy, and epistemology address many of the same questions in analogous terms" (*The Figure of the Theater* [New York: Columbia University Press, 1986], 3). Similarly Adela Pinch defends the inclusion of Hume in her study of eighteenth-century sentiment on the grounds that "questions about our knowledge of feelings ... structure both literary and philosophical works" (*Strange Fits of Passion* [Stanford: Stanford University Press, 1996], 8). While influential interpretations of Descartes, Locke, and Rousseau by Jacques Derrida and Paul de Man in the 1970s would appear to license rhetorical analysis of philosophical texts, the difficulty for literary critics of the enlightenment and romanticism such as Damrosch and Marshall lies in not losing sight of the other side of this interpretive imperative, and giving due emphasis to the manner in which literary texts participate in the articulation of philosophical concepts. Building on deconstructive readings, an exemplary recent analysis of how figuration alters lines of philosophical argument is Cathy Caruth, *Empirical Truths and Critical Fictions: Locke, Wordsworth, Kant, Freud* (Baltimore: Johns Hopkins University Press, 1991). Alternatively Damrosch's *Fictions of Reality* traces the shifting valuation of concepts such as "nature" by attending to the different ways in which philosophical assertions and rhetorical modes intersect at a particular historical moment. Important models for literary study of eighteenth-century philosophy, or of philosophy and literature together, include, in addition to those cited above, Hans Aarsleff, *From Locke to Saussure*; Carol Kay, *Political Constructions: Defoe, Richardson, and Sterne in Relation to Hobbes, Hume, and Burke* (Ithaca, N.Y.: Cornell University Press, 1988); Jules David Law, *The Rhetoric of Empiricism: Language and Perception from Locke to I. A. Richards* (Ithaca, N.Y.: Cornell University Press, 1993); Adam Potkay, *The Passion for Happiness: Samuel Johnson and David Hume* (Ithaca, N.Y.: Cornell University Press, 2000); John Richetti, *Philosophical Writing: Locke, Berkeley, Hume* (Cambridge, Mass.: Harvard University Press, 1983); and William Walker, *Locke, Literary Criticism, and Philosophy* (Cambridge: Cambridge University Press, 1994). Influential deconstructionist studies of enlightenment philosophers include Jacques Derrida (on Rousseau), *Of Grammatology*, 95–316, (on Descartes) *Writing and Difference*, trans. Alan Bass (Chicago: University of Chicago Press, 1978), 31–63; and "White Mythology: Metaphor in the Text of Philosophy," trans. F. C. T. Moore, *New Literary History* 6 (1974): 1; Paul de Man (on Locke) "The Epistemology of Metaphor," *Critical Inquiry* (1978): 13–30; (on Rousseau) *Allegories of Reading* (New Haven: Yale University Press, 1979).

20. Perhaps most familiar to literary scholars is Martha Nussbaum, *Love's Knowledge: Essays on Philosophy and Literature* (New York: Oxford University Press, 1990); but see also Richard Eldridge, *On Moral Personhood: Philosophy, Literature, Criticism, and Self-Understanding* (Chicago: University of Chicago Press, 1987); Colin McGinn, *Ethics, Evil, and Fiction* (Oxford: Clarendon, 1997); Robert Pippen, *Henry James and Modern Moral Life* (Cambridge: Cambridge University Press, 2000); Richard

Wollheim, *The Thread of Life* (New Haven: Yale University Press, 1984); and the many works of Stanley Cavell. Exemplary use of the realist novel is widespread, as is special emphasis on the "particularism" of literary representation in that genre. See, for example, Lorraine Code on the "value of the particular" (*Epistemic Responsibility* [Hanover, N.H.: University Press of New England, 1987], 201–226); Benhabib on narrative and the "art of the particular" (*Situating the Self*, 5–6, 127); and Naomi Scheman on the irreducible "contingencies and specificities" of novelistic representation (*Engenderings: Constructions of Knowledge, Authority, and Privilege* [New York: Routledge, 1993], 114–117). For thoughtful discussion of how the "varieties of moral thought found in literature" challenge modern philosophical models, see Cora Diamond, *The Realistic Spirit* (Cambridge: MIT Press, 1991), 301, 292–302, 367–381; and idem, "Losing Your Concepts," *Ethics* 98 (January 1988): 255–277.

21. Alasdair MacIntyre, *After Virtue: A Study in Moral Theory*, 2d ed. (Notre Dame: University of Notre Dame Press, 1981), 33, 221. The criticism is ventured as part of a broader argument for the constitutive role of history and social context in the formation of identity: "The notion of escaping" from the particular communal roles the self occupies "into a realm of entirely universal maxims which belong to man as such, whether in its eighteenth-century Kantian form or in the presentation of some modern analytical moral philosophies, is an illusion, and an illusion with painful consequences" (221).

22. Richard Rorty, *Consequences of Pragmatism* (Minneapolis: University of Minnesota Press, 1982), xix. Rorty's sustained anti-foundationalist indictment of "traditional philosophy as an attempt to escape from history—an attempt to find nonhistorical conditions of any possible historical development" is made in his earlier *Philosophy and the Mirror of Nature* (Princeton, N.J.: Princeton University Press, 1979).

23. Michael Sandel, *Liberalism and the Limits of Justice* (Cambridge: Cambridge University Press, 1982), 62, 178–179; see also 15–66, 147–153, 175–182.

24. Notable exceptions include Potkay and Damrosch (for the eighteenth century) and (for the nineteenth) Amanda Anderson (*The Powers of Distance* [Princeton, N.J.: Princeton University Press, 2001]). Some literary theorists have made an effort to draw connections between the post-Saussurian theories of language common among French thinkers and the Anglo-American analytic tradition (e.g., Charles Altieri and Austin Quigley on Wittgenstein, Judith Butler on Austin). Nevertheless, while philosophers have increasingly come to engage with what used to be called the "continental" tradition, even the broad outlines of contemporary debates in philosophy of mind, philosophy of language, and ethics remain largely beyond the purview of literary critics. A recent literature search of the MLA bibliography for articles, books, or dissertations written between 1985 and 2002 treating the work of several prominent Anglo-American philosophers (Jonathan Lear, Alasdair MacIntyre, Thomas Nagel, Bernard Williams, and Richard Wollheim) turned up fewer than fifty documents. A comparable search of the Philosopher's Index turned up hundreds of documents treating the work of French theorists who have been particularly influential in literary studies (Gilles Deleuze, Jacques Derrida, Michel Foucault, and Jacques Lacan). The disproportion is striking.

25. See Immanuel Kant, *Groundwork of the Metaphysics of Morals* (esp. sections 2 and 3) for Kant's famous argument for autonomy of the will. The Kantian usage is the first point of reference for definitions of autonomy in specialized reference works such as the *Oxford Companion to Philosophy* (ed. Ted Honderich [Oxford: Oxford University Press, 1995]) and the *Dictionary of Philosophy* (ed. Thomas Mautner [Cambridge, Mass.: Blackwell's, 1996]).

26. Schneewind, "The Use of Autonomy in Ethical Theory," in *Reconstructing Individualism*, 72.

27. Samantha Brennan, "Recent Work in Feminist Ethics," *Ethics* 109 (1999): 868. Marilyn Friedman usefully reviews evolving usage of the term in "Feminism in Ethics: Conceptions of Autonomy," *Cambridge Companion to Feminism in Philosophy*, ed. Miranda Fricker and Jennifer Hornsby (Cambridge: Cambridge University Press, 2000), 205–224.

28. Simon Blackburn, *Oxford Dictionary of Philosophy* (Oxford: Oxford University Press, 1994), 31. *Autonomy* is also frequently used as a contrasting term by psychoanalytically inclined theorists of a "relational self." So, for example, Nancy Chodorow credits Freud with "radically undermin[ing] notions of the unitary and autonomous individual" ("Toward a Relational Individualism," in *Reconstructing Individualism*, 198).

29. See, for example, Marilyn Friedman, "Autonomy and Social Relationships: Rethinking the Feminist Critique," in *Feminists Rethink the Self*, ed. Diana Tietjens Meyers (Boulder, Colo.: Westview, 1997), 40–61; and Nedelsky, "Reconceiving Autonomy"; and, on Kant, Onora O'Neill, *Constructions of Reason* (Cambridge: Cambridge University Press, 1989); and Christine Korsgaard, *Creating the Kingdom of Ends* (Cambridge: Cambridge University Press, 1996).

30. Although communitarian arguments arise in response to twentieth-century liberal theory (such as Michael Sandel's influential critique of Rawls's *Theory of Justice*), their elaboration has entailed significant engagement with the philosophical *sources* of twentieth-century views. In addition to Sandel, see Taylor, *Philosophy and the Human Sciences*; and MacIntyre, *After Virtue*.

31. For the general outlines of this critical perspective on contemporary moral theories, see Baier, *Moral Prejudices*, 1–32; and Christine Korsgaard, *The Sources of Normativity* (Cambridge: Cambridge University Press, 1996), 132–136.

32. Carole Pateman, *The Sexual Contract* (Stanford: Stanford University Press, 1988); Di Stefano, *Configurations of Masculinity*; Jane Flax, "Political Philosophy and the Patriarchal Unconscious," in the important collection *Discovering Reality: Feminist Perspectives on Epistemology, Methodology, and Philosophy of Science*, ed. Sandra Harding and Merrill Hintikka (Dordrecht: Reidl, 1983), 245–281. The appearance of numerous collections of essays on feminist approaches to mind, language, and ethics is indicative of the relatively rapid rise of feminism within the field (e.g., *A Mind of One's Own*, ed. Louise M. Antony and Charlotte Witt [Boulder: Westview, 1993]; *Feminist Ethics*, ed. Claudia Card [Lawrence: University Press of Kansas, 1991]; *Philosophy in a Feminist Voice*, ed. Janet A. Kourany [Princeton, N.J.: Princeton University Press, 1998]; *Feminist Social Thought*, ed. Diana T. Meyers [New York: Routledge, 1997]; a series of "Feminist Interpretations" of major philosophers

(including Plato, Kant, Descartes, Hegel, Foucault, Levinas, and Wittgenstein) [Pennsylvania State University Press, 1994–the present]; and large anthologies such as Blackwell's *Companion to Feminist Philosophy*, ed. Alison Jaggar and Iris Young [Oxford: Blackwell, 1998]).

33. Lorraine Code, *What Can She Know? Feminist Theory and the Construction of Knowledge* (Ithaca, N.Y.: Cornell University Press, 1991), 110–173; Sandra Harding, "The Social Function in Empiricist Conception of Mind," *Metaphilosophy* 10 (January 1979): 38–47. See also Bordo, *The Flight to Objectivity*; Harding and Hintikka, *Discovering Reality*; and *Gender/Body/Knowledge: Feminist Reconstructions of Being and Knowing*, ed. Alison Jaggar and Susan Bordo (New Brunswick, N.J.: Rutgers University Press, 1989).

34. The adoption of a perspective at once historical and synthetic (looking across ethics to epistemology, for example, or from analytic philosophy to questions in philosophy of mind) characterizes some of the most ambitious feminist analyses. See, for example, the exposition of the relationship between individualism in enlightenment political theories and empiricism, and the still influential "view of a separate, autonomous, sharply individuated self" on contemporary liberal theories and philosophies of mind in Scheman, *Engenderings*, 36–53. Cora Diamond traces "the philosophy of mind which is the source of our inarticulateness in ethics" back to "that picture of the human mind which our culture in general has inherited from the Enlightenment" in "Losing Your Concepts" (262). See also Lorraine Code's Wittgensteinian-inflected argument for intersections between ethics and epistemology, in *Epistemic Responsibility*, 165–197.

35. Baier, *Moral Prejudices*, 51–93. On Kantian reciprocity as effecting a "transformation" of identity and thereby making "relations... constitutive of our ongoing identities," a radical interpretation that takes issue with standard feminist criticisms of Kant, see Korsgaard, *Creating the Kingdom of Ends*, 208, 215–216.

36. Benhabib, *Situating the Self*, 223. Though common enough, the generalization about "sovereign rational consciousness" cited above is drawn from Jaggar and Young, *Companion to Feminist Philosophy*, 75. Arguably Benhabib's own grouping of a variety of theories under rubrics such as "postmodern" and "poststructuralist" is liable to the charge of generalization; see, for example, Judith Butler's response to Benhabib in *Feminist Contentions: A Philosophical Exchange*, ed. Seyla Benhabib, Judith Butler, Drucilla Cornell, and Nancy Fraser (New York: Routledge, 1995), 35–57.

37. Ludwig Wittgenstein, *Philosophical Investigations*, trans. G. E. M. Anscombe (New York: Macmillan, 1958), §§ 116, 90–133. It bears remarking that Wittgensteinian emphasis on the profoundly social and contextual constitution of linguistic meaning has shaped some of the most influential work in Anglo-American philosophy of language in recent decades (notably, W. V. Quine, *Word and Object* [Cambridge, Mass.: MIT Press, 1964]; and *Ontological Relativity* [Cambridge, Mass.: Harvard University Press, 1969]; and Donald Davidson, *Inquiries into Truth and Interpretation* [Oxford: Oxford University Press, 1980], and *Subjective, Intersubjective, Objective* [Oxford: Oxford University Press, 2001]). At the same time, Wittgenstein's "grammatical" investigations of key philosophical terms have obvious affinities with "anti-foundationalist" critiques associated with poststructuralism (see, for

example, Rorty's alignment of Wittgenstein with Heidegger, Habermas, and Derrida, among others, in *Philosophy and the Mirror of Nature*, 357–394). However, the demonstration of the necessary contingencies of meaning found in *Philosophical Investigations* unfolds alongside a critique of the drive toward theoretical explanation that might as easily be seen to challenge as to support current methodologies in literary and aesthetic study. For helpful discussions of this topic, see Austin Quigley, "Wittgenstein's Philosophizing and Literary Theorizing," *New Literary History* 19 (1988): 218; Charles Altieri's early essay, "Wittgenstein on Consciousness and Language: A Challenge to Derridean Literary Theory," *Modern Language Notes* 91 (1976): 1397–1423; and the thoughtful introduction by the editors of the collection *Wittgenstein, Theory, and the Arts*, ed. Richard Allen and Malcolm Turvey (New York: Routledge, 2001), 1–35.

38. Stanley Cavell, *Must We Mean What We Say?* (Cambridge: Cambridge University Press, 1976), 239; Wittgenstein, "an outburst of anger" and "resistances of the will": from remarks on philosophical method in the "Big Typescript," *Philosophical Occasions, 1912–1951*, ed. James C. Klagge and Alfred Nordmann (Indianapolis: Hackett, 1993), 161.

Victor Krebs describes Wittgenstein's "concern for the psychological dimension and depth of philosophical illusion," characterizing his method as one of *"empathically* placing oneself in the context where empty thinking acquires the feel of meaningful thinking" ("'Around the axis of our real need': On the Ethical Point of Wittgenstein's Philosophy," *European Journal of Philosophy* 9, no. 3 (2001): 351, 357. Jonathan Lear describes a Wittgensteinian "therapeutic model" of philosophy as "actively reenact[ing] the conflicts which led to the philosophical resolutions," in "On Reflection: The Legacy of Wittgenstein's Later Philosophy," *Ratio* (new series) 2 (June 1989): 44. Such a practice may be contrasted with what has come to be known as the "hermeneutics of suspicion"—not because of a failure to exercise suspicion, but because it compels critical awareness of shared susceptibility to illusion. See also Cavell's characterization of Freud and Wittgenstein as equally "intent upon unmasking the defeat of our real need in the face of self-impositions which we have not assessed, or fantasies which we cannot escape" (*Must We Mean What We Say?* 72). Wittgenstein himself identifies the idea that emotions (love, fear, anger, dread) are constitutive of philosophical beliefs as a psychoanalytic insight (*Philosophical Occasions*, 165); the suggestion that philosophical methods are like "therapies" is made in *Investigations*, § 133.

Although it is tempting to align Wittgenstein's famous assertion that "the thinking subject is surely a mere illusion" with Lacanian deconstruction of the *cogito* as a "grammatical fiction," the perspectives of these thinkers coincide only when the idea of the primacy of language in structuring thought, belief, and subjectivity is taken at the most general level. See Jacques Bouveresse, *Wittgenstein Reads Freud*, trans. Carol Cosman (Princeton, N.J.: Princeton University Press, 1995), 40–41; and Marcia Cavell, *The Psychoanalytic Mind* (Cambridge, Mass.: Harvard University Press, 1995), 5, 113–116, 244.

39. All these terms have to do with setting Wittgensteinian bounds on the reach of philosophical inquiries and investigations, with understanding the import of

statements such as, "We must do away with all explanation" (§ 109); "Philosophy simply puts everything before us, and neither explains nor deduces anything" (§ 126); and "What has to be accepted, the given, is—so one could say—*forms of life*" (II.226). The appeal to "form of life" is often misunderstood as naming the force of convention, but it evokes an almost anthropological view of human practices: "What we are supplying are really remarks on the natural history of human beings . . . observations which no one has doubted, but which have escaped remark only because they are always before our eyes" (§ 415). In the concept of "form of life," the terms *nature* and *culture*, or *nature* and *convention*, are bound up with each other, so much so that one cannot even say that the opposition between them is inoperative—for even to say that much is to imagine that they could be conceptualized apart from each other. On "form of life," see Stanley Cavell, *Claim of Reason* (Oxford: Oxford University Press, 1979), 111; Lear, "On Reflection," 37.

40. Cavell, *Must We Mean What We Say?* 61; Scheman, "Forms of Life: Mapping the Rough Ground," in *Cambridge Companion to Wittgenstein*, ed. Hans Sluga and David Stern (Cambridge: Cambridge University Press, 1996), 405.

41. Jessica Benjamin's cautionary argument against a "falsely totalizing" idea of the self as discursive construct is helpful in thinking through the relationship between fantasy and counter-fantasy. On her view psychoanalytic response to ethical questions must entail conceptions of self and intersubjective relations that will "speak to the concretes—fear, pain, loss." Benjamin worries that while deconstructions of the "language of unity, coherence, identity" normative for both philosophical and psychoanalytic conceptions of the ego properly focus on the "subject as a position of discourse," the "psychological production of self" in and through relationships with "real" others is all too often overlooked, "psychic agency" is eliminated, "motivation, need, and desire" disregarded (*The Shadow of the Other: Intersubjectivity and Gender in Psychoanalysis* [New York: Routledge, 1998], 86–105).

42. Hobbes, *De Cive*, 205. On Hobbes's metaphor as "expung[ing] human reproduction and early nurturance from [the] account of basic human nature," see Di Stefano, *Configurations of Masculinity*, 83–89. Charles Taylor makes a similar point about the obvious counterfactuality of the "atomistic" starting point of natural law theories, arguing that the key methodological innovation of thinkers such as Hobbes and Locke entails separating "normative questions" about individual rights from "adjudicat[ion] by factual considerations" (*Philosophy and the Human Sciences*, 190).

43. Descartes, *Discourse on Method*, 5; Immanuel Kant, "What Is Enlightenment?" in *Kant's Political Writings*, ed. Hans Reiss (Cambridge: Cambridge University Press, 1970), 55.

44. Locke, *Second Treatise*, § 4; *Essay*, 1.1.2 (emphasis added).

45. Sigmund Freud, *Introductory Lectures on Psychoanalysis*, trans. James Strachey (New York: Norton, 1966), 406–407. For further discussion, see Chapter 1. On the epistemological inflections of Freudian anxiety, see Adam Phillips, *Terrors and Experts* (Harvard, Mass.: Harvard University Press, 1995), 53; Marcia Cavell, *The Psychoanalytic Mind*, 228; and Lear, *Love and Its Place in Nature*, 107.

46. Insofar as a psychoanalytic conception of the subject typically begins (and is typically distinguished from a standard philosophical conception) by a powerful reimagination of the originary dependence of the human being, the works at the center of this book share (indeed anticipate) that fundamental insight. And, as is the case in much psychoanalytic theory, the acknowledgment of constitutive dependence is neither liberating nor comforting—but nor is it the basis for a static view of the individual as, for example, doomed to anxieties and uncertainties the generating conditions of which can never be removed, or driven by a desire that can never be met. A Lacanian model (or the Kojevian-Hegelian model so influential on Lacan) stakes its concept of the individual in the realization of a lack that might be seen, in terms of this book, to correspond to the unsentimental recognition of the individual's constitutive vulnerability to loss, betrayal, deception, and bereavement. However, that realization is but a *moment* in the works examined here; not forgotten, and certainly liable to repetition, the pang of lack is nevertheless not a fixation. And it is precisely in fixing, in generalizing as "law," the difference between individual need, demand, and desire that psychoanalysis crosses the threshold to metaphysics. Thus, for example, Judith Butler's compelling account of the self as formed in dependencies and attachments that must also be denied is arrested by the concept of repetition, where the "posture of the adult subject" consists precisely in its being "condemned to reenact" its earliest formation (*The Psychic Life of Power* [Stanford: Stanford University Press, 1997], 6–10). See Anthony Cascardi's interesting discussion of the "slippage from an analysis of subjectivity to a theory of inescapable subjection" in Lacanian theory (*The Subject of Modernity* [Cambridge: Cambridge University Press, 1992], 236–239), and Benjamin's related critique (specifically addressed to Butler) of a "regulatory counterideal" that "reifies" the split subject, allowing for no acknowledgment of "*ongoing* intrapsychic process" (102–103).

47. Anthony Ashley Cooper, third earl of Shaftesbury, *Characteristics of Men, Manners, Opinions, Times*, 3 vols. (1711; Hildsheim/New York: George Olms Verlag, 1978), 2:308–309.

48. "The original of all great and lasting societies consisted . . . in the mutual fear [men] had of each other" (Hobbes, *De Cive*, 113). On fear (rather than pure aggression or selfishness) as the psychological foundation of Hobbes's moral theory, see Schneewind, *Invention of Autonomy*, 84–91. See also Alan Ryan's argument that Hobbesian individuals are "essentially *anxious*" in "Hobbes' Political Philosophy," in *The Cambridge Companion to Hobbes*, ed. Tom Sorell (Cambridge: Cambridge University Press, 1996), 219.

49. Compare Hobbes's "the characters of man's heart blotted and confounded . . . with dissembling, lying, counterfeiting" with Rousseau's expansions, in the *Second Discourse*, on the idea that "to be and to appear became two different things": "Let us therefore look through our frivolous displays of beneficence to what goes on in the recesses of men's heart," the "deceitful cunning" and "secret jealousy" lurking under the "mask of benevolence" (*Discourse on the Origins of Inequality among Men*, in *The First and Second Discourses and Essay on the Origins of Languages*, trans. Victor Gourevitch [New York: Harper and Row, 1986], 208, 180–181).

50. Rousseau, *Discourse*, 182. For Hobbes, "the dominion of reason, peace, security, riches, decency, society, elegancy, sciences, and benevolence" is to be found in civil society, "out of it, there is the dominion of passions, war, fear, poverty, slovenliness, solitude, barbarism, ignorance, cruelty" (*De Cive*, 222).

51. Though I focus, for the purposes of this book, on his early writings, later works of Rousseau (*Social Contract, Emile, Nouvelle Héloïse*) may be seen to proceed where the *Second Discourse* leaves off: the acknowledged necessity of social dependence and the dangerous corruption of social life generating utopian fantasies of how society might be rearranged to reconstitute human beings in a way that would obviate anxieties by eliminating both the possibility and the necessity for deception. For further discussion, see Chapter 2.

1. Locke's Loneliness

1. John Locke, *An Essay concerning Human Understanding*, ed. Peter H. Nidditch (Oxford: Clarendon, 1975), 2.1.8. All quotations from the *Essay* are drawn from this edition, based on the fourth edition of 1700. Hereafter, quotations from the *Essay* are cited parenthetically in the text by book, chapter, and section number.

2. Derek Parfit, *Reasons and Persons* (Oxford: Oxford University Press, 1984), 205–208; Annette Baier, *Moral Prejudices: Essays on Ethics* (Cambridge, Mass.: Harvard University Press, 1995), 315–325. On Locke and contemporary views of "personal identity," see Michael Ayers, *Locke: Epistemology and Ontology*, 2 vols. (London: Routledge, 1991), 2:281–287. Ayers observes that "emphasis on the pure subject of thought as something at least conceptually distinct from the bodily self" is a cornerstone of "neo-Lockean theories of personhood" (2:287). It is precisely the disembodiment of the reasoning subject that feminist philosophers such as Baier criticize.

3. Alasdair MacIntyre, *After Virtue* (Notre Dame: University of Notre Dame Press, 1981), 33; Cathy Caruth, *Empirical Truths and Critical Fictions: Locke, Wordsworth, Kant, Freud* (Baltimore: Johns Hopkins University Press, 1991), 5. Caruth's work is evidently indebted to Paul de Man, see especially "The Epistemology of Metaphor," *Critical Inquiry* 5 (1978): 13–30. But, in response to the "deconstructive turn," it is worth keeping in mind William Walker's discussion of how attention to rhetoric has always been a "standard component of traditional 'philosophical' readings" of the *Essay* (*Locke, Literary Criticism, and Philosophy* [Cambridge: Cambridge University Press, 1994], 15–16).

4. John Richetti, *Philosophical Writing: Locke, Berkeley, Hume* (Cambridge, Mass.: Harvard University Press, 1983), 101–104; Richard Popkin, *The High Road to Pyrrhonism* (San Diego: Austin Hill, 1980), 63; Peter Nidditch, Foreword to *An Essay concerning Human Understanding* by John Locke, xxi; S. H. Clark, " 'The Whole Internal World His Own': Locke and Metaphor Reconsidered," *Journal of the History of Ideas* 59 (1998): 250.

5. The argument that classic empiricist theories such as Locke's "consistently bypass the epistemic significance of early experience with other persons" has been

forcefully made by a number of feminist thinkers. See especially Lorraine Code, *What Can She Know? Feminist Theory and the Construction of Knowledge* (Ithaca, N.Y.: Cornell University Press, 1991), 129, 110–144.

6. *Some Thoughts concerning Education* was first published in 1693, three years after the first edition of the *Essay* and, like the *Essay*, it was revised for subsequent publications, the final being the fifth edition of 1705. For the genesis of *Thoughts* in correspondence with Edward Clarke on the education of his son, and for a textual history of the book, see the introduction to *The Educational Writings of John Locke*, ed. James L. Axtell (Cambridge: Cambridge University Press, 1968), 3–17.

The relation between *Thoughts* and the *Essay* is vexed, and not only because of apparently superficial contradictions between the works (on, for example, the efficacy of association of ideas). John Yolton warns against "draw[ing] piecemeal connections between the two works," but his assertion that "the developmental psychology implicit in the *Essay*" is an "important, even foundational link" between them inevitably raises questions about the consistency of the account of "idea genesis" in both texts. More recently Alex Neill argues that the emphasis on influence and habit formation in *Thoughts* and on "epistemic autonomy" in the *Essay* constitutes "an important philosophical tension which threatens the overall coherence of Locke's account of education" (John Yolton, *John Locke and Education* [New York: Random House, 1971], 14). Alex Neill, "Locke on Habituation, Autonomy, and Education," *Journal of the History of Philosophy* 27, no. 2 (1989): 225.

7. Locke, *Some Thoughts concerning Education* and *Of the Conduct of the Understanding*, ed. Ruth Grant and Nathan Tarcov (Indianapolis: Hackett, 1996), § 115. Further citations from this edition are given parenthetically in the text.

8. "Tant de raisonneurs ayant fait le roman de l'âme, un sage est venu, qui en a fait modestement l'histoire"; "Il prend un enfant au moment de sa naissance; il suit pas à pas le progrès de son entendement" (Voltaire, "Sur M. Locke," *Lettres philosophiques* [1733; Paris: Garnier, 1964], 83–84]; *Letters on England*, trans. Leonard Tancock [New York: Penguin, 1980], 63–64). On the influence of Locke's "genetic" approach to philosophy of mind, pedagogy, and politics on French thinkers, in particular, see Hans Aarsleff, *From Locke to Saussure* (Minneapolis: University of Minnesota Press, 1982), 158–163.

9. Immanuel Kant, *Critique of Pure Reason*, trans. Norman Kemp Smith (1781; New York: St. Martin's, 1965), 8 and 122, respectively.

10. Jean-Jacques Rousseau, *Discourse on the Origins of Inequality among Men in the First and Second Discourses and Essay on the Origins of Languages*, trans. Victor Gourevitch (New York: Harper and Row, 1986), 143. See Chapter 3 for further discussion of the response to Locke in this text.

11. W. B. Carnochan, *Confinement and Flight: An Essay on English Literature of the Eighteenth Century* (Oxford: Oxford University Press, 1973), 15.

12. Richetti (*Philosophical Writing*, 61) and Caruth (*Empirical Truths and Critical Fictions*, 34) also read a highly personalized kind of case history within the impersonal form of Locke's philosophical argument. For both, the underlying narrative is not at odds with its empirical arguments but is inseparable from them, and this

is the case as well for the traces of the story I find about forgetting and yet not being able to forget the role of others in shaping the mind.

13. In both works influence is described as literally modifying the machinery of the mind. In *Education*, the fearful ideas "sink deep, and fasten themselves so as not easily, if ever, to be got out again" (§ 138; see also § 115). In the *Essay*, false ideas and superstitions "insinuated" into the young mind are "fastened by degrees" and "riveted there by long Custom and Education beyond all possibility of being pull'd out again" (4.20.9).

14. Sigmund Freud, *Three Essays on the Theory of Sexuality*, trans. James Strachey (New York: Avon, 1965), 127, 129; *Introductory Lectures on Psychoanalysis*, trans. James Strachey (New York: Norton, 1965), 407; *Inhibitions, Symptoms and Anxiety*, trans. Alix Strachey (New York: Norton, 1959), 66.

Contemporary psychoanalytic representations of others as "introjected" objects in the psyche bear a family resemblance to Locke's occluded representation of others as "phantasmic" presences within the individual mind, begging the question: to what extent do some forms of psychoanalytic theory share Locke's conceptualization of a private, immured experiential realm—even those that hold a relational view of the self? See Marcia Cavell, *The Psychoanalytic Mind* (Harvard, Mass.: Harvard University Press, 1995), 14; and Jessica Benjamin, *Like Subjects, Love Objects* (New Haven: Yale University Press, 1995), 28.

15. Attention to modulations and manipulations of affective response is central to the project of early education proposed in *Some Thoughts concerning Education*. See (in addition to § 9 on the "great principle" of love and fear) § 56 on the "pleasure of esteem" as a "great secret of education"; § 59 on the use of caresses and coldness; § 97 on fostering "love and esteem" by shows of "confidence and kindness."

16. According to Caruth, what Locke calls a "wrong and unnatural" combination of ideas can be as intransigent as a "natural" association because it seems right to the thinker, and thus "illness is not just the committing of error, but the unalterable experience of error as truth" (*Empirical Truths and Critical Fictions*, 29). This is true of one type of error Locke describes ("Education, custom, and the constant din of party" join certain ideas together so as to "captivate reason" and leave men unable to "see the falsehood of what they embrace for real truth" [2.33.18]), but the misconstrual of falsehood for truth does not seem to lie at the heart of those painfully troubling associations created by the emotions.

17. Discussion of passion in Locke has generally been limited to the well-known arguments about the will in book 2, section 21, "Of Power," and thus subordinated to analysis of Locke's arguments about motivation and their place among traditional philosophical treatments of weak will. Passion there plays the classic role of foil to rational judgment. Even within the context of the discussion in "Of Power," however, implicit shifts in Locke's view of the agent produce radically different characterizations of the relation between passion and will. Most familiarly, the workings of passion are represented as moving or compelling the agent as if from outside himself, neutralizing the will altogether (e.g., as "when the Ball obeys the stroke of a Billiard-stick, it is not any action of the Ball, but bare passion"; or as

when "a boisterous Passion hurries our Thoughts, as a Hurricane does our Bodies" [2.21.4, 12]). Elsewhere, however, particularly when Locke specifies the affective content of passion, its force appears as an extraordinary concentration of the will: "The ungovernable passion of a Man violently in love; or the impatient desire of revenge, keeps the *will* steady and intent; and the *will* thus determined, never lets the Understanding lay by the object, but all the thoughts of the Mind . . . are uninterruptedly employ'd that way" (2.21.38). I am primarily interested in how this latter characterization of passion can be seen to *coincide* with the workings of philosophical reflection. Common to both is the double sense of drivenness—a determination that is also compulsion.

Useful discussions of the will in Locke include Ayers, *Locke: Epistemology and Ontology*, 2:192–195; Vere Chappell, "Locke on the Freedom of the Will," in *Locke's Philosophy: Content and Context*, ed. G. A. J. Rogers (Oxford: Oxford University Press, 1994), 101–121; and John Colman, *John Locke's Moral Philosophy* (Edinburgh: Edinburgh University Press, 1983), 206–234. On the interplay between rational judgment, desire, and uneasiness in the *Essay*, see Jonathan Kramnick, "Locke's Desire," *Yale Journal of Criticism* 12, no. 2 (1999): 189–208.

18. David Hume, *A Treatise of Human Nature* (New York: Penguin, 1969), 315. Hereafter, page numbers from this edition are cited parenthetically in the text.

19. In the context of our discussion thus far, Hume's division between consideration of the "understanding" in book 1 and of the "passions" in book 2 distinguishes domains left fruitfully intermingled and obscure in Locke. For example, Hume's important innovation on Locke's arguments about motivation ("Of Power," 2.21) is to virtually eliminate the conflict between reason and passion by deriving moral inclination *from* the passions ("Morals excite passions, and produce or prevent actions," writes Hume, "Reason of itself is utterly impotent in this particular. The rules of morality, therefore, are not conclusions of our reason" [509]).

Adam Potkay offers a related reading of the stark alternatives Hume establishes at the end of book 1. Observing that "the inward turn of mind leads to states of solitude that are insupportable . . . to positions that are logically untenable," Potkay goes on to show how the dark meditations with which book 1 concludes "have no consequences in the following books," which are concerned with the "self in its passional, social, and ethical dimensions" (Adam Potkay, *The Passion for Happiness: Samuel Johnson and David Hume* [Ithaca, N.Y.: Cornell University Press, 2000], 52–53, 55). On the relationship between book 1, "Of the Understanding," and books 2 and 3, "Of the Passions" and "Of Morals," see Baier, *Moral Prejudices*, 78–79; and Donald Livingston, *Hume's Philosophy of Common Life* (Chicago: University of Chicago Press, 1984), 9–59.

20. An excess of similes illustrate the same point in Locke's first chapter. Just as our hands are not "big enough to grasp every thing," so the understanding "comes exceeding short of the vast Extent of Things"; yet despair is inappropriate because "if we will disbelieve every thing, because we cannot certainly know all things; we shall do much-what as wisely as he, who would not use his Legs, but sit still and perish, because he had no Wings to fly." We can and *ought* to seek to

improve our knowledge in spite of its limitations: "It will be no Excuse to an idle and untoward Servant, who would not attend his Business by Candlelight, to plead that he had not broad Sunshine. The Candle that is set up in us shines bright enough" (1.1.5).

21 Ayers, for example, sees that the tensions within Locke's argument on essences might generate *both* the "phenomenalistic or reductive empiricism" (with which Locke is still most frequently associated) *and* a Berkeleian or Kantian "conceptualism" (*Locke: Epistemology and Ontology*, 2:10–11). For a reading of the *Essay* as moving irresistibly toward idealism, see Clark, " 'The Whole Internal World His Own,' " 262–265.

22. In intimating that experience of the world would be fundamentally different if we had other senses, this example is not unrelated to what came to be known as "Molyneux's problem" in the eighteenth century. The well-known question of whether a blind man whose sight were suddenly restored would be able to judge that a flat circle is, in fact, a round globe touches on the complex problem of how immediate sensation itself is modified by judgment and experience, how the mind effectively *alters appearances*. Locke's answer to this question is that "Ideas we receive by sensation, are often in grown People, alter'd by Judgment," meaning that what we "see" is an amalgam of visual impression and judgment informed by experience (2.9.8). The Molyneux problem is later taken up by Leibniz in *Nouveaux Essais*, by Berkeley in *An Essay towards a New Theory of Vision*, by Diderot in *Lettre sur les aveugles*, and by Condillac in both the *Traité sur les connaissances humaines* and the *Traité des sensations*.

23. On the concepts of "substance," "essence," and "accident" in Locke, see especially Ayers, *Locke: Epistemology and Ontology*, 2:15–50. On Locke's use of "corpuscularianism," see Peter Alexander, *Ideas, Qualities, and Corpuscles: Locke and Boyle on the External World* (Cambridge: Cambridge University Press, 1985), 60–91, 117–130; and Lisa Downing, "Are Corpuscles Unobservable in Principle for Locke?" *Journal of the History of Philosophy* 30, no. 1 (1992): 33–52.

24. See Wittgenstein's investigation of the acts of interpretation and imagination implicit in the "reading" of facial expression, and of their difference from other kinds of "seeing" (*Philosophical Investigations*, trans. G. E. M. Anscombe [New York: Macmillan, 1958], 209–210). On the human face as locus for the imbrication of ethics and epistemology (from a phenomenological perspective), see Emmanuel Levinas, *Totality and Infinity*, trans. Alphonso Lingis (1961; Pittsburgh: Dusquesne University Press, 1969), 187–193.

25. Immanuel Kant, *Foundations of the Metaphysics of Morals*, trans. Lewis White Beck (New York: Macmillan, 1985), 5. But, on Kant's struggle to keep the anthropological and metaphysical domains of his investigation separate, see David Clark's provocative discussion, "Kant's Aliens: The *Anthropology* and Its Others," *New Centennial Review* 1 (2001): 206–209.

Locke's identification of the child along with the changeling as equally subject to law under the definition of man as "corporeal rational being" also stands in unresolved contradiction with the definition of full personhood that Locke proposes in the *Second Treatise*—a text precisely concerned with the constitution of legal subjects. (See, for example, §§ 60–63, on the exclusion of "idiots"—i.e., changelings—and children from the right to self-governance.) Recently attempting to align the *Essay*'s differing conceptions of the human by proposing a "continuum from man in a physical sense, to man as rational, to moral man," John Yolton is nevertheless led to Locke's own conclusion that "we only have the appearances to work with" in shaping an idea of man ("Locke's Man," *Journal of the History of Ideas* 62 (2001): 674, 677. See also Ruth Mattern, "Moral Science and Persons in Locke," in Chappell, *Locke*, 261–278.

26. See also the examples of the talking parrot at 2.27.8 and Balaam's ass at 3.6.29.

27. Cf. Stanley Cavell's related thought experiment exploring the suspicion that "something humanoid or anthropomorphic lacks something; that one could have all the characteristics of a human being *save one*." Imagining a robot that not only looks just like a human being but that has "for all the world, the insides of a human being" does not do away with the suspicion of a hidden non-human-ness but shifts attention away from the idea that it might be resolved by "looking inside" (*The Claim of Reason* [Oxford: Oxford University Press, 1979], 404–407). On the body as literalized figuration of intersubjective impenetrability, see ibid., 368.

28. On Hobbesian fear, see Bernard Gert, "Hobbes' Psychology," in *The Cambridge Companion to Hobbes*, ed. Tom Sorell (Cambridge: Cambridge University Press, 1996), 157–175; and, in the same collection, Alan Ryan, "Hobbes' Political Philosophy," 208–245. The mind's inability to penetrate "inside" other bodies and recognize others places the epistemic experience analyzed in the *Essay* in relation to the "fears and continual dangers" to which natural man is exposed in the *Second Treatise*.

29. The notion that language makes social life possible is a claim consistent with and relevant to Locke's political theory. Cf. the *Second Treatise* § 77, and *Essays on the Law of Nature*: "[man] feels himself . . . urged to enter into society by a certain propensity of nature, and to be prepared for the maintenance of society by the gift of speech and through the intercourse of language" (*Essays on the Law of Nature*, ed. W. von Leydon [Oxford: Clarendon, 1954], 157).

30. See, for example, the contrast drawn between the view of language "inherited from Locke," where there is "an immediate connection, in each *individual* speaker's mind or brain, between word and idea" and an alternative view that "agreement in judgments [among speakers in a given community] . . . is what makes any language possible" (Naomi Scheman, "Forms of Life: Mapping the Rough Ground," in *The Cambridge Companion to Wittgenstein*, ed. Hans Sluga and David Stern [Cambridge: Cambridge University Press, 1996], 400).

31. Jonathan Bennett, *Locke, Berkeley, Hume: Central Themes* (Oxford: Clarendon, 1971), 27. Here the *Essay* follows Hobbes's reasoning that the imperfections of language are necessarily owing to variation and dissimilarity in perceptions: "Though the nature of that we conceive, be the same; yet the diversity of our reception of it, in respect of different constitutions of body . . . gives everything a tincture of our different passions" (*Leviathan*, ed. C. B. Macpherson [New York: Penguin, 1981],

109). Although the topic of Hobbes's influence on Locke is vexed, Hobbes's discussion "Of Speech" in *Leviathan* is generally recognized as a significant precedent; see especially Paul Guyer, "Locke's Philosophy of Language," in *The Cambridge Companion to John Locke*, ed. Vere Chappell (Cambridge: Cambridge University Press, 1994), 115–145.

32. Guyer, "Locke's Philosophy of Language," 120.

33. "If we ask whether our ideas are qualitatively similar to [others], the answer is: 'Perhaps not, and in any case it does not matter' so long as speakers use words consistently" (E. J. Ashworth, "Locke on Language," in *John Locke: Critical Assessments*, ed. Richard Ashcraft, 4 vols. [New York: Routledge, 1991], 2:250).

34. Richetti, *Philosophical Writing*, 93. See also Guyer, "Locke's Philosophy of Language," 120–121.

35. John Locke, *Two Treatises of Government*, ed. Peter Laslett (Cambridge: Cambridge University Press, 1960), 283; *Second Treatise*, § 22. Further quotations from this edition are cited parenthetically by section number.

36. On the seventeenth-century context of this discussion—in particular, Locke's argument against the "Adamic doctrine"—see Aarsleff, *From Locke to Saussure*, 42–83.

37. Locke frequently evokes a sense of being *physically* suited to inhabit the world ("the all-wise Architect has suited our Organs, and the Bodies, that are to affect them, one to another") alongside and as if conceptually akin to claims that we are well-*equipped* for our "business" in this world ("the infinite wise Contriver of us... hath fitted our Senses, Faculties, and Organs, to the conveniences of Life, and the Business we have to do here"). Both these forms of suitability are contrasted to a "perfect, clear, and adequate Knowledge" of the world, which Locke assumes "would be inconsistent with our Being" (3.23.12). Subsumed by this contrast to an unimaginable, perhaps undesirable, omniscience is the difference between being instrumentally fit for commerce with the world and organically suited to the world—a difference that is all the more crucial to consider if we think of ourselves as inhabiting a *social* world.

38. Cf. Hobbes, *Leviathan*: "A man must take heed of words, which besides the signification of what we imagine of their nature, have a signification also of the nature, disposition, and interest of the speaker; such as are the names of Vertues and Vices; for one man calleth Wisedome what another calleth fere, and one cruelty, what another justice" (109).

39. Ibid.

40. Marquis de Sade, *Justine, Philosophy in the Bedroom, and Other Writings*, trans. Richard Seaver and Austryn Wainhouse (New York: Grove, 1965), 283.

41. Dolmancé further reasons that if a "tie of brotherhood and the virtues it enjoins" existed, then "men would be aware of them at birth"; given that they are not, neither affection nor obligation to others can be derived from the facts of parental care (ibid., 284; see also 253). In his introductory essay to this edition of Sade, Maurice Blanchot describes Sadean "morality [as] based upon the primary fact of absolute solitude.... Nature wills that we are born alone, there is no real

contact or relationship possible between one person and another" (40). See also Claude Lefort, "Sade: The Boudoir and the City," *South Atlantic Quarterly* 95 (1996): 1009–1028.

42. Thomas Hobbes, *De Cive*, in *Man and Citizen (De Homine and De Cive)*, ed. Bernard Gert (Indianapolis: Hackett, 1991), 205.

43. Anthony Ashley Cooper, third earl of Shaftesbury, "The Moralists: A Philosophical Rhapsody," in *Characteristics of Men, Manners, Opinions, Times*, 3 vols. (1711; Hildsheim/New York: Georg Olms Verlag, 1978), 2:308–309. See also Shaftesbury's explicit criticism of Hobbes for presenting "the *Rough-Draft* of Man . . . a Kind as yet *unform'd* not in its *natural State*" (2:313).

44. From, respectively, Adam Ferguson, *An Essay on the History of Civil Society*, ed. Fani Oz-Salzberger (1767; Cambridge: Cambridge University Press, 1995), 21–22; and idem, *Principles of Moral and Political Societies*, 2 vols. (Edinburgh: A. Strahan and T. Cadell, 1792), 1:24. On Hume, Hutcheson, Ferguson, and other enlightenment proponents of the "priority of the social," see David Carrithers, "The Enlightenment Science of Society," in *Inventing Human Science: Eighteenth-Century Domains*, ed. Christopher Fox, Roy Porter, and Robert Wokler (Berkeley: University of California Press, 1995), 232–270.

45. Hume, *Treatise*, 544. See also pages 537–538 and Hume's evocation of the "length and feebleness of human infancy" to argue that "there must be an union of male and female for the education of the young" (621). Hobbes is explicitly addressed in the *Enquiry concerning the Principles of Morals*, where Hume insists, "Men are necessarily born in a family-society at least" (§3).

46. Shaftesbury, *The Moralists*, 2:308–309. See also Francis Hutcheson's complaint that "many of our moralists, after Mr. Hobbs . . . never talk of any kind instincts to associate; of natural affections, of compassion, of love of company, a sense of gratitude . . . which yet all may be observed to prevail exceedingly in humane life" ("Reflections on the Common Systems of Morality" [1724] in *On Human Nature*, ed. Thomas Mautner [Cambridge: Cambridge University Press, 1993], 100). See also Hutcheson, *An Essay on the Nature and the Conduct of the Passions and Affections* (1728; Gainesville: Scholar's Facsimiles and Reprints, 1969), 201. On the split between adherents of Hobbes's view of fundamentally self-interested creatures and those who developed a countervailing view of a sympathetic and sociable human being, see J. B. Schneewind, *The Invention of Autonomy* (Cambridge: Cambridge University Press, 1998), 295–310 (on Shaftesbury); and 333–353 (on Hutcheson and Butler).

47. David Hume, *An Enquiry concerning the Principles of Morals* (Indianapolis: Hackett, 1983), 24–25; see also idem, *Treatise*, 544–546.

48. Hume concedes that "there is no such passion in human minds, as the love of mankind, merely as such," because "man in general, or human nature" is too abstract an object to arouse passion. He proceeds to argue, however, that any individual—indeed, any *creature*—immediately present will arouse sympathy. "There is no human, and indeed no sensible, creature, whose happiness or misery does not, in some measure, affect us when brought near to us"—a response Hume holds to offer "no proof of . . . an universal affection to mankind" but which he uses as

evidence of the more ambitious claim that sympathy "extends itself beyond our own species" (533).

49. Hume designates sympathy a "natural virtue" but refrains from representing it in the naturalizing terms used by others. Shaftesbury, for example, habitually equates the impulses of affection with a physiological process: "If *Eating and Drinking* be natural, *Herding* is so too. If any *Appetite or Sense* be natural, the *Sense of Fellowship* is the same" (*Sensus Communis* in *Characteristics*, 1:110); affection "is as *proper and natural* to [man] as it is to any Organ, Part or Member of an Animal-Body, or mere Vegetable, to work in its own course.... 'Tis not more *natural* for the Stomach to digest, the Lungs to breathe" (*An Inquiry concerning Virtue and Merit*, in *Characteristics*, 2:78). By comparison, Hume's figures for the operations of sympathy (the mirror, the "strings equally wound up") are insistently artificial. This is not to say, however, that Hume's descriptions belie his insistence on the natural-ness of sympathy. The *Treatise* itself instructs its readers on the different conceptual deployments of the term *natural*, particularly in the analysis of virtues and vices (524–527). Under different definitions it is possible to assert that moral sentiments are both natural and unnatural ("in the first sense of the word... both vice and virtue are equally natural; and in the second sense... virtue will be found to be the most unnatural"), leading Hume to conclude that "'Tis impossible... that the character of natural and unnatural can ever, in any sense, mark the boundaries of vice and virtue" (526–527).

50. Sade, *Justine, Philosophy in the Bedroom, and Other Writings*, 284; see also 354. Sade's reasoning that "it is far less for our sake than for their own" that parents raise children follows Hobbes's explanation of the mother's self-interested nurture of a child in the state of nature. Nothing obliges a woman to care for her offspring ("she may rightly, and at her own will, either breed him up or adventure him to fortune"); her choice to parent the child is conditional and implicitly contractual: "If therefore she breed him, because the state of nature is the state of war, she is supposed to bring him up on this condition; that being grown to full age he become not her enemy" (*De Cive*, 212). Locke, by way of contrast, is led to invoke God's "great design" to ground the mutual obligations binding parents and children: "as [God] hath laid on them an obligation to nourish, preserve, and bring up their Offspring; So he has laid on the Children a perpetual Obligation of *honouring their parents*, which containing in it an inward esteem and reverence to be shewn by all outward Expressions, ties up the Child from any thing that may ever injure or affront" his parents (*Second Treatise*, § 66).

51. Sade, *Justine, Philosophy in the Bedroom, and Other Writings*, 340, 342.

52. Hume, *Treatise*, 402. It bears emphasis that the company of others is not only an "entertainment" or pleasure but also an absolute necessity for human beings as Hume imagines them. "We can form no wish which has not a reference to society," he famously writes, "A perfect solitude is, perhaps, the greatest punishment we can suffer.... Let all the powers and elements of nature conspire to serve and obey one man: Let the sun rise and set at his command: The sea and rivers roll as he pleases. ... He will still be miserable, till you give him some one person at least, with whom he may share his happiness" (412).

2. Rousseau's Autonomous Beast

1. Cora Diamond, "The Importance of Being Human," in *Human Beings*, ed. David Cockburn, *Royal Institute of Philosophy Supplement: 29* (Cambridge: Cambridge University Press, 1991), 47. On the way that conceptions of human/animal difference may be seen to underlie ethical expectations and appeals, see Cora Diamond, "Eating Meat and Eating People," in *The Realistic Spirit: Wittgenstein, Philosophy, and the Mind* (Cambridge, Mass.: MIT Press, 1991), 319–334.

2. For a philosophical and historical overview of the many conceptual "differentia" between human beings and animals, as well as the theoretical assumptions behind them, see Mary Midgely, *Beast and Man* (1979; London: Routledge, 1995). On the use of "animals, or rather cultural constructions of them" as metaphors for aspects of human social and moral conduct, see Richard Tapper, "Animality, Humanity, Morality, Society," in *What Is an Animal?*, ed. Tim Ingold (New York: Routledge, 1984), 47–62.

3. Durkheim writes, "Il y a longtemps que Rousseau l'a démontré: si l'on retire de l'homme tout ce qui lui vient de la société, il ne reste qu'un être réduit à la sensation, et plus ou moins indistinct de l'animal." "Determination du fait moral," *Bulletin de la Société française de Philosophie* 6 (1906): 132.

4. Jean-Jacques Rousseau, "Discourse on the Origins of Inequality among Men," in *The First and Second Discourses and Essay on the Origin of Languages*, trans. Victor Gourevitch (New York: Harper and Row, 1986), 209. For the sake of readability, most quotations from the *Discourse* will be drawn from this translation, and the original text used only when the French expression is pertinent to the argument. Hereafter page references are cited parenthetically in the text to both the Gourevitch translation and (*in italics*) to the standard edition of the *Discours*, in volume 3 of *Oeuvres complètes de Jean-Jacques Rousseau*, ed. Bernard Gagnebin and Marcel Raymond, 4 vols. (Paris: Gallimard, 1964).

5. Victor Goldschmidt, *Anthropologie et politique: Les principes du système de Rousseau* (Paris: Librairie Philosophique J. Vrin, 1974), 261, my translation ("De plus, l'opposé de l'homme civilisé n'est pas tant l'homme naturel que la condition animale de celui-ci"), and 175–219. See also Victor Gourevitch, "Rousseau's Pure State of Nature," *Interpretation* 16 (1988): 41; and Heinrich Meier, "The Discourse on the Origin and Foundation of Inequality among Men: On the Intention of Rousseau's Most Philosophical Work," *Interpretation* 16 (1988): 220.

6. A. O. Lovejoy was first to argue that the *Discourse* anticipates the theory of human evolution out of a "state of pure animality" in "The Supposed Primitivism of Rousseau," *Essays in the History of Ideas* (New York: George Braziller, 1955). More generally, Lovejoy describes a "temporalizing of the great chain of being" as "one of the principal happenings in eighteenth-century thought" (*The Great Chain of Being* [Cambridge, Mass.: Harvard University Press, 1936], 244). For a review of the critical debate on Rousseau's relation to eighteenth-century evolutionism, see Asher Horowitz, *Rousseau, Nature, and History* (Toronto: University of Toronto Press, 1987), 50–73.

7. Robert Wokler, "Perfectible Apes in Decadent Cultures: Rousseau's Anthropology Revisited," *Daedalus* 107 (1978): 115. See also Wokler, "The Ape Debates in Enlightenment Anthropology," *Studies on Voltaire and the Eighteenth Century* 192 (1980): 1164–1175; Wokler and Christopher Frayling, "From the Orang-utan to the Vampire: Towards an Anthropology of Rousseau," in *Rousseau after Two Hundred Years: Proceedings of the Cambridge Bicentennial Colloquium*, ed. R. A. Leigh (Cambridge: Cambridge University Press, 1982), 109–129; and Wokler, "Anthropology and Conjectural History in the Enlightenment," in *Inventing Human Science: Eighteenth-Century Domains*, ed. Christopher Fox, Roy Porter, and Robert Wokler (Berkeley: University of California Press, 1995), 31–52.

8. For a thorough account of scientific study of and philosophical speculation about primates in the eighteenth century, see Franck Tinland, *L'Homme sauvage: Homo ferus et Homo sylvestris de l'animal à l'homme* (Paris: Payot, 1968), 89–130.

9. Roger D. Masters, "Jean-Jacques Is Alive and Well: Rousseau and Contemporary Sociobiology," *Daedalus* 107 (1978): 97–98, 99.

10. Wokler and Frayling, "From the Orang-utan to the Vampire," 125–126. The objection is made by C. Berry in a printed transcript of discussion following the presented paper. Wokler has more recently repeated the contention that Rousseau's "conjectural history . . . in fact turns out to be a very good piece of empirical primatology . . . [his] portrayal of the solitary, frugivorous, indolent and itinerant creature described in [the *Discourse*] actually accords rather well with the true orangutan of Southeast Asia, and indeed forms one of the best such descriptions available in the West until the fieldwork . . . [of] the late 1960s" (Wokler, "Anthropology and Conjectural History," 43).

11. Frans de Waal, *Good Natured: The Origins of Right and Wrong in Humans and Other Animals* (Cambridge, Mass.: Harvard University Press, 1996), 166–167, 63. The complex uses of anthropomorphism to describe animal behavior, and the attribution (or failure to attribute) states of mind to animals, are lively areas of debate in the fields of philosophy, anthropology, biology, and cognitive psychology. For an introduction to the topic, see Ingold, *What Is an Animal?*

12. The passage quoted from *Histoire générale des voyages*, vol. 5 (1748), on the "Orang-Outang" is drawn from a chapter on animal species found in the Congo based largely on four sources: a French translation of *Purchas, His Pilgrimage*, Dapper's *Description de l'Afrique*, Merolla's *Breve e succinta relatione del viaggio*, and Pigafetta's sixteenth-century *Viaggio attorno il mondo* (1550). The majority of the physical and behavioral details about "orang-outangs" in this section of the *Histoire* derives from a scant page or so from Purchas, now thought to describe a gorilla (see Tinland, *L'Homme sauvage*, 99). For an informative discussion of eighteenth-century texts and illustrations of anthropoids, see Francis Moran, "Between Primates and Primitives: Natural Man as the Missing Link in Rousseau's *Second Discourse*," *Journal of the History of Ideas* (1993): 37–58.

13. The notion that anthropoids must be the satyrs of the ancient world was long-lived, part of what Tinland terms the "halo de représentations les unes vraies, les autres fantaisistes" surrounding these animals in the early modern period. See

Tinland, *L'Homme sauvage*, 30–41, 101–104. Purchas, incidentally, straightforwardly categorized apes as a type of satyr, and the *Histoire*'s account of "orang-outangs" in the Congo (in vol. 5), and of bogos, mandrills, and other anthropoform monkeys found on the Ivory Coast (in vol. 4), not only emphasizes the uncanny mélange of human and animal *physical* features typical of satyrs but also attributes the powerful sexual and aggressive energies symbolized by that mythical creature to (for example) male monkeys who "se saisissent des femmes . . . et les caressent jusqu'à l'excès" (Samuel Purchas, *Purchas, His Pilgrimage* [London, 1626], 623; *Histoire générale des voyages* [Paris, 1748], 4:240).

14. Noting that "Rousseau was most impressed by the extent to which his authorities were agreed about the orangutan's 'human countenance' and its striking 'exact' physical resemblance to man," Wokler takes the purpose of this material to be that of advancing the "hypothesis" that further research would prove these creatures to be men rather than beasts (Wokler, "Rousseau's Anthropology Revisited," 113). Leaving aside the fact that the "authorities" in this case are simply those sources cited in the *Histoire*, it is not clear why Rousseau would have chosen the "orang-outang" to venture this kind of hypothesis when other entries in the *Histoire* (to which Rousseau later alludes) contain descriptions of other monkeys that would more easily accommodate such a hypothesis. The monkeys of the Ivory Coast "approchent beaucoup de la forme humaine, les Nègres sont persuadés que c'est une race d'hommes"; the species called bogos is described as having "véritablement la figure humaine, que dans toute sa grandeur on le prendroit pour un homme de la taille moienne"; one monkey that an officer purchased "avoit une parfaite ressemblance avec un enfant," and another, transported to London and displayed to the public, was much admired for "son visage, sa petite chevelure, & ses parties naturelles, qui ne differoient pas de l'espèce humaine" (*Histoire générale*, 4:239–241). The *Histoire*'s entry on Ivory Coast monkeys is lengthier, more detailed, and insistently anthropomorphizing than its entry on the "orang-outang," and it is mentioned by Rousseau as a further description of what he takes to be the same "species of Anthropomorphic animals" passing under different names. In other words, more and stronger evidence for the notion that these creatures might be a type of human being might easily have made its way into this discussion, but it does not, which indicates that its argumentative direction may lie beyond the intriguing suggestion that observers have confounded men with beasts. See also Rousseau's reply, in the "Letter to Philopolis," to the criticism of the naturalist Charles Bonnet: "That the monkey is a beast, I believe it. . . . you are good enough to inform me that the Orang-outang also is one, but I must admit that *given the facts I cited, that seemed to me to be a difficult fact to prove*. You philosophize too well to settle such questions as lightly as do our travelers" (235, 234; emphasis added).

15. The passage Rousseau cites testifies to a series of notable behavioral resemblances between "orang-outangs" and human beings, including upright posture, their construction of shelters in the trees as a protection from the rain, crude burial practices ("when one of these animals dies, the others cover its body with a heap of branches and boughs"), and legends of their adoption and care of a young Negro child.

16. See, for example, in note 5 of the *Discourse*, the odd blend of evidence on the vegetarianism of natural man where the movement from mundane facticity to fabulism to theoretical claim underscores the malleability of facts and their role in bolstering a conceptual scheme. Rousseau states that the blunt shape of the teeth of human beings is more "like" that of frugivorous animals than of carnivores—an anatomical fact that is itself of dubious significance, since it is easy enough to see that human beings have both flat and pointed teeth. But the note does not offer this fact alone, for "not only do anatomical observations confirm [the] opinion" that man is naturally frugivorous; "the monuments of antiquity" also support the position. The observable physical fact of tooth size is thus supplemented and supported by a quotation from St. Jerome that passes on Dicaearchus's claim that "under the reign of Saturn" the earth was naturally fertile and man ate only fruits. The anatomical fact and the fanciful citation are taken together, on the same evidentiary plane, to support the *idea* of natural man as frugivorous and therefore peaceful: "since prey is almost the only object about which Carnivores fight, and frugivores live in constant peace with one another, it is clear that if the human species were of the latter kind, it could have subsisted much more easily in the state of nature" (204, *199*).

17. Gourevitch translates into English the French translation of Locke as it appears in the *Discourse*. The passage appears in the *Second Treatise of Government*, §§ 79–80.

18. That the status of Rousseau's information about animals is, at the very least, ambiguous, is suggested by the uneven treatment of that information in the meticulous notes to the Pléiade edition. The scholarly apparatus to note 5 (on vegetarianism), for example, traces Rousseau's possible sources to Buffon's *Histoire naturelle*, and to a debate between Wallis and Tyson reprinted in the *Journal Economique* of 1754 but offers no possible sources for the information Rousseau deploys in note 12, leaving unresolved the disagreements of "fact" between Locke and Rousseau in this important discussion of parenting and nurture. Elsewhere in the *Discourse* Rousseau does cite Buffon and others to support claims far less contentious and central to the argument than the claims of note 12; see, for example, note 7 on the relative life spans of animals.

19. A quality operative in "the species as well as in the individual," perfectibility is the capacity to alter oneself for better or for worse in response to circumstance and experience, the condition for the possibility of all intellectual and moral development, that which "causes [man's] enlightenment and his errors, his vices and his virtues" (149, *142*). Rousseau is credited with coining the term *perfectibilité*, which soon came to be commonly used in eighteenth-century social theory and natural history. For careful reconstruction of its earliest usages, see Starobinski's note in the Pléiade edition (3:1317–1319). See also John Passmore, "The Malleability of Man in Eighteenth-century Thought," in *Aspects of the Eighteenth Century*, ed. E. Wasserman (Baltimore: Johns Hopkins University Press, 1965); and *The Perfectibility of Man* (London: Duckworth. 1970). On the role of perfectibility in the *Discourse*, see Victor Goldschmidt's argument that "la majeure partie de l'enquête métaphysique, après avoir indiqué la 'qualité très spécifique' qui distingue l'homme de l'animal, s'emploie à montrer que cette qualité est à peine active et reste en sommeil"

(*Anthropologie et politique*, 274). He further suggests that perfectibility can only come into play in tandem with socialization, that it cannot, in and of itself, motivate the invention of language and the other humanizing faculties (306).

20. For related arguments about the constitutive and humanizing force of dependence in the *Discourse* and in Rousseau's work generally, see N. J. H. Dent, *Rousseau: An Introduction to His Psychological, Social, and Political Theory* (New York: Basil Blackwell, 1988), 30ff.; Guy Besse, *Jean-Jacques Rousseau: L'Apprentissage de l'humanité* (Paris: Messidor/Editions Sociales, 1988), 163ff. For related arguments that focus on the *Discourse*, see especially Gourevitch, "Rousseau's Pure State of Nature"; and Meier, "*The Discourse on the Origin and Foundation of Inequality among Men:* On the Intention of Rousseau's Most Philosophical Work."

Rousseau's insistence on the limitation and stasis of the autonomous individual's understanding—of how little he can realize "by his own strength alone"—bears comparison to Locke's depiction of autonomous intellectual development in the *Essay concerning Human Understanding*—of how much the mind achieves "from powers intrinsical and proper to itself." See chapter 1 for further discussion.

21. Moran, "Between Primates and Primitives," 53.

22. From the article "Homme," in *Questions sur l'Encyclopédie* (1771), cited in Starobinski's notes to the *Discourse* (1375; my translation).

23. According to Hume, "the first and original principle of human society . . . is no other than that natural appetite betwixt the sexes, which unites them together, and preserves their union, till a new tie takes place in their concern for their common offspring" (*A Treatise of Human Nature* [New York: Penguin, 1969], 538). See also Shaftesbury's enumeration of "parental kindness, zeal for posterity, concern for the propagation and nurture of the young" among the "natural affections" implanted in the species in his *Inquiry concerning Virtue or Merit*, in *Characteristics*, 3 vols. (Hildsheim / New York: Georg Olms Verlag, 1978), 2:78. While attention to parental care is understandably central to theorists of natural sociability, it bears emphasizing that even a forceful opponent of Shaftesburian notions of virtuous inclination such as Mandeville is compelled to account for parental nurture. Although he maintains that human beings are not originally social, he finds the origins of social interaction in familial relations: "Natural affection would prompt a wild man to love and cherish his child" (Bernard Mandeville, *The Fable of the Bees or Private Vices, Public Benefits*, ed. Irwin Palmer [New York: Capricorn, 1962], 169, 199, 209–210).

24. The urge to align Rousseau's conjectures with those of contemporary science leads Masters to a decontextualized misrepresentation of this part of the argument. Giving Rousseau credit for "granting the vulnerability of such relatively helpless infants," Masters claims that Rousseau actually "stresses the maternal bond as a means of assuring the survival of the young," adding that "once again, contemporary research on primates reinforced the essential accuracy of Rousseau's insight" ("Jean-Jacques Is Alive and Well," 97). The "maternal bond" in the context of the *Discourse* means no more and no less than the act of not abandoning a newborn infant, but Masters would like to ally the account of infancy in the *Discourse* with current theories linking the prolonged period of gestation and infancy common to

primates with the development of culture (indeed, his sources on this topic all have to do with the "social preconditions of neoteny," or the prolongation of the period of pregnancy and infancy).

25. The "knowledge" of natural man is insistently physical, limited to what the body is capable of learning: "his knowledge is restricted to jumping, running, fighting, throwing a stone, climbing a tree" (205).

26. John Locke, *Two Treatises of Government*, ed. Peter Laslett (Cambridge: Cambridge University Press, 1960), 320 (*Second Treatise*, § 80).

27. Locke's arguments on this point in the two *Treatises* are complicated and somewhat inconsistent. In the *Second Treatise* Locke attributes the birth of affectionate and moral bonds between man, woman, and offspring to a prolonged interaction made necessary not by nature alone but also by divine design. "God having made Man such a Creature, that, in his own Judgment, it was not good for him to be alone" drives him first into "Conjugal Society," the primary end of which is not only procreation but a lasting union (§§ 77–80). Divine design seemingly redresses the ignorance about the ends and consequences of sexual relations and thus supplies natural man with the "foresight and an Ability to lay up for the future" that a solitary creature occasionally moved by mere sexual appetite would lack. Locke himself presents this knowledge as lacking in natural man when he argues against parental "ownership" of children in the *First Treatise:* "What Father of a Thousand, when he begets a Child, thinks farther than the satisfying his present Appetite?" (§ 54). On the contradictions in Locke's account of conjugal and paternal societies in both *Treatises*, see especially Gordon J. Schochet, "The Family and the Origins of the State in Locke's Political Philosophy," in *John Locke: Problems and Perspectives*, ed. John Yolton (Cambridge: Cambridge University Press, 1969), 81–99.

28. I borrow this term from Annette Baier's essay on the occlusion of interdependence in philosophies of mind and morals ("A Naturalist View of Persons," in *Moral Prejudices: Essays on Ethics* [Cambridge, Mass.: Harvard University Press, 1995], 313–326).

29. A. O. Lovejoy was perhaps the first to see a "Darwinian" explanation for the transition from state of nature to society, reading the "*concours fortuit*" of the *Discourse* as a "law of necessary and gradual progress through natural causes." More recently Asher Horowitz describes an interruption in the "static equilibrium" of the species and of Rousseau's recognition of "the activity of natural selection as an agency of organic transformation" (Lovejoy, "The Supposed Primitivism of Rousseau," 23–24; Horowitz, *Rousseau, Nature, and History*, 74).

Other readers struck by the radical contingency of the transition described in the text treat it as a problematic or unsuccessful point in the argument, "the weakest part of Rousseau's system," according to Robert Derathé (*Jean-Jacques Rousseau et la science politique de son temps* [Paris: Presses Universitaires de France, 1950], 19; my translation). More recently Jim Macadam has written that the "two problems with Rousseau's account of the state of nature" are that "there is nothing in it to explain historical development and, nothing to explain human development" ("Rousseau's Criticism of Hobbesian Egoism," in *Trent Rousseau Papers*, ed. Jim Macadam, Michael Neumann, and Guy Lafrance [Ottawa: University of Ottawa Press, 1980],

123); and, according to Jean Terrasse, "the cause of the mutation" from independence to social life "escapes us, its cause, material and contingent, is steeped in mystery" ("La Statue de Glaucus," in *Etudes sur les Discours de Rousseau*, ed. Jean Terrasse [Ottawa: North American Association for the Study of Rousseau, 1988], 70; my translation). Cf. Rousseau's linking of providence and the contingencies of nature in a similar conjectural narrative in the *Essay on the Origin of Languages*: "Human associations are in large measure the work of accidents of nature: local floods, overflowing seas, volcanic eruptions, major earthquakes.... The traditions about natural disasters which were so common in ancient times show what instruments providence used to force humans to come together" (268).

30. *Oeuvres complètes*, 3:1328; my translation of Jean Starobinski's note.

31. Gourevitch, "Rousseau's Pure State of Nature," 54; and Charles Hendel, *Jean-Jacques Rousseau, Moralist* (New York: Bobbs-Merrill, 1934), 51. See also Goldschmidt, who characterizes the argument regarding language as "une nouvelle et dernière aporie, elle aussi de structure circulaire, et qui nous ramène au début même de l'analyse" (*Anthropologie et politique*, 303). In the same interpretive line, Terrasse counts the origin of language as one of a series of *"coupures internes"* in the state of nature ("La Statue de Glaucus," 69), and Jim Macadam proposes that the question the *Discourse* raises is how "a human creature lacking social relations [can be] understood as human at all?" ("Rousseau's Criticism of Hobbesian Egoism," 127).

32. For a discussion of the possible biblical allusions in this passage, see Starobinski's note in *Oeuvres complètes*, 1368; and Gourevitch's note in *The First and Second Discourses*, 353.

33. Rousseau represents this age of the "first developments of the human heart" as the "happiest and longest-lasting epoch" of human history, and in spite of the bleak elements it includes (and not to mention the brevity of Rousseau's account) many readers have viewed this primitive society as the true object of nostalgia in the *Second Discourse*. See, for example, Judith Shklar, *Men and Citizens: A Study of Rousseau's Social Theory* (Cambridge: Cambridge University Press, 1969), 23–29. Anthony Skillen describes this phase more accurately, in my view, as initiating a "dialectics of despair, whereby in the very act of coming together in the fullest desire for community, human beings are impelled into a decline . . . marked by radical self-estrangement and misery" ("Rousseau and the Fall of Social Man," *Philosophy* 60 [1985]: 109).

34. Other readers have not failed to observe that the *Discourse* ends with a Hobbesian vision, though the tendency is to associate the final state of war with Rousseau's arguments about the moral corruption of civilization. See especially Lovejoy, "The Supposed Primitivism of Rousseau," 26–27; Starobinski, Introduction to the *Second Discourse* in *Oeuvres complètes*, 3:lxiv–lxviii; and Derathé, *Rousseau et la science politique de son temps*, 176. My emphasis falls on the epistemic assumptions that lead Hobbes (and Rousseau) to imagine human beings as inevitably and constantly vulnerable to one another.

35. Thomas Hobbes, *Leviathan*, ed. C. B. Macpherson (New York: Penguin, 1981), 82.

36. Jean-Jacques Rousseau, *Emile*, trans. Allan Bloom (New York: Basic Books, 1979), 226, 319; *Oeuvres completes*, 4:511, 4:642. Hereafter page numbers from both these editions are cited parenthetically in the text.

37. The conceptual equivalence between privacy and particularity in Rousseau's writings, and the need to drastically restrict the particular in creation of an ideal social order, is most evident in the *Social Contract*. The "social bond begins to grow slack . . . when private interests begin to make themselves felt," he writes there. As in the *Second Discourse*, the corrosive effect of the conflict between individual interests is imagined as a proliferation of deceit and dissimulation ("everyone [is] guided by secret motives")—a cleavage between being and appearance that makes it possible for "the meanest interest [to] brazenly flaunt the sacred name of the public good" (*On Social Contract* in *Rousseau's Political Writings*, trans. Julia Conaway Bondanella [New York: Norton, 1988], 149; *Oeuvres complètes*, 3:438).

38. Jean-Jacques Rousseau, *La Nouvelle Héloïse*, in *Oeuvres complètes*, 2:424; my translation. *Letter to M. D'Alembert on the Theatre*, trans. Allan Bloom (Ithaca, N.Y.: Cornell University Press, 1960), 59; and *Lettre à d'Alembert sur les spectacles*, ed. Léon Fontaine (Paris: Garnier, 1889), 182. Subsequent references to these editions are cited parenthetically in the text.

That both Clarens and the small villages described in the *Letter to d'Alembert* are communities in which conformity and participation are assured by the constant mutual surveillance of its own members will inevitably strike many as related to the social world that Foucault describes in (especially) *Discipline and Punish*. My interest here lies not in the various practices of control Rousseau takes no pains to conceal—indeed, indulgently and delightedly describes—but rather in the epistemological problem of intersubjectivity that drives the representation of these social arrangements as *utopian* rather than dystopian.

39. Closely related to the dependable predictability instilled in Emile is the extreme conformity prevailing in the communities of Emile-like beings described in the *Letter to d'Alembert*, whose "hearts are in their eyes as they are always on their lips." In the *Social Contract*, this same predictability is present in the idea of "moral habit" (*moeurs*), which Rousseau calls the "unshakable keystone" and "most important kind of law" (118, 394). For an excellent discussion of moral habit and public festivals in Rousseau's middle works, see Jean Starobinski, *Transparency and Obstruction*, trans. Arthur Goldhammer (Chicago: University of Chicago Press, 1988), 92–111. Even a reader eager, as James Miller is, to maintain that individuals lead "autonomous" and "independent" lives in Rousseau's utopian communities concedes the central role of homogeneity; each citizen "has relations only with those like himself" (*Rousseau: Dreamer of Democracy* [New Haven: Yale University Press, 1984], 46).

40. Jean-Jacques Rousseau, *Emile et Sophie, ou Les Solitaires*, in *Oeuvres complètes*, 4:890; my translation. In all of Rousseau's middle works (as well as in part 2 of the *Discourse on Inequality*), the family is seen as the "oldest" form of social organization, its legitimacy based on the marital bond between two individuals, the "purity" of which is of special concern to Rousseau. His emphasis on female chastity is most often seen as exemplary of what Carole Pateman has described as a patriarchal

"sexual contract." In the terms of our discussion, the implications Rousseau draws from sexual difference can also be related to his effort to curtail epistemic uncertainty. The moral habits he prescribes for women are designed to spare men from what he describes, in *Emile*, as the "most frightful condition in the world": that of the "unhappy father who, lacking confidence in his wife ... doubts, in embracing his child, whether he is embracing another's" (361, 698). The ideal wife, as Rousseau imagines her, internalizes not only the moral imperative to *be* faithful to her husband but also what may be called the epistemological imperative of being *apparently* faithful, an object of her husband's confidence: "What is thought of her is no less important than what she actually is" (361, 698). On sexual difference in Rousseau's social thought, see Carole Pateman, *The Sexual Contract* (Stanford: Stanford University Press, 1988), 96–102.

41. Insofar as Rousseau's imagination of the ideal marriage takes as its aim the transformation of one partner into a reliable object of knowledge for the other, it attempts and fails to transform love into a form of security. Mary Wollstonecraft's critique of *Emile* in the *Vindication of the Rights of Woman* is based precisely on the poverty of the fantasy of substituting an epistemic quality (confidence, certitude) for the ethical substance of relationship. As I argue elsewhere, this incisive criticism is of a piece with her sympathetic diagnosis of Rousseau as tormented by suspicion. See Nancy Yousef, "Wollstonecraft, Rousseau, and the Revision of Romantic Subjectivity," *Studies in Romanticism* 38 (1999): 538–541. On Rousseauvian marriage as an effort to secure the other as an object, see also Skillen, "Rousseau and the Fall of Social Man," 112.

3. Natural Man in the Wild

1. The details of Victor's "capture" (in Lacaune, in the south of France), as well as letters and documents concerning his discovery, are to be found in Thierry Gineste, *Victor de l'Aveyron: Dernier enfant sauvage, premier enfant fou* (Paris: Hachette, 1993), 20–25, 113–131, and Harlan Lane, *The Wild Boy of Aveyron* (Cambridge, Mass.: Harvard University Press, 1979), 3–29. Hereafter references to these two works are cited parenthetically in the text with G (Gineste) or L (Lane) and the relevant page numbers. See also Roger Shattuck, *The Forbidden Experiment: The Story of the Wild Boy of Aveyron* (New York: Farrar, Straus and Giroux, 1980).

2. Carl von Linné (Linnaeus), *Systemae naturae*, 13th ed. (Leipzig, 1788), 1:21. On Linnaeus's sources, see Lucien Malson, *Wolf Children and the Problem of Human Nature*, trans. Edmund Fawcett, Peter Ayrton, and Joan White (London: NLB, 1972), 38–42. Hereafter references to this work are cited parenthetically in the text with M (Malson) and the relevant page number. The most useful study of *Homo ferus* in European intellectual history (from medieval myth to enlightenment scientific and anthropological writing) remains Franck Tinland, *L'Homme sauvage: Homo ferus et Homo sylvestris, de l'animal à l'homme* (Paris: Payot, 1968). On Linnaeus, Buffon, and classification of the human species in eighteenth-century scientific discourse, see Phillip Sloan, "The Gaze of Natural History," in *Inventing Human Science: Eighteenth-*

Century Domains, ed. Christopher Fox, Roy Porter, and Robert Wokler (Berkeley: University of California Press, 1995), 112–152. On the eighteenth-century fascination with feral children, see Julia Douthwaite, "*Homo ferus:* Between Monster and Model," *Eighteenth-Century Life* 20 (1997): 176–202; and *The Wild Girl, Natural Man, and the Monster: Dangerous Experiments in the Age of Enlightenment* (Chicago: University of Chicago Press, 2002), 11–69.

3. Roch-Ambroise Sicard (Abbé), *Comte-rendu de l'abbé Sicard dans la Gazette de France (9 Aout 1800)*, reproduced in its entirety in Gineste, *Victor de l'Aveyron*, 142–144; quoted and translated in Lane, *The Wild Boy of Aveyron*, 18.

4. Jean-Marc-Gaspard Itard, *De l'éducation d'un homme sauvage ou des premiers développements physiques et moraux de jeune sauvage de l'Aveyron* (Paris: Gouyon, 1801); quoted in Malson, *Wolf Children*, 93. The behavior Itard describes is consistent with that observed by others who had access to the boy in the months after his "discovery," making him a more credible source than Sicard. The entirety of Itard's report is reprinted in Gineste, *Victor de l'Aveyron*, 279–325, and, in English translation, in Malson, *Wolf Children*, 91–140.

5. Louis-Constant Wairy, *Mémoires sur la vie privée de Napoléon, sa famille et sa cour*, 3 vols. (Paris: Ladvocat, 1830), 48–58; extracted in Gineste, *Victor de l'Aveyron*, 331–333; quoted in translation in Lane, *The Wild Boy of Aveyron*, 108–109. Wairey recounts a society dinner party hosted in Victor's honor and attended by powerful politicians and generals, famous artists, and intellectuals. Characteristically Victor was more "occupied with the abundant things to eat, which he devoured with startling greed" than with the company around him. Later in the evening the boy was found in the garden, half-naked, perched in the branches of a chestnut tree, "leaving the guests . . . to draw a sweeping and useful comparison between the perfection of civilized life and the distressing picture of nature untamed, which this scene had so strikingly contrasted."

6. Jean-Jacques Rousseau, "Discourse on the Origins of Inequality among Men," in *The First and Second Discourses and Essay on the Origins of Languages*, trans. Victor Gourevitch (New York: Harper and Row, 1986), 213. For the sake of readability, quotations from the *Discourse* will be drawn from this translation. Hereafter page references are cited parenthetically in the text to both the Gourevitch translation and (*in italics*) to the standard edition of the *Discours*, in volume 3 of *Oeuvres complètes de Jean-Jacques Rousseau*, ed. Bernard Gagnebin and Marcel Raymond, 4 vols. (Paris: Gallimard, 1964).

Rousseau's remarks anticipate reactions to the *Discourse* such as that of Voltaire: "On n'a jamais tant employé d'esprit à vouloir nous rendre bêtes. Il prend envie de marcher à quatre pattes quand on lit votre ouvrage" (letter to Rousseau, 30 August 1755; reprinted in the notes to the *Discourse*, in *Oeuvres complètes*, 3:1379).

7. Pierre-Joseph Bonnaterre, *Notice historique sur le sauvage de l'Aveyron et sur quelques autres individus qu'on a trouvé dans les forêts à différentes époques* (Paris: Panckoucke, 1800); reprinted in Gineste, *Victor de l'Aveyron*, 180–211, and translated and reproduced in its entirety in Lane, *The Wild Boy of Aveyron*, 33–48. Julien-Joseph Virey, *Dissertation sur un jeune enfant trouvé dans les forets du département de l'Aveyron, avec des remarques sur l'état primitif de l'homme*, in *Histoire naturelle du genre*

humain, 2 vols. (Paris: F. Dufart, 1800), 2:289–350; reprinted in Gineste, *Victor de l'Aveyron*, 225–248. Parts of the *Dissertation* are incorporated into the translation of Bonnaterre's *Notice* reproduced in Lane, *The Wild Boy of Aveyron*. When not otherwise identified, quotations in English from Virey's and Bonnaterre's reports are from Lane, *The Wild Boy of Aveyron*.

8. See chapter 2 above.

9. Irreversible inability to learn language, cognitive retardation, impairment in the capacity to interact with others similar to that seen in cases of autism, inability to smile or recognize mirror reflection—these are some of the characteristics common both to feral children and to so-called closet children imprisoned within their own homes by abusive or disturbed parents. See Malson, *Wolf Children*, 10. The case of a young Californian child known as "Genie" (discovered in 1970) offers a remarkable twentieth-century parallel to that of Victor. Although Victor was isolated in a forest and Genie was confined to a small room, they presented virtually the same array of emotional, cognitive, and even motor disabilities. See Russ Rymer, *Genie: A Scientific Tragedy* (New York: Harper, 1993), 52–78.

10. All three scientists also point to the remarkable insensitivity to heat and cold that the boy exhibited, interpreting it as a likely adaptation to the extremes of cold and heat he would have endured unclothed and unsheltered. Itard, for example, observes that he could pick up live coals that tumbled off a fire "with the most perfect indifference," and that, semi-nude and barefoot, he could take pleasure in running and rolling around in new-fallen snow (G, 293; M, 104–105).

11. See also Virey's judgment that the scar on Victor's throat "annonce qu'on a voulu le tuer" (G, 232).

12. Victor's real origins remained a mystery. Two fathers who lost children during violent disturbances related to the Revolution traveled to Rodez in early 1800, but neither claimed the boy as his own (L, 17). On Rousseau's treatment of infancy in the state of nature, see chapter 2 above.

13. Itard's conjecture is strikingly consistent with what has come to be known as the "critical period hypothesis" of language acquisition (see Eric Lenneberg, *Biological Foundations of Language* [New York: Wiley, 1967], 127–142). Even in adults, prolonged periods of solitary confinement result in degradation of linguistic capacity. Bonnaterre cites the famous example of the Scottish mariner Selkirk (model for Defoe's Robinson Crusoe), abandoned on the island of Juan Fernandez in 1709 and, when rescued four years later, reported to have "forgot" his language for lack of use (G, 202; L, 38). Rousseau also alludes to the case in his *Essay on the Origin of Languages*, in which he notes: "Isolated individuals living on desert islands have been known to forget their own language" (264).

14. Virey persistently returns to this theme: "Let him be shown the heavens, the green fields, the works of Nature," he writes. "He does not see anything in all that if there is nothing there to eat; and there you have the sole route by which external objects penetrate his consciousness. It is astonishing how thoroughly this one idea absorbs him completely; he is always looking for something to eat and he eats a lot" (G, 242; L, 39).

15. Like Virey, Bonnaterre also observed: "His affections are as limited as his knowledge; he loves no one; he is attached to no one; and if he shows some preference for his caretaker, it is an expression of need and not the sentiment of gratitude; he follows the man because the latter is concerned with satisfying his needs" (L, 39).

16. *Rapport fait à s.e. le Ministre de l'Intérieure sur les nouveaux développements et l'état actuel du sauvage de l'Aveyron* (Paris: Imprimerie impériale, 1807), in Malson, *Wolf Children*, 168. The entire report is reprinted in Malson, *Wolf Children*, 149–179.

17. Uta Frith, *Autism: Explaining the Enigma* (Oxford: Basil Blackwell, 1989), 16–24; see also 24–26, for the debate over etiology. On "mind-blindness," see Simon Baron-Cohen, *Mindblindness: An Essay on Autism and Theory of Mind* (Cambridge: MIT Press, 1995).

18. For detailed discussion of Itard's efforts to instruct Victor in the use of language, see Lane, *The Wild Boy of Aveyron*, 133–182.

19. On Pinel's report, see Lane, *The Wild Boy of Aveyron*, 57–69; and Douthwaite, *The Wild Girl, Natural Man, and the Monster*, 59–60.

20. Claude Lévi-Strauss, *Les Structures élémentaires de la parenté* (Paris: Presses Universitaires de France, 1949), 3–4; quoted in Tinland, *L'Homme sauvage*, 79. Maurice Merleau-Ponty, quoted in Malson, *Wolf Children*, 56. Contemporary scholars of the literature on feral children tend to agree that the ability of these children to survive in the wild suggests a resourcefulness and acumen inconsistent with severe mental retardation. See Robert M. Zingg, "Feral Man and Extreme Cases of Isolation," *American Journal of Psychology* 53, no. 4 (1940): 487–517; and Arnold Gesell, *Wolf Child and Human Child* (New York: Harper & Brothers, 1941), 67–86. For the debate on etiology as it bears on Victor's case in particular, see Lane, *The Wild Boy of Aveyron*, 174–179.

21. Lévi-Strauss, quoted in Tinland, *L'Homme sauvage*, 79.

22. Lord Monboddo (James Burnett), *Antient Metaphysics* (London, 1784), 3.2.1.

23. For Locke's image of the "mind as a dark room," see *An Essay concerning Human Understanding* (2.11.17) and my discussion in chapter 1 above. E. B. Condillac's statue rendered gradually sentient is the subject of his *Traité des Sensations* (1754).

24. E. B. Condillac, *Treatise on the Sensations*, in *Philosophical Writings of Etienne Bonnot, Abbé de Condillac*, trans. Franklin Philip, with the collaboration of Harlan Lane (Hillsdale, N.J.: Erlbaum, 1982), 330–331. Condillac is especially relevant in this context because Itard openly acknowledges his debt to the philosopher's theories in formulating an approach to Victor's education (G, 323; M, 143). It is precisely this passage regarding the developmental consequences of prolonged preoccupation with survival that appears as the opening epigraph of Itard's first report: "Quand on dit que cet enfant ne donnait aucun signe de raison, ce n'est pas qu'il ne raissonât suffisamment pour veiller à sa conservation; mais c'est que la réflexion, jusqu'alors appliquée à ce seul objet, n'avait point eu occasion de ce porter sur ceux dont nous nous occupons" (G, 303).

25. Douthwaite views Condillac's narrative of the statue as typical of a genre of thought experiment designed to "elid[e] the barriers between fiction and reality";

the "social isolation" of the figure is but one feature of the "theatricality" and "abstraction" marring the experiment. Douthwaite's generally helpful discussion of the interpenetration of speculative fiction and fact in scientific and philosophical writings of the eighteenth century is flawed, however, in presenting a theorist of natural sociability such as Adam Ferguson as engaged in the same kind of work as a thinker such as Condillac (each taking "similar liberties in their treatment of evidence") (*The Wild Girl, Natural Man, and the Monster*, 73–78, 82–86). The status of myth, hearsay, conjecture, and fiction in scientific discourse is certainly an important and underexplored topic in eighteenth-century studies, but focus on formal and rhetorical methods should illuminate rather than cast into shadow the radically opposed positions about human origins that shaped debate in the period. See, for example, David Carrithers's account of the split between "methodological individualism" and a proto- "sociological" starting point in enlightenment theories of human nature—an account that pays special attention to explicit anxieties about the status of evidence, conjecture, and fiction in scientific writing ("The Enlightenment Science of Society," in *Inventing Human Science*, 232–270). See also Mary Poovey's study of the use of evidence by Scottish natural historians (*A History of the Modern Fact: Problems of Knowledge in the Sciences of Wealth and Society* [Chicago: University of Chicago Press, 1998], 220–223).

4. "Unfathered Vapour"

1. On Wordsworth and enlightenment thought, see Alan Bewell, *Wordsworth and the Enlightenment: Nature, Man, and Society in the Experimental Poetry* (New Haven: Yale University Press, 1989); and Alan Grob, *The Philosophic Mind: A Study of Wordsworth's Poetry and Thought, 1797–1805* (Columbus: Ohio State University Press, 1973). The concluding chapters of Basil Willey's *The Seventeenth-Century Background* and *The Eighteenth-Century Background* ("Wordsworth and the Locke Tradition" and "'Nature' in Wordsworth," respectively) are still useful introductions to the topic.

2. William Wordsworth, *The Prelude, 1799, 1805, 1850*, ed. Jonathan Wordsworth, M. H. Abrams, and Stephen Gill (New York: Norton, 1979). Unless otherwise specified, all citations from this edition are drawn from the 1805 version of the poem and are cited parenthetically in the text with the relevant book and line numbers from the poem.

3. Francis Jeffrey, "The Prelude," *Eclectic Review* 28 (November 1850): 556.

4. Anon., "The Prelude," *Graham's Magazine* 37 (1850): 323.

5. A. C. Bradley's "English Poetry and German Philosophy in the Age of Wordsworth" contains the most influential (if not the earliest) account of Wordsworth's poetry "as an imaginative expression of the same mind which, in his day, produced in Germany great philosophies" (A. C. Bradley, *Oxford Lectures on Poetry*, 2d ed. [London: Macmillan, 1909], 105–138). The correspondence between *The Prelude* and German metaphysics is perhaps most forcefully elaborated by M. H. Abrams, who, nevertheless, also relies on the historical coincidence of the

poem and the philosophy to establish the connection between them. The "affinities" and "likeness" Bradley observes become, in Abrams's work, "a comprehensive intellectual tendency" of the age (M. H. Abrams, *Natural Supernaturalism: Tradition and Revolution in Romantic Literature* [New York: Norton, 1971], 11, 90–93, 236, 280–284). Both critics also note that Wordsworth and Hegel coincidentally share the same year of birth, Abrams adding that Wordsworth completed the 1805 *Prelude* just one year before Hegel completed the *Phenomenology of Mind*.

6. Abrams, *Natural Supernaturalism*, 91.

7. Bradley, *Oxford Lectures on Poetry*, 122; Abrams, *Natural Supernaturalism*, 286; and Geoffrey Hartman, "A Poet's Progress: Wordsworth and the *Via Naturaliter Negativa*," *Modern Philology* 59 (1962): 220.

8. Jeffrey, "The Prelude," 551; Abrams, *Natural Supernaturalism*, 92, 77.

9. David Masson, "The Prelude," *British Quarterly Review* 12 (1850): 577. Similarly *The Examiner*'s reviewer complained that Wordsworth "lives alone in a world of mountains, streams, and atmospheric phenomena . . . rarely encountered by even shadowy specters of beings outwardly resembling himself" (*The Examiner*, no. 2217 (July 1850): 478. Although this is an exaggeration, in reviewing the "characters" presented in this eerily unpopulated poem, it is nevertheless clear that strangers (such as the discharged soldier, the blind beggar, the fallen woman, the "hunger-bitten girl") figure more prominently than family; emblematic types (the solitary shepherd, the Arab horseman, the boy of Winander) are more fully realized than friends of childhood and youth; and the fictional lovers Vaudracour and Julia render the poet's silence about his own loves and longings all the more apparent.

10. On traumatic loss in the poem, see Richard J. Onorato's still influential account, *The Character of the Poet: Wordsworth in "The Prelude"* (Princeton, N.J.: Princeton University Press 1971). See also James A. W. Heffernan, "The Presence of the Absent Mother in Wordsworth's *Prelude*," *Studies in Romanticism* 27 (Summer 1988): 253–272. For sophisticated interpretations combining psychoanalytic concerns and a deconstructive approach, see Thomas Weiskel, *The Romantic Sublime: Studies in the Structure and Psychology of Transcendence* (Baltimore: Johns Hopkins University Press, 1976); Frances Ferguson, *Wordsworth: Language as Counter-Spirit* (New Haven, Conn.: Yale University Press, 1977); and Cathy Caruth, *Empirical Truths and Critical Fictions: Locke, Wordsworth, Kant, Freud* (Baltimore: Johns Hopkins University Press, 1991). On guilt and repression in *The Prelude* (particularly concerning Wordsworth's abandonment of Annette Vallon), see Gayatri Spivak, "Sex and History in *The Prelude*," *Texas Studies in Literature and Language* 23 (1981): 324–360; and W. J. T. Mitchell, "Influence, Autobiography, and Literary History: Rousseau's *Confessions* and Wordsworth's *Prelude*," *ELH* 57 (1990): 643–664.

11. Susan Wolfson, *The Questioning Presence* (Ithaca, N.Y.: Cornell University Press, 1986) 166; for an effective challenge to Abrams's interpretation of *The Prelude* as "spiritual autobiography," see also 138–139. William Galperin makes a related argument about the contradictions that necessarily complicate the poem's "'humanistic' or 'progressive' argument," in his *Return of the Visible in British Romanticism* (Baltimore: Johns Hopkins University Press, 1993), 103–111, 128.

12. Hartman, "A Poet's Progress," 220; and Ferguson, *Wordsworth: Language as Counter-Spirit*, 149.

13. Abrams, *Natural Supernaturalism*, 119. The claim is part of a broader argument that in the final books of the poem the imagination "plays a role equivalent to that of [Milton's] Redeemer," and that the conclusion of *The Prelude* offers a kind of "theodicy" (an identification that is, in turn, part of the effort to align Wordsworth's project with Hegel's *Phenomenology of Spirit*). Compare the related argument that "to justify evil by placing it in a larger conceptual overview is not to annul it" (443–445) and Bradley's earlier characterization of Wordsworth's "optimism" as a recognition of human power to "win glory out of agony" (131–133).

14. David Ferry, *The Limits of Mortality* (Middletown, Conn.: Wesleyan University Press, 1959), 173. Ferry's still bracing indictment of Wordsworth's social "antipathy," abstract perspective on human life ("it is only when men are least men that they are most man"), "withdrawal," and "quiescence" may be placed in a critical tradition that extends back to Hazlitt ("It is as if there were nothing but himself and the universe") and also anticipates Marxist and new historicist arguments emphasizing Wordsworth's political "apostasy" (E. P. Thompson) and his "selective and enabling blindness" to social and historical reality (Marjorie Levinson) (William Hazlitt, "Character of Mr. Wordsworth's New Poem, *The Excursion*," *The Examiner* 21 (August 1814); E. P. Thompson, *The Making of the English Working Class* (New York: Vintage, 1963), 175; and Marjorie Levinson, *Wordsworth's Great Period Poems* (New York: Cambridge University Press, 1986), 44. See also Marilyn Butler, *Romantics, Rebels, and Reactionaries* (Oxford: Oxford University Press, 1981), 39–69; and James K. Chandler, *Wordsworth's Second Nature: A Study of the Poetry and Politics* (Chicago: University of Chicago Press, 1984).

15. Geoffrey Hartman, *Wordsworth's Poetry, 1787–1814* (New Haven, Conn.: Yale University Press, 1964), 209–210; Abrams, *Natural Supernaturalism*, 92, 281.

16. Onorato, *Character of the Poet*, 111. See also Heffernan's argument that Wordsworth's memory of "the fairest of all rivers ... blend[ing] his murmurs with my nurse's song" (1:273–275) is a re-creation of intimate union with his mother: "To speak of his mother directly [in the opening book of the poem] would only be to signify her absence. He can intimate her remembered presence more subtly and powerfully by recalling her surrogates, the nurse and the stream" ("The Presence of the Absent Mother," 258).

17. Barbara Schapiro, *Literature and the Relational Self* (New York: New York University Press, 1994), 31. Inspired by "relational models" of psychological development, Schapiro's argument that *The Prelude* presents an "intersubjective, profoundly social view of mental development" requires that nature be seen not as on object but as the "m/other." However, in making no distinction between relationship *with* persons and *to* inanimate nature, the distinction between an "intersubjective" dynamic and a "subject/object dynamic" is lost.

18. A related *apparent* contrast between "natural" and "scientific" representations is to be found in book 5's juxtaposition of the "infant prodigy" (immersed in

books) and the boy of Winander (educated by nature). Galperin argues that the two figures are, in fact, counterparts in his reading of the insistently deliberate contradictions the poem presents (*The Return of the Visible*, 103–111). On the infant prodigy, see also Adam Potkay, "A Satire on Myself," *Nineteenth-Century Literature* 49 (1994): 149–166.

19. Heffernan, "The Presence of the Absent Mother," 255. Heffernan admits that "it is probably impossible to prove that the passage refers to the death of Wordsworth's mother," but his own argument, like so many others that attempt to establish a maternal presence in *The Prelude*, inclines him to "believe it does" (255). Heffernan is not alone in making the assumption that the indeterminate "trouble" of mind in book 2 refers to the death of the poet's mother. For example, Margaret Homans's influential argument that "language and culture depend on the death or absence of the mother and on the quest for substitutes of her" is introduced and illustrated by a reading of the "trouble" as both the death of Wordsworth's mother and the "acquisition of language" (Margaret Homans, *Bearing the Word: Language and Female Experience in Nineteenth-Century Women's Writing* (Chicago: University of Chicago Press, 1986), 3–5. And prior to Homans, Frances Ferguson proposed that "book 2 links the death of the poet's mother to the trauma of the poet's birth into language and the visible world" (*Wordsworth: Language as Counter-Spirit*, 138). The question here concerns the degree to which larger arguments rely on this instance of evidence. My own interpretation of *The Prelude* is indebted to Ferguson's argument that Wordsworth presents his readers with a subjectivity evolved "from a passion which it could not choose or avoid" (150), but what it means to arrive at similar conclusions from different paths is another matter.

20. The intellectual-historical context is worth reviewing. Newton's discovery of the law of universal gravitation was an inaugural event, so compelling in its explanatory force as to offer an inspiring model not only for natural scientists but also for philosophers pursuing many lines of inquiry in the human sciences—hence Hume's express aspiration to become a kind of "Newton of the moral sciences" by applying "experimental philosophy to moral subjects" (as he states in the introduction to the *Treatise of Human Nature*, 1739–1740) and endeavoring (in his *Enquiry concerning the Principles of Morals*, 1751) to follow "Newton's chief rule of philosophizing" (*Enquiry*, §3). Earlier the moral philosopher Francis Hutcheson compared the "universal benevolence" moving all individuals to "that principle of *gravitation*, which perhaps extends to all bodies" (*An Inquiry into the Original of Our Ideas of Beauty and Virtue*, 1725; 2.5.2). Kant also employed a Newtonian idiom in his writing and lecturing on ethics (as in, for example, the *Metaphysics of Morals*: "We consider ourselves in a moral world, where by analogy with the physical world, *attraction* and *repulsion* bind together rational beings").

On Newton as a "cultural symbol" for enlightenment thinkers, see Francis Haskell, "The Apotheosis of Newton in Art," *Past and Present in Art and Taste* (New Haven, Conn.: Yale University Press, 1987), 1–15; and Simon Schaffer, "Natural Philosophy," in *The Ferment of Knowledge*, ed. G. S. Rousseau and Roy Porter (Cambridge: Cambridge University Press, 1980). See also the three chapters on gravitation, optics, and infinity that Voltaire devotes to Newton in his *Lettres philosophiques*.

Wordsworth, it is worth recalling, had been well educated in mathematics and science at Hawkshead. In his biography of the poet, Stephen Gill notes that "firsthand acquaintance with Newton's *Principia* and *Optiks* and with Euclidean mathematics seem to have carried Wordsworth . . . into an imaginative response to the beauty revealed by Newtonian physics" (*William Wordsworth: A Life* [Oxford: Oxford University Press, 1990], 28).

21. Hartman, *Wordsworth's Poetry*, 219. On the "visionary power" as perception of a "transcendental reality," see also Abrams, *Natural Supernaturalism*, 91–92; and Herbert Lindenberger, *On Wordsworth's Prelude* (Princeton, N.J.: Princeton University Press, 1963), 71.

22. Jean-Jacques Rousseau, *Reveries of the Solitary Walker*, trans. Charles E. Butterworth (1778; New York: Harper, 1979), 69, 1; *Les Rêveries du promeneur solitaire*, in *Oeuvres complètes de Jean-Jacques Rousseau*, ed. Bernard Gagnebin and Marcel Raymond, 4 vols. (Paris: Gallimard, 1959), 1:1047, 995.

23. René Descartes, *Meditations on First Philosophy*, trans. Donald A. Cress (1641; Indianapolis: Hackett, 1980), 60; idem, *Discours de la méthode et Méditations* (Paris: Garnier, 1960), 125. Jane Worthington Smyser long ago established the presence of Descartes in *The Prelude*, tracing the source of book 5's dream of the Arab horseman (racing to spare Euclid's *Elements* and a volume of poetry) to a dream recorded by Descartes ("Wordsworth's Dream of Poetry and Science," *PMLA* 71 [1956]: 269–275). Also relevant here are Wordsworth's recollections of solipsistic experiences in early childhood (see note 24 below).

24. In the Fenwick note to the "Ode: Intimations of Immortality," Wordsworth recalls: "I was often unable to think of external things as having external existence, and I communed with all that I saw as something not apart from, but inherent in my own immaterial nature. Many times, while going to school have I grasped at a wall or tree to recall myself from this abyss of idealism to the reality" (quoted in Wordsworth, *Selected Poems and Prefaces*, ed. Jack Stillinger [Boston: Houghton Mifflin, 1965], 537).

25. Wolfson's exposition of the "texture of contrary tendencies" running through *The Prelude*, and thus admitting into it "fears of vain hopes . . . awful irresolution and self-doubt" (*The Questioning Presence*, 165–166), is one among several sophisticated recent analyses of Wordsworth's rhetorical complexity. See, for example, Brooke Hopkins's view of the poem as presenting the "past recaptured in a certain form of ironic self-reflexivity," in "Wordsworth's Voices: Ideology and Self-Critique in *The Prelude*," *Studies in Romanticism* 33 (1994): 279–299. See also Don H. Bialostosky's studies of the dialogics of Wordsworth's poetry in *Making Tales: The Poetics of Wordsworth's Narrative Experiments* (Chicago: University of Chicago Press, 1984); and idem, *Wordsworth, Dialogics, and the Practice of Criticism* (Cambridge: Cambridge University Press, 1992). Also see Galperin, *Return of the Visible*, 99–128. In crediting Wordsworth with varying degrees of ironic insight into his own blindness, these readers develop and complicate the work of Paul de Man, especially *Blindness and Insight* (Minneapolis: University of Minnesota Press, 1983).

26. Rousseau's direct "influence" on Wordsworth remains a puzzle for interpretation. For a recent compelling treatment of the problem, see W. J. T. Mitchell's argument that, even though the "coordination of literary and psychological issues with political ones" makes "Rousseau the exemplary figure of English Romanticism's most thorough repression," he nevertheless remained a "monumental cultural presence" for the English Romantics ("Influence, Autobiography, and Literary History," 651–652). See also Jacques Voisine, *J.-J. Rousseau en Angleterre à l'époque romantique* (Paris: Didier, 1956), 202–222; and Henri Roddier, *J.-J. Rousseau en Angleterre au XVIIIe siècle* (Paris, n.d.), 99–104.

5. Fantastic Form

1. Mary Shelley, *Frankenstein, or the Modern Prometheus*, ed. M. K. Joseph (1831; Oxford: Oxford University Press, 1969), 24. Subsequent references to this edition are cited parenthetically in the text. I follow Shelley's 1831 edition, but see also James Reiger's edition of the 1818 text, with the revisions of 1823 and 1831 (Chicago: University of Chicago Press, 1982). The focus of this essay—the creature's autobiography—is, in any case, among the least revised sections of the novel.

2. Ellen Moers, "Female Gothic," in *The Endurance of Frankenstein*, ed. George Levine and U. C. Knoepflmacher (Berkeley: University of California Press, 1979), 77–87; Mary Jacobus, "Is There a Woman in This Text?" *New Literary History* 14, no. 1 (1982): 117–141; Margaret Homans, *Bearing the Word: Language and Female Experience in Nineteenth-Century Women's Writing* (Chicago: University of Chicago Press, 1986), 100–119.

3. Feminist approaches to the autonomous subject in philosophy that are of particular relevance to this discussion include Annette Baier, "A Naturalist View of Persons," in *Moral Prejudices: Essays on Ethics* (Cambridge, Mass.: Harvard University Press, 1994), 313–326; Seyla Benhabib, "The Generalized and Concrete Other: The Kohlberg-Gilligan Controversy and Moral Theory," in the important collection *Women and Moral Theory*, ed. Eva Feder Kittay and Diana T. Meyers (Totowa, N.J.: Rowman and Littlefield, 1987), 154–177; and Lorraine Code, *What Can She Know? Feminist Theory and the Construction of Knowledge* (Ithaca, N.Y.: Cornell University Press, 1991), 71–172.

4. Etienne Bonnot, abbé de Condillac, *Treatise on Sensations* (1754), in *Philosophical Writings of Condillac*, trans. Franklin Philip, with the collaboration of Harlan Lane (Hillsdale, N.J.: Erlbaum, 1982), 155–156.

5. An important, early, and still useful essay on the sources of *Frankenstein* is Burton R. Pollin, "Philosophical and Literary Sources of *Frankenstein*," *Comparative Literature* 17 (1965): 97–108. Among other works that identify enlightenment philosophy as source material unproblematically incorporated into the narrative are Christopher Small, *Mary Shelley's 'Frankenstein': Tracing the Myth* (Pittsburgh: University of Pittsburgh Press, 1973); and Peter Brooks, "Godlike Science/Unhallowed Arts," in *The Endurance of Frankenstein*, 208–209. In an important recent essay, Lawrence Lipking observes that the creature's autodidactic acquisition of human

faculties has rarely been regarded as a fantastic element of the fiction ("*Frankenstein, the True Story; or, Rousseau Judges Jean-Jacques,*" in Mary Shelley, *Frankenstein*, ed. J. Paul Hunter [New York: Norton, 1996], 313–331).

6. John Locke, *An Essay concerning Human Understanding*, ed. Peter Nidditch (Oxford: Clarendon, 1975), 2.1.6. Subsequent references to book, chapter, and section numbers of the *Essay* are given parenthetically in the text. The *Essay* appears on Mary Shelley's reading list in November and December 1816 and in January 1817 (*The Journals of Mary Shelley, 1814–1844*, ed. Paula R. Feldman and Diana Scott-Kilvert [Baltimore: Johns Hopkins University Press, 1987], 1:146–153; see also Pollin, "Philosophical and Literary Sources of *Frankenstein*," 107).

7. William Wordsworth, *The Prelude, 1799, 1805, 1850*, ed. Jonathan Wordsworth, M. H. Abrams, and Stephen Gill (New York: Norton, 1979), 2:229; citation drawn from the 1805 version of the poem.

8. Condillac, *Treatise on Sensations*, 158; Baier, "A Naturalist View of Persons," 323; Benhabib, "The Generalized and Concrete Other," 162.

9. Compare Condillac: "A baby learns only because he feels the need to instruct himself.... The knowledge a baby has of his *wet nurse or of anything else* only amounts to a knowledge of sensory qualities" (*Treatise on Sensations*, 348; emphasis added). According to Lorraine Code, such an amalgamation of persons and things is typical of how a certain form of empiricist inquiry "bypasses the epistemic significance of early experience with other people" (*What Can She Know?* 129). See chapter 1 for further discussion of the occlusion of human influence on the early development of the mind in Locke's *Essay*.

10. Jean-Jacques Rousseau, *The First and Second Discourses and Essay on the Origin of Languages*, trans. Victor Gourevitch (New York: Harper, 1990), 141–142. Subsequent references are cited parenthetically in the text. The presence of Rousseau's *Discourse* in Shelley's novel has not escaped critical notice. The clear allusion to the earlier work's image of natural man "trouvant son lit au pied du même arbre qui lui a fourni son repas" appears first in Jean de Palacio, *Mary Shelley dans son oeuvre: Contribution aux études shelleyennes* (Paris: Editions Klincksieck, 1969), 210. See also Paul Cantor, *Creature and Creator: Myth-Making and English Romanticism* (Cambridge: Cambridge University Press, 1984), 103–132. David Marshall's bibliography of scholarship on Rousseau and Mary Shelley is especially useful (*The Surprising Effects of Sympathy: Marivaux, Diderot, Rousseau, and Mary Shelley* [Chicago: University of Chicago Press, 1988], 265–266). The significance of Rousseau's works generally in Mary Shelley's intellectual formation is well established in scholarship by Burton Pollin, James O'Rourke, and Alan Richardson, as well as in those studies listed above. In addition to reading Rousseau's works, Shelley also would have been exposed to interpretations of his ideas in writings by her parents. Mary Wollstonecraft's engagement with Rousseau is evinced by his presence in both of her *Vindications*, in her reviews for the *Analytical*, and in her autobiographical *Letters from Sweden*. He is of principal importance to Godwin and is frequently cited in Godwin's *Enquiry concerning Political Justice*. Rousseau is also a powerful presence in Percy Shelley's poetry and prose.

11. Mary Shelley, "Rousseau," in *Lives of the Most Eminent Literary and Scientific Men of France* (London: Longman, 1839), 2:134. Mary Wollstonecraft, *Vindication of the Rights of Woman* (1792; New York: Penguin, 1975), 93–94.

12. Shelley, "Rousseau," 134. Shelley returns to this theme later in the essay, insisting that although "[Rousseau] would not allow a man to be a father, scarcely a woman to be a mother . . . such are the natural and imperative duties of life, even in the most primitive states of society" (173). James O'Rourke reads these criticisms in biographical terms, linking Rousseau's notorious abandonment of his own children to Shelley's own sense of aggrievement and neglect, but the substance of her engagement with Rousseau's writing stands apart from the details of both authors' lives (James O'Rourke, " 'Nothing More Unnatural': Mary Shelley's Reading of Rousseau," *ELH* 56 [1989]: 543–569).

13. Christine Di Stefano, *Configurations of Masculinity: A Feminist Perspective on Modern Political Theory* (Ithaca, N.Y.: Cornell University Press, 1991), 82; see also Benhabib on the figure of the noble savage as one that "frees the male ego from the most natural and basic bond of dependence" ("The Generalized and Concrete Other," 161). These and other studies of masculinist bias in the philosophical canon, such as Carol Pateman's *The Sexual Contract* (Stanford: Stanford University Press, 1988), and Genevieve Lloyd's *The Man of Reason: "Male" and "Female" in Western Philosophy* (Minneapolis: University of Minnesota Press, 1984), should be read alongside feminist interpretations of countercurrents in the tradition (such as Annette Baier's reading of Hume in *Moral Prejudices*, Martha Nussbaum's reading of Aristotle in *The Fragility of Goodness* [Cambridge: Cambridge University Press, 1986], and Christine Korsgaard's reading of Kantian autonomy in *Creating the Kingdom of Ends* [Cambridge: Cambridge University Press, 1996]). On the diversity of feminist approaches from "wholesale repudiation" to revisionary recognition of "counterthemes" within the canon, see Alison M. Jaggar, "Feminist Ethics: Projects, Problems, Prospects" in *Feminist Ethics*, ed. Claudia Card (Lawrence: University Press of Kansas, 1991), 87–88; and Genevieve Lloyd, "Feminism in History of Philosophy: Appropriations of the Past," *Cambridge Companion to Feminism in Philosophy*, ed. Miranda Fricker and Jennifer Hornsby (Cambridge: Cambridge University Press, 2000), 243–263.

14. Reference to the *Discourse* in the context of *Frankenstein* criticism is generally limited to evocations of the state of nature, natural man, and the corruptions of civil society. David Marshall sees the direct borrowings from the *Discourse* as evidence of Shelley's interest in tracing the creature's "elevation from his original state to civil society" but without confronting the problem of socialization in Rousseau's text. After criticizing Marshall, Christian Bok proposes that Shelley's "narrative about the evolution of the Monster is fraught with the same kinds of aporias that plague Rousseau's narrative," yet he credits neither the *Discourse* nor *Frankenstein* with insights into the tensions, contradictions, and discontinuities traversing them (Marshall, *The Surprising Effects of Sympathy*, 183–184). See also Christian Bok, "The Monstrosity of Representation: *Frankenstein* and Rousseau," *English Studies in Canada* 18, no. 4 (December 1992): 416.

15. Marshall, *The Surprising Effects of Sympathy*, 214.

16. Lipking argues that the creature's acquisition of moral sentiment strains Locke's theories beyond recognition: "Locke would not have recognized the result. Put simply, the Creature is just too good" ("*Frankenstein*, the True Story," 325).

17. Anonymous review of *Frankenstein*, *Knight's Quarterly* (August 1824): 195–199; reprinted in Shelley, *Frankenstein*, ed. J. Paul Hunter, 197–200.

18. Peter Brooks and David Marshall (among others) have adduced Rousseau's *Essay on the Origins of Language* as a source for the creature's tale. Brooks understands Rousseau's hypothesis that the "figurative word arises before the literal word does when passion holds our eyes spellbound" to mean that the "sign is not consubstantial with the thing it names" and attributes a similar discovery to the creature. In being struck by the "mystery of reference," the creature "uncovers the larger question of the arbitrariness or immotivation of the linguistic sign" ("Godlike Science / Unhallowed Arts," 209). Marshall suggests that the creature's "more or less simultaneous discovery of music, language, and then poetry provides a condensed tableau" of Rousseau's theories (*The Surprising Effects of Sympathy*, 185). While highly suggestive, such interpretations make it seem as if the creature learns a theory of language rather than a language—and perhaps the wrong theory. Like the *Second Discourse*, the *Essay on the Origin of Languages* is a genealogical argument speculating about the history of the species rather than the development of the individual. When Rousseau does turn his attention to the instruction of the individual in *Emile; or, On Education*, he emphasizes the child's constant exposure to speakers of language ("Children hear speech from their birth. They are spoken to not only before they understand what is said to them, but before they can reproduce the voices they hear"); it is this social habitat that the creature exists outside of, and the lack of which makes his acquisition of language so unrealistic (Jean-Jacques Rousseau, *Emile*, trans. Allan Bloom [New York: Basic Books, 1979], 68). Because of its focus on individual development, and because of the isolation of the subject whose development it traces, Locke's account of language learning seems a more appropriate source for these scenes in *Frankenstein*, as well as being an object of Shelley's critical revision.

19. Ludwig Wittgenstein, *Philosophical Investigations*, trans. G. E. M. Anscombe (New York: Macmillan, 1953), § 1. For an invaluable discussion of the scene of instruction with which the *Investigations* begins, see Stanley Cavell, *Philosophical Passages: Wittgenstein, Emerson, Austin, Derrida* (Oxford: Blackwell, 1995), 125–186.

20. On the growing body of philosophical argument that makes use of literary works—especially novels—for their particularized, multi-perspectival presentation of moral questions and identity, see note 20 in the introduction to this volume.

21. Stanley Cavell, *The Claim of Reason* (Oxford: Clarendon, 1979), 177. Compare Locke's account of how the child learns the difference between particular and abstract nouns: "The Names of *Nurse*, and *Mamma*, the Child uses, determine themselves to those Persons. Afterwards, when time and a larger Acquaintance has made them observe, that there are a great many other Things in the World, that . . . resemble their Father and Mother, and those Persons they have been used to, they frame

an *Idea* . . . and to that they give . . . the name *Man*, for Example" (3.3.7). Typically, for Locke, abstract "time" and the mind's "larger acquaintance" with the world deepens and extends understanding; "nurse," "mamma," "mother," and "father" are merely some among many "things" about which the child forms ideas and names. For further discussion, see chapter 1.

22. Bok, "The Monstrosity of Representation," 426.
23. Wittgenstein, *Philosophical Investigations*, § 32.
24. Alasdair MacIntyre, *After Virtue* (Notre Dame: University of Notre Dame Press, 1981), 33.
25. Benhabib, "The Generalized and Concrete Other," 162.
26. Marshall, *The Surprising Effects of Sympathy*, 191; Lipking, "*Frankenstein*, the True Story," 327.
27. Marshall, *The Surprising Effects of Sympathy*, 206–207.
28. See, for example, Laura Claridge, "Parent-Child Tensions in *Frankenstein*: The Search for Communion," *Studies in the Novel* 17 (1985): 14.
29. Jean Hall, "*Frankenstein*: The Horrifying Otherness of Family," *Essays in Literature* 17 (1990): 181.
30. For a related argument about how Victor is "doomed to community . . . to the impossibility of his ever being alone," see Frances Ferguson, *Solitude and the Sublime: Romanticism and the Aesthetics of Individuation* (New York: Routledge, 1992), 105–112.
31. After a first and final description of the creature's face, the only illustration of the horrible shape is the consistency of the responses it evokes: fear, shock, flight, attack. In the first dwelling the creature enters, an old man "shrieked loudly" on "perceiving [him] . . . and, quitting the hut, ran across the fields" (105); in the second, the creature had "hardly placed [his] foot within the door before the children shrieked and one of the women fainted" (106). As James A. Heffernan argues, "a faithful [cinematic] re-creation of the novel's central narrative . . . would never show the monster at all—would give us only the sound of his voice over shots of what he perceives, such as the roaring crowd of torch-bearing villagers charging up a mountain after him" ("Looking at the Monster: *Frankenstein* and Film," *Critical Inquiry* 24 [1997]: 142).
32. One significant line of criticism views the monster as a victim of the failure of sympathy, excluded from human communities because "prejudice clouds their eyes" (as the creature complains) (134). Such an interpretation underlies readings of the monster as a figure for cultural constructions of the Other as outsider, deviant, fiend. See, for example, Sandra M. Gilbert and Susan Gubar, "Mary Shelley's Monstrous Eve," in *The Madwoman in the Attic* (New Haven, Conn.: Yale University Press, 1979), 241 (for the creature as monstrous woman); Gayatri Chakravorty Spivak, "Three Women's Texts and a Critique of Imperialism," *Critical Inquiry* 12 (Autumn 1985): 243–261 (for the creature as colonized subject); and Lee Sterrenburg, "Mary Shelley's Monster: Politics and Psyche in *Frankenstein*," in Levine and Knoepflmacher, *The Endurance of Frankenstein*, 143–171 (for the creature as unruly proletariat). In arguing that the physical deformity of the creature is both the visible sign and necessary implication of the fundamental flaw in Frankenstein's effort to

autonomously create life, I follow the insights of readers such as Mary Poovey, who see the creature as an embodiment of the deformity of a certain ideal of masculine self-sufficiency (*The Proper Lady and the Woman Writer* [Chicago: University of Chicago Press, 1984], 120–123).

33. Wittgenstein, *Philosophical Investigations*, II.iv.

34. MacIntyre describes the relationship between narrative structure and the conceptualization of individual identity as follows: "The story of my life is always embedded in the story of those communities from which I derive my identity. I am born with a past; and to try to cut myself off from that past, in the individualist mode, is to deform my present relationships. The possession of a historical identity and the possession of a social identity coincide" (*After Virtue*, 221).

6. MILL ALONE

1. Although German idealism has a powerful impact on post-Romantic English philosophy and is the dominant influence on the most innovative cultural thinkers of the period (from Coleridge to Carlyle to Pater), eighteenth-century English empiricism still provides the basic presuppositions and vocabulary shaping investigations of knowledge, motivation, and behavior. On Locke's presence in nineteenth-century intellectual culture, see Hans Aarsleff, *From Locke to Saussure* (Minneapolis: University of Minnesota Press, 1982), 120–145. Jules Law traces the persistence of empiricism in understanding the "physiology and psychology of perception" through to Ruskin in *The Rhetoric of Empiricism* (Ithaca, N.Y.: Cornell University Press, 1993), 204–234. The term *science of morality* comes from Leslie Stephens, *English Thought in the Eighteenth Century*, 2 vols. (1876; New York: Harcourt, 1962), 2:108. Stephens's discussion of the Utilitarians begins with their "primary influence," John Locke (2:68).

2. James Mill, *Analysis of the Phenomena of the Human Mind*, 2 vols., ed. John Stuart Mill (London: Longmans, Green, Reeder & Dyer, 1869). This second edition of the 1829 *Analysis* includes substantive critical notes and additions by Alexander Bain, Andrew Findlater, and George Grote, as well as by John Stuart Mill. On the *Analysis* as a "complete codification of the English empirical tradition," see W. H. Burston, *James Mill on Philosophy and Education* (London: Athlone, 1973), 233.

3. George Henry Lewes, *Biographical History of Philosophy* (London: C. Cox, 1851), 3:191. John Stuart Mill, "Professor Sedgwick's Discourse" (1835), in *Essays on Ethics, Religion, and Society*, ed. J. M. Robson, in *Collected Works of John Stuart Mill* (Toronto: University of Toronto Press, 1969), 10:46.

4. John Stuart Mill, "Bentham," in *Collected Works*, 10:96, 98, respectively.

5. Fred Wilson, *Psychological Analysis and the Philosophy of John Stuart Mill* (Toronto: University of Toronto Press, 1990), 234; see also 224–235, for a discussion of Mill's moral psychology in the context of debates in eighteenth-century philosophy.

6. Wendy Donner, *The Liberal Self* (Ithaca, N.Y.: Cornell University Press, 1991), 146. See also Donner, "Mill's Utilitarianism," and Mary Lyndon Shanley, "The

Subjection of Women," in *Cambridge Companion to John Stuart Mill*, ed. John Skorupski (Cambridge: Cambridge University Press, 1998), 255–292, 396–442.

7. Robert Paul Wolff, *The Poverty of Liberalism* (Boston: Beacon, 1968), 141.

8. See, for example, Charles Taylor's discussion of the paradoxical relationship between the "reductive ontology" and "moral impetus" of utilitarian theories in *Sources of the Self* (Cambridge, Mass.: Harvard University Press, 1989), 332–339.

9. John Stuart Mill, *Autobiography*, ed. Jack Stillinger (Boston: Houghton Mifflin, 1969), 3. Further page references to this edition are cited parenthetically in the text.

10. On the early response to the *Autobiography*, see Francis E. Mineka, "The *Autobiography* and the Lady," *University of Toronto Quarterly* 32, no. 3 (1963): 301–306. Jack Stillinger traces the apparent deliberation with which Mill altered the "public voice" of the manuscripts composed between 1853 and 1856 to the still *"more* public voice" of the final version in his introduction to *The Early Draft of John Stuart Mill's Autobiography* (Urbana: University of Illinois Press, 1961), 11. More recently Jonathan Loesberg describes how "abstract intellectuality is completely thematized" in Mill (*Fictions of Consciousness* [New Brunswick: Rutgers University Press, 1986], 64).

11. F. A. Hayek, *John Stuart Mill and Harriet Taylor: Their Correspondence and Subsequent Marriage* (Chicago: University of Chicago Press, 1951), 17.

12. On Mill's mother, see Christine Di Stefano, "Reading J. S. Mill: Interpolations from the (M)Otherworld," in *Discontented Discourses: Feminism, Textual Intervention, Psychoanalysis*, ed. M. S. Barr and R. Feinstein (Urbana: University of Illinois Press, 1989), 163. On Mill's frustration with the career chosen for him, see Janice Carlisle, "J. S. Mill's *Autobiography*: The life of a 'Bookish Man,'" *Victorian Studies* 27 (1983): 7–23.

13. Two typical passages from the *Autobiography*: "I learnt no Latin until my eighth year. At that time I had read, under my father's tuition, a number of Greek prose authors, among whom I remember the whole of Herodotus, and of Xenophon's Cyropaedia and Memorials of Socrates; some of the lives of the philosophers by Diogenes Laertius; part of Lucian, and Isocrates ad Demonicum and ad Nicoclem. I also read, in 1813, the first six dialogues (in the common arrangement) of Plato, from the Euthyphron to the Theaetatus inclusive" (5).

"From about the age of twelve, I entered into another and more advanced stage of my instruction.... This commenced with Logic, in which I began at once with the Organon, and read it to the Analytics inclusive, but profited little by the Posterior Analytics.... Contemporaneously with the Organon, my father made me read the whole or parts of several of the Latin treatises on the scholastic logic.... After this, I went in a similar manner, through the 'Computatio sive Logica' of Hobbes" (12).

14. A canceled passage of the *Early Draft* contains Mill's only sustained remarks about his mother, and yet the dismissive brevity of those comments is at least as remarkable as the absence of anything resembling them, or replacing them, in the final version: "That rarity in England, a really warm-hearted mother, would ... have made my father a totally different being, and would have made the children grow up loving and being loved. But my mother with the very best intentions only

knew how to pass her life in drudging for them. Whatever she could do for them she did & they liked her, because she was kind to them, but to make herself loved, looked up to, or even obeyed, required qualities which she unfortunately did not possess" (*Early Draft*, 184).

15. See also the *Early Draft*, where the lack of intimacy in the Mill household is similarly generalized and impersonally extended to "most English families": "genuine affection is altogether exceptional; what is usually found being more or less of an attachment of mere habit, like that to inanimate objects. . . . I believe there is less personal affection in England than in any other country of which I know anything, and I give my father's family not as peculiar in this respect" (184).

16. As in chapter 5 I use the phrase "form of life" in a Wittgensteinian sense in order to indicate the whole range of learned practices, subtle gestures, facial expressions, habits, contextual cues, and history of shared responses that are, along with grammar and syntax and vocabulary, constitutive of our language and our means of mutual understanding.

Alan Ryan credits Mill with self-consciously crafting himself as "more object than subject" of the *Autobiography* but not with control over the emotions displayed "by the smooth didactic prose" and "strained coolness" of his narrative ("Sense and Sensibility in Mill's Political Thought," in *A Cultivated Mind: Essays on John Stuart Mill Presented to John M. Robson*, ed. Michael Laine [Toronto: University of Toronto Press, 1991], 122–124).

17. For a discussion of how accurately Mill presented the punishing rigidity of his father's educational schedule and the quantity of material the young Mill read and understood, see Jack Stillinger, "John Mill's Education: Fact, Fiction, and Myth," in Laine, *A Cultivated Mind*, 42.

18. J. S. Mill, *Utilitarianism* (1863), in *Collected Works*, 10:228.

19. See, for example, Mill's correspondence with Thomas Carlyle during the spring and summer of 1833—a full six years after the events recorded in the "Crisis" chapter of the *Autobiography* and three years prior to the depression that would follow the death of his father. "I believe I am the least *helpable* of mortals," Mill writes in one letter, "I have always found that when I am in any difficulty or perplexity of a spiritual kind . . . I should shut myself up from the human race, and not see the face of man until I had got firm footing" (*The Earlier Letters of John Stuart Mill, 1812–1848*, ed. Francis Mineka, in *Collected Works*, 12:154). See also Carlyle's responses, almost always counseling Mill to seek relief by communicating with others rather than remaining in "self-seclusion": "If you know any heart that can understand you," urges Carlyle, "to that heart speak; the very act of such speaking brings assuagement, almost healing" (*Letters of Thomas Carlyle to John Stuart Mill, John Sterling, and Robert Browning*, ed. Alexander Carlyle [New York: Frederick A. Stokes, 1923], 56).

20. See, for example, John Durham's early psychoanalytic interpretation, "The Influence of John Stuart Mill's Mental Crisis on His Thoughts," *American Imago* 20 (1963): 369–384; and Adam Phillips's account of Mill's "accumulation of fathers living and dead" in the *Autobiography*, in *On Flirtation* (Cambridge, Mass.: Harvard University Press, 1994), 42–46.

21. Linda M.-G. Zerilli, "Constructing 'Harriet Taylor': Another Look at J. S. Mill's *Autobiography*," in *Constructions of the Self*, ed. George Levine (New Brunswick, N.J.: Rutgers University Press, 1992), 204, 206.

22. Quoted in Hayek, *John Stuart Mill and Harriet Taylor*, 85.

23. I borrow this usage from D. W. Winnicott's surprising argument that "at the center of each person is an incommunicado element, and this is sacred and worthy of preservation." Winnicott calls this "permanently non-communicating" core a "hard fact . . . softened by the sharing that belongs to the whole range of cultural experience," but he also identifies intimacy as the condition for the possibility of its coming into being ("Communicating and Not Communicating Leading to a Study of Certain Opposites," in *The Maturational Processes and the Facilitating Environment* [London: Hogarth, 1965], 180–187).

24. Typical is Francis Mineka's characterization of Mill's "fulsome praise" as "the harmless aberration of a love-blinded husband" ("The *Autobiography* and the Lady," 302). For a useful review of recent scholarship on the Mill-Taylor relationship, see Zerilli, "Constructing 'Harriet Taylor,' " 209.

25. William Godwin, *Memoirs of the Author of "The Rights of Woman,"* ed. Richard Holmes (New York: Penguin, 1987), 258. The rational Godwin, like the analytical Mill, found in his companion an intellect enlivened by feeling, sensibility, and imagination—though Godwin exaggerates, to the point of distortion, those elements of Wollstonecraft's thought, and his account serves, in this respect, as a more revealing memoir of the author of *Political Justice*.

26. Mill, "Bentham," in *Collected Works*, 10:91.

27. Mill, "Professor Sedgwick's Discourse," in *Collected Works*, 10:49.

28. Mill, "Bentham," in *Collected Works*, 10:93.

29. Mill, "Thoughts on Poetry and Its Varieties" in *Collected Works*, 1:348–349.

30. Isobel Armstrong, *Victorian Poetry: Poetry, Poetics and Politics* (London: Routledge, 1993), 137.

31. Mill, *Utilitarianism*, in *Collected Works*, 10:228.

32. Ibid.

33. Cf. Isobel Armstrong's interpretation of Mill's poetics as "transcend[ing] the immediate social order" and pitting "the solitary work of the speaking subject over against communality" (*Victorian Poetry*, 134–135).

34. William Wordsworth, *The Prelude, 1799, 1805, 1850*, ed. Jonathan Wordsworth, M. H. Abrams, and Stephen Gill (New York: Norton, 1979), 3:186–187 (1805 version); Winnicott, "Communicating and Not Communicating," 187; Wittgenstein, *Philosophical Investigations*, trans. G. E. M. Anscombe (New York: Macmillan, 1953), § 299. Pain is the exemplum of irreducibly private experience for both Mill and Wittgenstein, though Mill embraces it as such whereas Wittgenstein would have us reflect on what it means to imagine it as such. Elsewhere Wittgenstein observes that "outside philosophy" statements such as "of course only he knows how he feels" or "I can't know what you feel" are meaningful expressions of "helplessness," but "this helplessness isn't due to an unfortunate metaphysical fact, 'the privacy of personal experience,' or it would worry us constantly" ("Notes for Lectures on Private Experience and Sense Data," in *Philosophical Occasions*,

1912–1951, ed. James Klagge and Alfred Nordmann [Indianapolis: Hackett, 1993], 228).

35. Christopher Bollas, *The Mystery of Things* (New York: Routledge, 1999), 11. Without "denying the interpersonal element or the comforting contexts" of the analytic relationship, Bollas maintains that the patient and the analyst "acknowledge the indisputable fact that the other is ultimately beyond knowing" (13).

36. Stanley Cavell, *The Claim of Reason* (Oxford: Oxford University Press, 1979), 115.

37. Review of Tennyson's *Poems, Chiefly Lyrical* (1830) and *Poems* (1833), *London Review*, July 1835.

38. I am indebted here to Armstrong's observation that, in the final version of the refrain, one may read the word "will" as having "the force of prediction" (*Victorian Poetry*, 51).

39. On the complex hermeneutic dynamic contained by the double structure of the poem, see Armstrong's argument that "Mariana" doubles back on itself, framing the lover's utterance as "solipsistic construction" while also reflecting on the "process which presents that self-enclosed utterance" (*Victorian Poetry*, 17). See also Armstrong's reading of two dramatic monologues by Browning as critical responses to Mill's theory of poetry as soliloquy (ibid., 137–145).

Index

○ ○ ○

Aarsleff, Hans, 199 n.8, 210 n.8, 215 n.36, 240 n.1
Abrams, M. H., 116, 119, 121, 230 n.5, 232 n.13
Adorno, Theodor, 198 n.1
Altieri, Charles, 203 n.24, 206 n.37
Ambivalence, 14, 91–92, 135, 145, 193–195
Anderson, Amanda, 203 n.24
Animals:
 as conceptual category, 63, 74–76, 83–85, 218 nn.1, 2
 interpretation of behavior, 68–72, 219 n.11, 220 nn.13, 14, 15
 natural man and, 21, 64–65, 75–76
 in Rousseau's *Discourse on the Origins of Inequality*, 69–75
 See also Facts; Orangutans; Primates
Anxiety:
 as compelling imagination of autonomy, 3, 19, 23, 62, 114, 197
 Freudian account of, 22–23, 31, 35, 207 n.45
 intersubjective, 22, 24–25, 33–34, 39, 50–51, 58, 62, 90–95
 in Locke, 28, 33–34, 37–39, 50–51, 55, 193
 See also Fear; Vulnerability
Armstrong, Isobel, 243 n.33, 244 nn.38, 39
Ashworth, E. J., 215 n.33
Atomism, 2, 15, 26, 207 n.42
Autism, 108
Autobiography (John Stuart Mill), 9, 114, 170, 172–189
 crisis in, 182–184, 242 n.19
 education in, 173, 176–177, 180–181, 241 nn.13, 14

 emotion in, 178–180, 183, 186–189
 impersonality of, 173–179, 184–185, 187–190
 interpretation of, 174–175, 184, 241 nn.10, 12
Autonomy:
 as absence of relation to others, 21–22, 27–30, 75–76, 78–85, 104, 112–113, 126–127, 154, 164–165, 193
 contemporary critique of, 5–7, 11–12, 15, 151
 definitions of, 12–14, 204 n.25, 204 n.28
 epistemic, 15, 29–31, 151, 193
 imagined as original condition, 1–4, 19–21, 61–62, 75–79, 114–115, 117–118, 131, 144–145
 repudiation of, 2–3, 7–9, 20–23, 25, 76–78, 84–86, 95, 172, 192–193
 See also Independence; Isolation; "State of nature"
Axtell, James, 210 n.6
Ayers, Michael, 209 n.2, 212 n.17, 213 nn.21, 23

Babbitt, Irving, 201 n.18
Baier, Annette, 5–6, 15, 26, 204 n.31, 209 n.2, 212 n.19, 223 n.28
Battel, Andrew, 70, 72, 81
Benhabib, Seyla, 6, 15, 165, 199 n.12, 203 n.20, 205 n.36, 237 n.13
Benjamin, Jessica, 207 n.41, 208 n.46, 211 n.14
Bentham, Jeremy (Benthamite), 14
 J. S. Mill on, 171–172, 190
Berkeley, George, 213 n.22

Besse, Guy, 222 n.20
Bewell, Alan, 230 n.1
Bialostosky, Don H., 234 n.25
Blackburn, Simon, 13
Blanchot, Maurice, 215 n.41
Bloom, Harold, 200 n.15
Body, human:
   as concealing, 45–51, 53, 58–59, 90–93, 168
Bok, Christian, 163, 237 n.14
Bollas, Christopher, 244 n.35
Bonnaterre, Pierre-Joseph, 100–101, 103–108, 112–113, 228 n.13, 229 n.15
Bordo, Susan, 15, 198 n.7
Bradley, A. C., 116, 119, 230 n.5, 232 n.13
Bromwich, David, 201 n.17
Brooks, Peter, 235 n.5, 238 n.18
Brown, Marshall, 10, 201 n.17
Burnett, James (Lord Monboddo), 110
Burston, W. H., 240 n.2
Butler, Judith, 203 n.24, 205 n.36, 208 n.46
Butler, Marilyn, 232 n.14

Calvert, Raisley, 141
Carlyle, Thomas, 184, 242 n.19
Carrithers, David, 216 n.44, 230 n.25
Caruth, Cathy, 27, 202 n.19, 209 n.3, 210 n.12, 211 n.16, 231 n.10
Cascardi, Anthony, 208 n.46
Cassirer, Ernst, 198 n.1, 199 n.8
Cavell, Marcia, 207 n.45, 211 n.14
Cavell, Stanley, 16–17, 163, 195, 206 n.38, 214 n.27, 238 n.19
Chandler, James K., 232 n.14
Childhood, Child:
   representations of, 26, 28–30, 34–36, 54–55, 153–155 (Locke), 176, 180–182 (Mill), 117–118, 121–123, 143–144 (Wordsworth)
   weakness of, 19, 22–23
   "wild child." *See* Victor of Aveyron
   See also Infancy, Infant; "State of nature," parenting in
Chodorow, Nancy, 204 n.28
Clark, David, 213 n.25
Clark, S. H., 27, 213 n.21
Code, Lorraine, 15, 203 n.20, 205 n.34, 210 n.5, 236 n.9
Coleridge, Samuel Taylor, 141–142
Communitarianism, 11, 13–14, 204 n.30
Condillac, Etienne Bonnot de, 5, 63, 111–112, 151, 153, 171, 213 n.22, 229 nn.23, 24, 25, 236 n.9
Conduct of the Understanding (Locke), 32, 37

Confessions (Rousseau), 31, 94, 165
Corpuscularianism, 44, 213 n.23

Damrosch, Leo, 201 n.19, 203 n.24
Dapper, Olfert, 70
Davidson, Donald, 205 n.37
De Cive (Hobbes), 1–2, 4, 19, 118, 209 n.50, 217 n.50
De Man, Paul, 202 n.19, 209 n.3, 234 n.25
Dent, N. J. H., 201 n.16, 222 n.20
Dependence:
   acknowledgment of, 21, 95, 126–127, 140–143, 145, 147, 166–167, 185, 187–189
   neglected in philosophy, 1, 3, 5–6, 22, 29, 31, 62, 112–114, 151, 165, 169
   in theories of natural sociability, 18–19, 24, 59–61, 82, 155, 170, 172
   See also Childhood, Child; Infancy, Infants
Derathé, Robert, 223 n.29, 224 n.34
Derrida, Jacques, 201 n.16, 202 n.19
Descartes, René (Cartesian), 4–5, 12, 15, 19, 129–130, 199 n.8, 234 n.24
Diamond, Cora, 17, 63, 203 n.20, 205 n.34, 218 n.1
Diderot, Denis, 5, 65, 213 n.22
Discourse on the Arts and Sciences (*First Discourse*) (Rousseau), 90–91, 94
Discourse on the Origins of Inequality (*Second Discourse*) (Rousseau), 8–9, 25, 31, 63–89, 92, 94, 96–97, 111–114, 145–146, 193
   animals in, 69–75, 220 n.15, 221 n.18
   facts, use of, 69–75, 87, 220 n.14, 221 nn.16, 18
   language, mysterious origin of, 79, 88
   Locke in, 72–74, 83–85
   natural man, figure of, 21, 74–79, 87
   nature, conception of, 64, 79–80, 82, 86–88
   origins in, 65, 79–80, 85–88
   paradoxes of, 64, 87–88, 96–97, 103, 112–113
   perfectibility, 75–76, 79, 221 n.19
   Shelley's *Frankenstein* and, 155–157
   state of nature, impossibility of evolving from, 73, 76, 78–80, 82–87, 95
   state of nature, impossibility of returning to, 89, 99, 145–146
   state of nature, interpretation of, 64–66, 86, 88, 99, 218 nn.5, 6, 222 nn.20, 24, 223 n.29, 224 nn.31, 33, 34

246   Index

state of nature, reproduction in, 73–74, 79–84
Victor of Aveyron and, 99–105, 111–113
Wordsworth's *The Prelude* and, 114, 145–146
Dissimulation, 25, 90–94, 225 n.37
See also Intersubjectivity
Di Stefano, Christine, 14, 199 n.12, 207 n.42, 241 n.12
Douthwaite, Julia, 227 n.2, 229 n.25
Durham, John, 242 n.20
Durkheim, Emile, 63–64, 201 n.16, 218 n.3

Education:
  in Locke's *Essay concerning Human Understanding*, 28–30
  in Mill's *Autobiography*, 173, 176–177, 180–181, 241 nn.13, 14
  in Shelley's *Frankenstein*, 157–165
Egoism, 2, 60, 62, 116
  See also Individualism
Emile (Rousseau), 31, 92–94, 226 nn.40, 41, 238 n.18
Emile et Sophie, ou Les Solitares (Rousseau), 93–94
Emotion:
  in philosophical writing, 17–18, 31, 34–40, 178–180, 206 n.38, 211 n.16
  See also Anxiety; Fear; Passion; Vulnerability
Empiricism:
  Locke and, 5, 30–31, 41–43, 46–48, 210 n.5, 213 n.22
  J. S. Mill and, 171–172, 191, 193, 240 n.1
  Shelley's *Frankenstein* and, 152–154, 157, 160–161, 169, 236 nn.6, 9
  Victor of Aveyron and, 110–112
  Wordsworth and, 117–118, 123–124
  See also Epistemology; Perception
Enlightenment, 1–3, 5–7, 11–12, 14–16, 19, 114, 198 n.1, 199 nn.8, 12, 230 n.25
  romanticism and, 9–11, 21–22, 114–115, 117–118, 129–130, 144–146, 151–152, 155–157, 160–161, 169
  See also Philosophy, history of
Epistemology:
  ethics and, 25, 39–41, 45–51, 57–59, 91–94, 191
  isolation and, 4–5, 32–34, 40–41, 62, 99, 110–112, 152–154, 157
  See also Empiricism; Mind
Essay concerning Human Understanding (Locke), 5, 9, 20, 26–57, 171, 190, 193, 209 n.1
  anxiety in, 33–34, 37–39, 55

association of ideas, 36, 211 n.16
child, figure of, 26, 28–30, 34–36, 54–55, 153–154
emotion in, 31, 34–40, 211 n.16
fear in, 34–36, 38–39, 51, 57
influence in, 29, 32, 34–36, 39, 54–55, 211 n.13
interpretation of, 26–27, 43, 52, 209 nn.2, 3, 4, 5, 210 nn.6, 12
knowledge, limits of, 27, 42–46, 49–50, 55–56, 215 n.37
language, 51–56, 214 nn.29, 31, 215 n.36
mind, as "dark room," 32, 38–39, 111, 157, 191
passion, 36–37, 211 n.16
perception of persons, 26–28, 32–34, 39, 45–50, 213 n.25
Second Treatise of Government and, 54, 56–57
self-determination in, 29, 31, 53–56
Shelley's *Frankenstein* and, 152–154, 157, 160, 162, 169
skepticism of, 27, 33–34, 38–39, 41–42
vision, 32, 43–45, 213 n.22
Essays on the Law of Nature (Locke), 214 n.29
Essay on the Origin of Languages (Rousseau), 224 n.29, 228 n.13, 238 n.18
Ethics:
  epistemology and, 25, 39–41, 45–51, 57–59, 91–94, 191
  See also Philosophy, moral
Ethology, 65–69
Evolution, 65–66, 75, 86, 218 n.6, 223 n.29
Facts:
  status of in philosophical argument, 5–6, 18–19, 60, 63, 65–74, 229 n.25
  use of, in Rousseau's *Discourse on the Origins of Inequality*, 69–74, 221 n.16
Fear, 22–25
  in Hobbes, 24, 51, 208 n.48, 214 n.28
  in Locke, 34–36, 38–39, 51, 57
  See also Anxiety; Vulnerability
Feminism:
  philosophical interpretation and, 12–15, 26, 150–151, 155, 199 n.12, 204 n.32, 205 n.34, 237 n.13
Ferguson, Adam, 59, 216 n.44, 230 n.25
Ferguson, Frances, 201 nn.15, 17, 231 n.10, 233 n.19, 239 n.30
Ferry, David, 232 n.14
Fichte, Johann Gottlieb, 116

Index **247**

"Form of life," 159, 164, 178–179, 186–187, 206 n.39, 242 n.16
See also Wittgenstein, Ludwig
Foucault, Michel, 198 n.1, 225 n.38
Frankenstein (Shelley), 8–9, 24, 30, 114, 149–169, 174, 193
  creature, difference from human beings, 165–169
  creature, gigantic size of, 149, 155, 165
  creature, implausible self-education of, 157–164
  creature, narrative of, 151–165
  fantastic, use of, 149, 152, 157, 163
  interpretation of, 150, 158–160, 165–167, 235 n.3, 239 nn.30, 32
  language learning in, 161–164, 238 n.18
  Locke and, 152–154, 157, 160, 162, 164, 169, 236 n.6, 238 n.16
  as philosophical critique, 10, 149–157, 161–162, 169, 235 n.5
  Rousseau and, 155–157, 236 n.10, 237 n.14, 238 n.18
  sympathy in, 158–159, 166–168, 239 n.32
Freud, Sigmund, 16, 22–23, 31, 35, 200 n.14, 206 n.38, 207 n.45
Friedman, Marilyn, 204 n.27

Galperin, William, 231 n.11, 233 n.18, 234 n.25
Gert, Bernard, 214 n.28
God:
  in Locke, 51–52, 56, 217 n.50, 223 n.27
  in Rousseau, 88–89
Godwin, William (Godwinian), 136, 151, 186–188, 236 n.10, 243 n.25
Goldschmidt, Victor, 64, 221 n.19, 224 n.31
Gourevitch, Victor, 65, 201 n.16
Gravity:
  as metaphor in moral philosophy, 233 n.20
  in Wordsworth's *The Prelude*, 126–127, 132–133, 138–139, 143–148
Grob, Alan, 230 n.1
Guyer, Paul, 215 n.31

Harding, Sandra, 15
Hartley, David, 171
Hartman, Geoffrey, 116, 121, 129
Hayek, F. A., 174–175
Hazlitt, William, 232 n.14
Heffernan, James A. W., 232 n.16, 233 n.19, 239 n.31
Hegel, G. W. F. (Hegelian), 10, 116, 231 n.5, 232 n.13
Henderson, Andrea, 201 n.15

History:
  conjectural, 1–3, 19–20, 86–87. See also "State of nature"
  intellectual, 1, 7, 10, 115–116, 150–151, 171. See also Philosophy, history of
Hobbes, Thomas (Hobbesian), 1–5, 12, 18–21, 23–25, 51, 58–60, 68–69, 85, 91, 95, 118, 172, 214 n.31, 216 nn.45, 46, 217 n.50
  Hobbesian fear, 24, 51, 208 n.48, 214 n.28
  Rousseau and, 25, 208 n.49, 224 n.34
  —Works:
    De Cive, 1–2, 4, 19, 118, 209 n.50, 217 n.50
    Leviathan, 25, 59, 214 n.31, 215 n.38
Homans, Margaret, 150, 233 n.19
Hopkins, Brooke, 234 n.25
Horkheimer, Max, 198 n.1
Horowitz, Asher, 218 n.6, 223 n.29
Human beings:
  concealed by body, 45–51, 53, 58–59, 90–93, 168, 214 n.28
  as dissimulators, 25, 90–91
  distinctive faculties of, 63–64, 87–88, 95
  as originally autonomous, 1–4, 19–20, 61–62
  as originally social, 18–19, 24, 59–61, 155, 170, 172, 216 n.46, 217 n.52, 222 n.23
  See also Intersubjectivity; Mind; Perception; "State of nature"
Hume, David, 15, 18, 39–42, 51, 56–62, 82, 91, 115, 192, 212 n.19, 216 nn.45, 48, 217 n.49, 222 n.22, 233 n.20
  Treatise of Human Nature, 39–41, 56–58, 212 nn.18, 19, 216 nn.45, 48, 217 n.49, 217 n.52, 222 n.22
Hutcheson, Francis, 18, 24, 216 n.46, 233 n.20

Imagination, in philosophical argument, 3, 5, 19–22, 44–45, 63, 74–75, 80–82, 86–87
Independence:
  ideal of, 1, 3–4, 19, 29–30, 54, 115, 192
  imagined as original condition, 1–5, 19–21, 61–62
  repudiated as original condition, 5–9, 20–24, 76–79, 84–86, 95, 172, 192–193
  See also Autonomy; Dependence; "State of nature"
Individualism, 2, 7, 12, 14–15, 26–27, 68, 172, 191–192, 194–196
  See also Independence, ideal of; Isolation

Infancy, Infants:
  "blessed babe" (Wordsworth), 21, 23, 122–127, 145
  in Locke, 3–4, 27–28, 152–153
  philosophical representation of, 3–6, 18–19, 22–24, 216n.45, 236n.9
  in Rousseau, 80–83, 105, 222n.24
  See also Childhood; Children; Dependence; "State of nature," parenting in
Ingold, Thomas, 219n.11
Interdisciplinarity, 10–12, 201n.19, 202n.20, 203n.24
  See also Literature: philosophy and; Philosophy: literature and
Interpretation, 7, 9–11, 15–18
Intersubjectivity:
  limits of: in Hobbes, 24–25; in Locke, 45–46, 50–52, 55; in Rousseau, 62, 90–95; in Sade, 59–61
  See also Anxiety, intersubjective; Perception; Sympathy
Isolation:
  as affliction, 21–22, 31, 76–78, 104, 106, 154, 166–167, 181–183, 217n.52
  epistemology and, 4–5, 15, 32–34, 39–41, 62, 111–112
  privacy and, 16, 185, 191–197
  See also Autonomy: as absence of relation to others; Independence; Solitude
Itard, Jean-Marc-Gaspard, 98–109, 112, 227n.4, 228n.13, 229n.24

Jacobus, Mary, 150
Jagger, Alison M., 237n.13
Jeffrey, Francis, 116

Kant, Immanuel (Kantian), 12–16, 19, 30–31, 48, 115–116, 204n.25, 205n.35, 233n.20
Korsgaard, Christine, 15, 205n.35, 237n.13
Kramnick, Jonathan, 212n.17
Krebs, Victor, 206n.38

Lacan, Jacques (Lacanian), 200n.14, 206n.38, 208n.46
"Lack," 18, 208n.46
Language:
  as expression of hidden ideas, 52–53, 214n.31, 215n.38
  learning of, 161–164, 178–180, 238nn.18, 21
  in Locke, 51–56, 238n.21

in Rousseau, 79, 88, 238n.18
in Shelley's *Frankenstein*, 161–164, 238n.18
and Victor of Aveyron, 106, 228n.13
in Wittgenstein, 16–17, 162, 164, 195, 205n.37, 206n.38
Law, Jules, 240n.1
Lear, Jonathan, 200n.14, 206n.38
Leibniz, G. W., 213n.22
Letter to d'Alembert (Rousseau), 92–93, 225nn.38, 39
Leviathan (Hobbes), 25, 59, 214n.31, 215n.38
Lévi-Strauss, Claude, 110
Levinas, Emmanuel, 213n.24
Levinson, Marjorie, 200n.15, 232n.14
Lewes, George Henry, 171
Linnaeus (Carl von Linné), 97
Lipking, Lawrence, 165, 235n.5, 238n.16
Literature:
  philosophy and, 7–11, 114–118, 129–130, 151–152, 162–163, 168–169, 190–192, 195–197, 201n.19, 202n.20, 240n.34
  See also Interdisciplinarity; Philosophy: literature and
Livingston, Donald, 212n.19
Lloyd, Genevieve, 237n.13
Locke, John, 2–5, 7, 9–11, 15, 20–22, 26–58, 62, 69, 72–74, 82–85, 93, 95, 97, 111, 114–115, 152–154, 157, 171–172, 174, 222n.20, 223n.27
  J. S. Mill on, 171–172, 190–193
  Rousseau and, 72–74, 83–85
  Shelley's *Frankenstein* and, 152–154, 157, 160, 162, 164, 169, 236n.6, 238n.16
  —Works:
    Conduct of the Understanding, 32, 37
    Essay concerning Human Understanding, 5, 9, 20, 26–57, 171, 190, 193, 209n.1
    Essays on the Law of Nature, 214n.29
    Second Treatise of Government, 3–4, 20, 54, 56–57, 83–84, 213n.25, 214n.28, 217n.50, 223n.27
    Some Thoughts concerning Education, 28–29, 35–36, 210n.6, 211n.13
Loesberg, Jonathan, 241n.10
Lovejoy, A. O., 218n.6, 223n.29, 224n.34

Macadam, Jim, 223n.29, 224n.31
MacIntyre, Alasdair, 11, 27, 165, 203n.21, 240n.34
Mandeville, Bernard, 69, 82, 222n.23
Marshall, David, 158, 165–166, 201n.17, 202n.19, 237n.14, 238n.18

Index   249

Masson, David, 116
Masters, Roger, 66, 222 n.24
McGann, Jerome, 200 n.15
Meier, Heinrich, 65, 218 n.5
Merleau-Ponty, Maurice, 110
Merolla, Jerome, 70
Midgely, Mary, 218 n.2
Mill, James, 171–172, 176–178, 180, 183
Mill, John Stuart, 2, 9, 21–22, 24, 114–115, 170–197
  on Locke, 171–172, 190–193
  on poetry, 185, 191–197
—Works:
  Autobiography, 172–189
  "Bentham," 171–172, 190
  Utilitarianism, 170, 182, 194
Miller, James, 225 n.39
Mind:
  as "dark room" (Locke), 32, 38, 111, 157, 191
  as isolated, 32–34, 39–41, 151–154, 174, 192, 195–197
  as "mirror" (Hume), 57–59, 62, 91, 192
  See also Body: human; Empiricism; Epistemology
Mitchell, W. J. T., 201 n.18, 235 n.26
Moers, Ellen, 150
Monsters, Monstrosity:
  in Locke's *Essay concerning Human Understanding*, 49–51
  in Shelley's *Frankenstein*, 10, 155, 165–168
Moran, Francis, 81, 219 n.12

"Natural Man":
  as animal, 64–67
  as imaginary animal, 74–77
  in Rousseau's *Discourse on the Origins of Inequality*, 63–89, 114
  Shelley's *Frankenstein* and, 155–157
  Victor of Aveyron and, 99–104, 111–113
  See also "State of nature"
Nedelsky, Jennifer, 199 n.12
Neill, Alex, 210 n.6
Newton, Isaac, 233 n.20
Nidditch, Peter, 27
Nietzsche, Friedrich, 16
Nouvelle Héloïse (Rousseau), 92–93, 225 n.38
Nussbaum, Martha, 202 n.20, 237 n.13
"Obvious," the
  philosophical affirmation of, 16–17
  philosophical departures from, 1–5, 18–19

Onorato, Richard J., 122, 231 n.10
O'Rourke, James, 236 n.10, 237 n.12
Orangutans, as model for "natural man," 65–68, 70–71, 219 nn.10, 12, 220 nn.14, 15
  See also Animals; Primates
Origins:
  imagination of, in philosophy, 1–3, 5, 19–24, 59–62, 65, 79–80, 85–88, 114, 199 n.8
  imagination of, in Wordsworth's *The Prelude*, 117–118, 120–121, 123–126, 131, 140–141
  See also "State of nature"

Parfit, Derek, 26
Passion, 36–38, 61, 211 n.17, 212 n.19
  See also Emotion
Pateman, Carole, 14, 225 n.40, 237 n.13
Perception:
  of persons, opposed to things, 26–28, 32–34, 39, 45–50, 58, 92–93, 154, 160
Perfectibility, 75–76, 79, 221 n.19
Phillips, Adam, 207 n.45, 242 n.20
Philosophy:
  feminist interpretation and, 12–15, 26, 150–151, 155, 199 n.12, 204 n.32, 205 n.34, 237 n.13
  history of, 1–2, 5–7, 11–16, 240 n.1
  literature and, 7–11, 114–118, 129–130, 151–152, 162–163, 168–169, 190–192, 195–197, 201 n.19, 202 n.20, 240 n.34
  moral, 11–15, 17, 39, 41, 57–58, 61, 89, 171–172, 190–192, 194, 217 n.49
  Wordsworth's *The Prelude* and, 114–118, 129–130, 144–146
  See also Empiricism; Enlightenment; Epistemology; Ethics
Philosophy in the Bedroom (Sade), 59, 61–62
Pinch, Adela, 202 n.19
Pinel, Philippe, 109
Pollin, Burton, 235 n.5
Poovey, Mary, 230 n.25, 240 n.32
Popkin, Richard, 27
Poststructuralism, 12, 15, 203 n.24, 205 nn.36, 37
Potkay, Adam, 203 n.24, 212 n.19, 233 n.18
Prelude, The (Wordsworth), 8–9, 114–148, 153, 193
  autonomy in, 115–118, 126, 131, 135, 138, 140–145
  "blessed babe," figure of, 21, 23, 122–127, 145
  crisis, 135–138, 142

gravity and weight in, 126–128,
132–133, 137–139, 143–144, 146–148,
233 n.20
imagination of origins in, 117–118,
120–121, 123–126, 131, 140–141
interpretation of, 115–117, 119, 121–122,
129, 230 nn.1, 5, 231 nn.9, 10, 11,
232 nn.13, 14, 16, 234 n.25
moral perception in, 118–120, 127–128,
132–139, 232 n.14
philosophy and, 114–118, 129–130,
230 n.1, 234 n.23
as self-critical, 117–120, 122, 133–135,
141–142, 145, 234 n.25
solitude in, 117, 128–131
"spots of time," 143–144
Primates, 65–69, 71–72, 219 nn.8, 10
See also Animals; Orangutans
Psychoanalysis, 6, 17, 22–23, 37, 194–195,
200 n.14, 207 n.41, 208 n.46, 211 n.14,
243 n.23, 244 n.35
in literary criticism, 116–117, 122, 150,
184, 232 n.17, 242 n.20
See also Freud, Sigmund
Purchas, Samuel, 70, 72, 220 n.13

Quigley, Austin, 203 n.24, 206 n.37
Quine, W. V., 205 n.37

Rawls, John, 11, 204 n.30
Reveries of a Solitary Walker (Rousseau),
94, 129–130, 165
Richetti, John, 27, 210 n.12
Romanticism:
critical conceptions of, 7, 9–10, 200 n.15
enlightenment and, 9–11, 21–22,
114–115, 117–118, 129–130, 144–146,
151–152, 155–157, 160–161, 169,
201 n.17, 202 n.19
Rorty, Richard, 11, 203 n.22, 206 n.37
Rousseau, Jean-Jacques, 2, 7–10, 16,
21–22, 25, 30–31, 62–95, 114–115, 151,
193–195
"being" opposed to "appearing" in,
90–94, 225 n.37
Hobbes and, 25, 85, 208 n.49, 224 n.34
imagination of utopia in, 92–94,
225 nn.37, 38, 39
infidelity in, 92–94, 225 n.40
Locke and, 72–74, 83–85, 222 n.20
Romanticism and, 10, 201 n.18
Shelley's *Frankenstein* and, 155–157,
165, 236 n.10, 237 n.14, 238 n.18
Victor of Aveyron and, 99–105, 111–113

Wordsworth's *The Prelude* and, 129–131,
145–146, 235 n.26
—Works:
Confessions, 31, 94, 165
Dialogues, Rousseau juge de Jean-Jacques,
94
*Discourse on the Arts and Sciences (First
Discourse)*, 90–91, 94
*Discourse on the Origins of Inequality
(Second Discourse)*, 8–9, 25, 31, 63–89,
92, 94, 96–97, 111–114, 145–146,
193
Emile, 31, 92–94, 225 nn.40, 41, 238 n.18
Emile et Sophie, ou Les Solitares, 93–94
Essay on the Origin of Languages, 224
n.29, 228 n.13, 238 n.18
Letter to d'Alembert, 92–93, 225 nn.38,
39
"Letter to Philopolis," 220 n.14
Nouvelle Héloïse, 92–93, 225 n.38
Reveries of a Solitary Walker, 94, 129–130,
165
Social Contract, 92, 225 nn.37, 39
Ryan, Alan, 208 n.48, 242 n.16
Rymer, Russ, 228 n.9

Sade, Marquis de, 59, 61–62, 215 n.41,
217 n.50
Sandel, Michael, 11, 204 n.30
Satyr, 71, 219 n.13
Schapiro, Barbara, 232 n.17
Scheman, Naomi, 17, 203 n.20, 205 n.34,
214 n.30
Schneewind, J. B., 5, 13, 216 n.46
Schochet, Gordon, 223 n.27
Second Treatise of Government (Locke), 3–4,
20, 54, 56–57, 83–84, 213 n.25,
214 n.28, 217 n.50, 223 n.27
Self:
autonomous, conceptions of, 13, 19–20,
30, 54–55, 117, 123, 126–127
autonomous, repudiations of, 5–7,
11–15, 21–25, 29–30, 122–125, 151,
192–193
contradictory representation of
(Wordsworth), 117–120, 125–128,
134–135, 140–142
Self-sufficiency. *See* Autonomy;
Independence
"Sentiment of being," 64, 101, 129–130
Shaftesbury (Anthony Ashley Cooper),
18, 24, 59–61, 82, 91, 216 n.43,
217 n.49, 222 n.22
Shakespeare, William, 183

Index 251

Shelley, Mary, 2, 7–10, 21–22, 30–31, 97, 114–115, 149–169, 172, 193, 195
  Frankenstein, 149–169
  "Rousseau," 155, 237 n.12
Shklar, Juduth, 224 n.33
Sicard, Roch-Ambroise, 98–99
Simpson, David, 201 n.15
Skepticism:
  in Hume's *Treatise of Human Nature*, 40–41
  in Locke's *Essay concerning Human Understanding*, 27, 33–34
  in Wordsworth's *The Prelude*, 130, 234 n.24
  See also Epistemology; Intersubjectivity: limits of
Skillen, Anthony, 224 n.33, 226 n.41
Sloan, Phillip, 226 n.2
Small, Christopher, 235 n.5
Smyser, Jane Worthington, 234 n.23
Social Contract (Rousseau), 92, 225 nn.37, 39
Sociality:
  anxieties about, 19, 22–25, 50–51, 62, 89–95
  as natural to human beings, 18–19, 24, 59–61, 170, 172, 216 nn.44, 46, 217 nn.49, 52, 222 n.23
  unsentimental affirmation of, 3, 24–25, 64, 89–91, 94–95, 195
  See also Dependence
Sociobiology, 65–69
Solitude, 74–80, 104, 128–131, 160, 166–167, 194–197
  See also Isolation
Some Thoughts concerning Education (Locke), 28–29, 35–36, 210 n.6, 211 n.13
Spivak, Gayatri, 231 n.10, 239 n.32
Starobinski, Jean, 88, 221 n.19, 224 n.34, 225 n.39
"State of nature," 1–4, 18–20, 24–25, 57, 59–62, 95, 102–104
  in Hobbes, 1–2, 18–19, 24, 60, 95, 208 n.48, 209 n.50, 217 n.50
  in Locke, 3–4, 57, 73–74, 83–84, 217 n.50, 223 n.27
  parenting in, 73–74, 79–85, 217 n.50, 222 nn.23, 24, 223 n.27
  in Rousseau, 8, 63–89
Stephens, Leslie, 240 n.1
Stillinger, Jack, 241 n.10
Sympathy:
  Hume on, 41, 58, 60–62, 216 n.48, 217 n.49

  Mill on, 171–172, 190, 194
  in Shelley's *Frankenstein*, 158–159, 166–168
  See also Intersubjectivity; Perception

Tapper, Richard, 218 n.2
Taylor, Charles, 2, 198 n.4, 207 n.42, 241 n.8
Taylor, Harriet, 185–189, 243 n.24
Tennyson, Alfred, 196
Terrasse, Jean, 224 nn.29, 31
Thompson, E. P., 232 n.14
Thought experiments, 49, 214 n.27, 229 n.25
Tinland, Franck, 219 nn.8, 12, 13, 226 n.2
Todorov, Tzvetan, 5–6, 199 n.12
Treatise of Human Nature (Hume), 39–41, 56–58, 212 nn.18, 19, 216 nn.45, 48, 217 n.49, 217 n.52, 222 n.22
Trust. *See* Dissimulation

Utilitarianism, 14, 170–172, 190–194
Utilitarianism (John Stuart Mill), 170, 182, 194

Victor of Aveyron, 96–113
  discovery of, 97
  etiological debate on, 108, 110–111, 229 n.20
  impairments of, 100–101, 104, 106–110, 228 n.9
  as philosophical test case, 97–99, 109–111, 113
  physical description of, 104–106
  Rousseau's *Discourse on the Origins of Inequality* and, 99–105
Virey, Julien-Joseph, 100–108, 228 n.14
Voisine, Jacques, 201 n.18
Voltaire, 5, 30, 82, 227 n.6, 234 n.20
Vulnerability, 22–25, 193–195, 208 n.46
  to deception, 50–51, 62, 90–91, 94–95, 208 n.49
  to loss, 37–38, 143–144, 197
  See also Anxiety; Fear

Waal, Frans de, 68
Walker, William, 209 n.3
Weiskel, Thomas, 231 n.10
Willey, Basil, 230 n.1
Wilson, Fred, 240 n.5
Winnicott, D. W., 194, 200 n.14, 243 n.23
Wittgenstein, Ludwig (Wittgensteinian), 12, 16–18, 43, 69, 162, 164, 168, 195, 205 n.37, 206 nn.38, 39, 213 n.24, 243 n.34

Wokler, Robert, 65–68, 70, 219n.10, 220n.14
Wolfson, Susan, 231n.11, 234n.25
Wollstonecraft, Mary, 155, 186, 226n.41, 236n.10
Wordsworth, Dorothy, 141–142
Wordworth, William, 2, 7–9, 21–24, 37, 114–148, 153, 193–195
  "Ode: Intimations of Immortality," 127
  The Prelude, 8–9, 114–148, 153, 193
  "Tintern Abbey," 127, 200n.15

Yolton, John, 210n.6, 214n.25

Zerilli, Linda, 184